TRAN NGUYEN

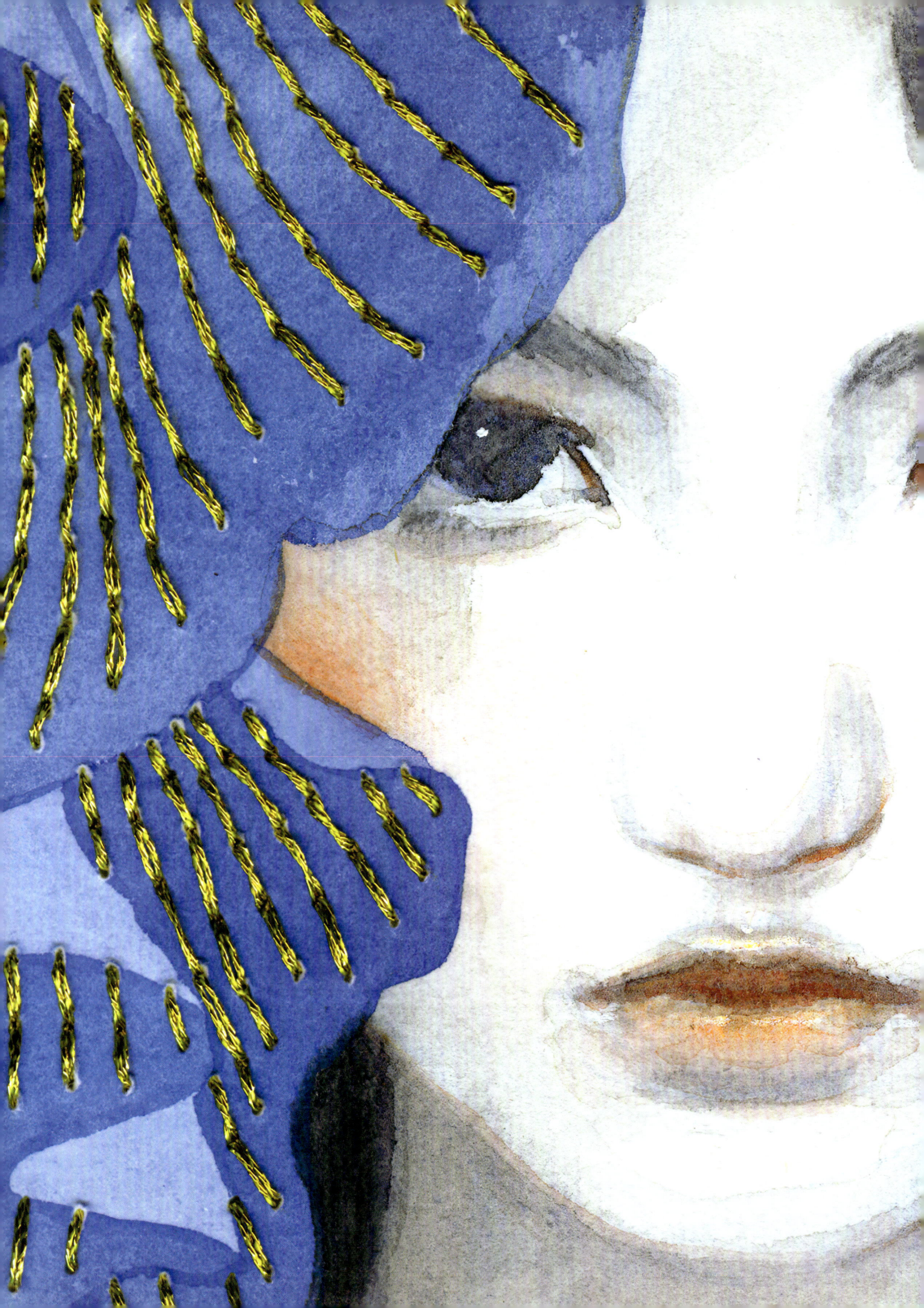

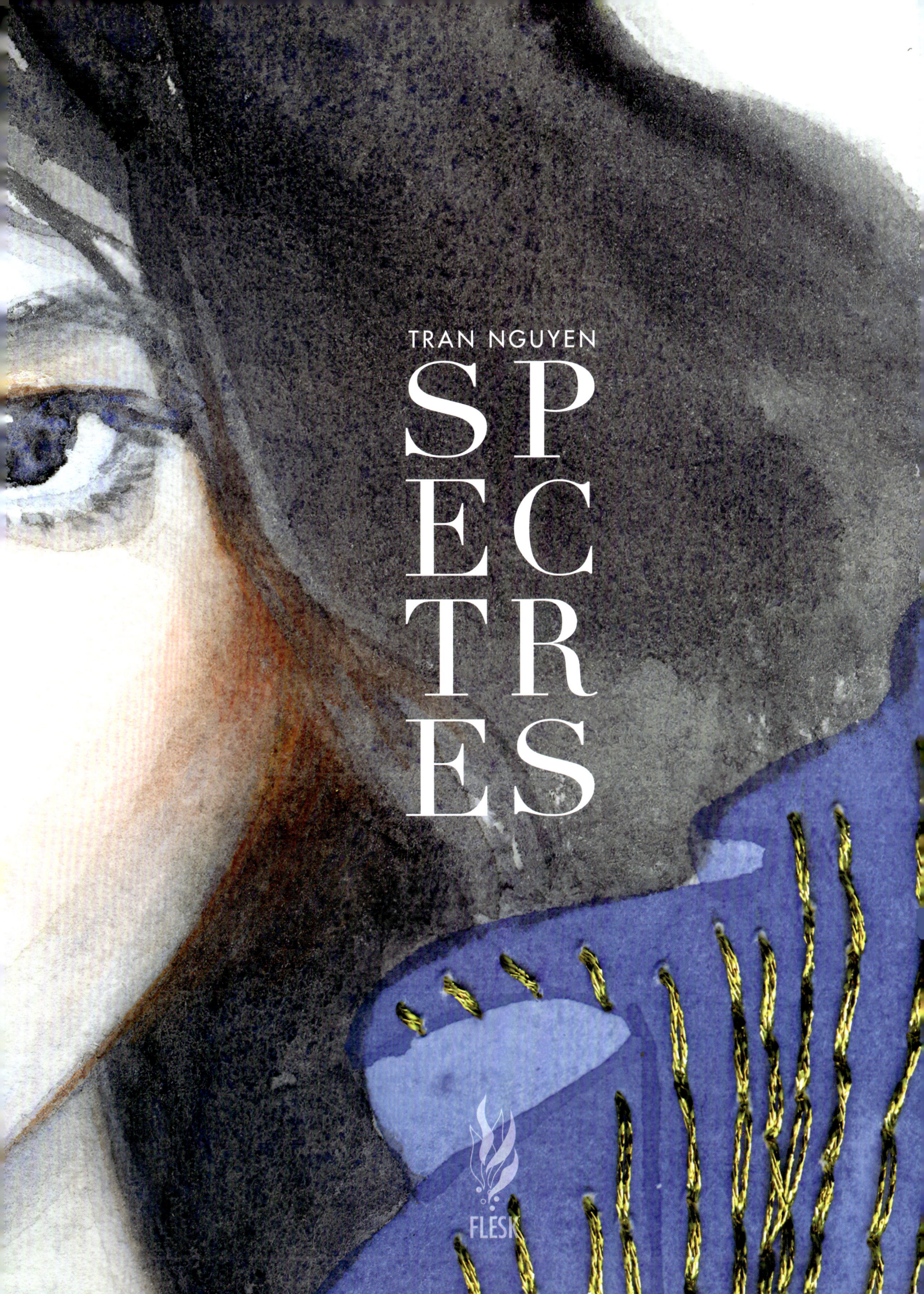

TRAN NGUYEN

SPECTRES

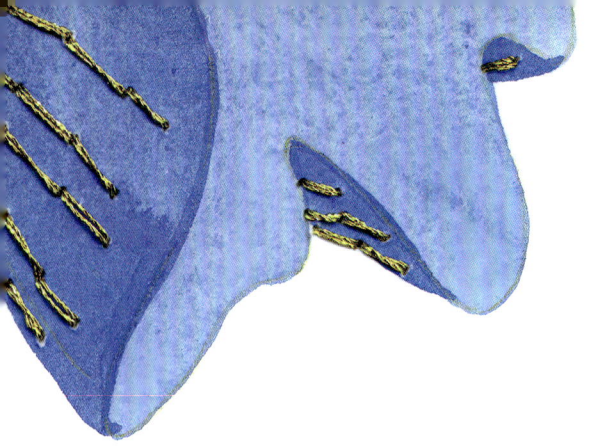

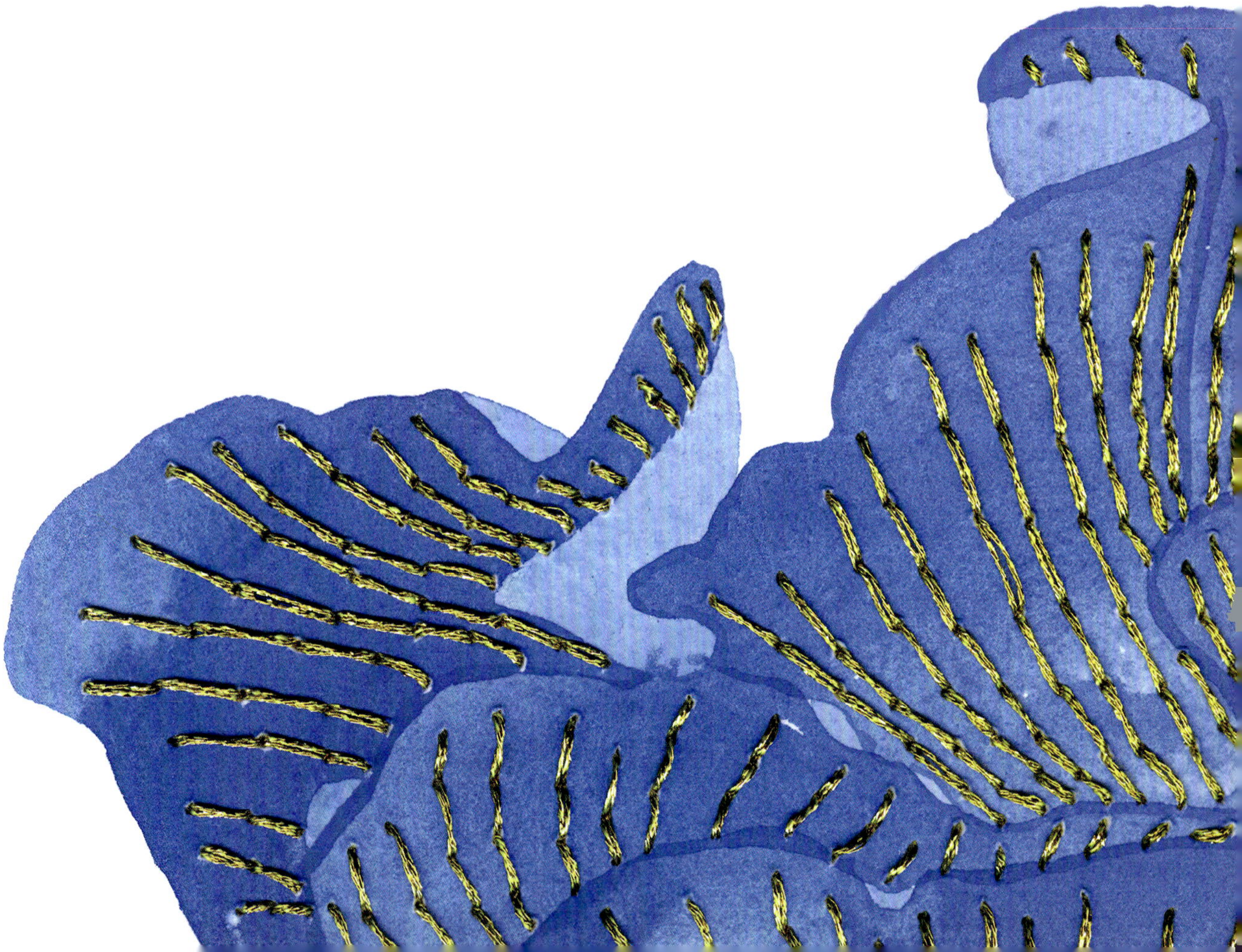

INTRO

Growing up in a first-generation immigrant household, I found that my parents saturated my everyday routine with the rich tapestry of Vietnamese culture and its traditional beliefs. Many of these routines revolved around honoring the dead to help them find passage to the afterlife. One belief in particular has stuck with me through adulthood: This is the enchanting symbolism of moths—creatures deeply embedded in Vietnamese folklore as the messenger of a loved one's spirit or spectre. Moths are believed to have a spiritual connection to the dead, and my parents made it known that moths were not to be bothered or misfortune would visit the family. Along with its grim colors, the mystical-yet-formidable aura that my culture ascribed to these insects spooked me as a kid. My encounters with them were fleeting, and it was rare to come across the same moth twice. The uneasiness I felt from the mysticism surrounding these creatures turned into fascination as I grew older, and it has made its way into my art throughout the years.

Similar to this cultural belief is the idea that paintings can also possess the intangible essence of a being. A painting portrays a precise moment in the subject matter's life via brushstrokes, tells its story and character, embodies its spirit and conveys a definite feeling to the viewer. I believe art can transcend into the metaphysical realms of the afterlife and act as a conduit for ethereal energies.

Spectres is a curated collection of over 110 small artworks made in the past decade. Each painting is a means of exploration—a study whose purpose is to develop a deep understanding of new media.

The works depict loosely rendered female portraits or, on seldom occasions, animals. Unlike my large-scale paintings, they were created without the restraints imposed by extensive preliminaries that I often adhere to as part of my standard illustration process. This study series started out as an outlet for trying new ideas, materials, color palettes and substrates, without the looming pressure of perfection or deadlines. They fulfill my need to be adventurous, which allows me to stumble with my brushstrokes and evolve as an artist.

Like my encounters with moths, the time spent with each piece was brief—to capture the fleeting moments of my artistic curiosity. In recent years, my fixation to over-render has become increasingly stifling. Instead of focusing on composition and the overall dynamism within it, I'm imprisoned by an urge to render each asset photo-realistically. Limiting the experiments preserves the raw execution of its form. These art studies help me take a step back, put away excess reference materials and celebrate the simplicity of creative expression.

This series has helped me to freely discover unconventional and unique methods of art-making, which has been incorporated into my gallery and illustration work. This includes the application of pressed flowers and embroidery. What began with a few small-scale portrait paintings has become the stepping stones to hone the technical skills that inform my larger pieces. Much like moths and the spectres that they embody, the works in this book serve as guides into my artistic exploration.

—*Tran Nguyen*

Designed by John Fleskes and Tran Nguyen
Copyedited by Martin Timins
Production assistance by Vicky Lien
First Printing, October 2025
Hardcover ISBN: 978-1-64041-097-8
Deluxe Signed Hardcover in Slipcase. Limited to 500 copies
ISBN: 978-1-64041-098-5
Library of Congress Control Number: 2024949441
Printed in China
Asia One Printing Limited, Hong Kong
www.fleskpublications.com
www.mynameistran.com

CONTENTS

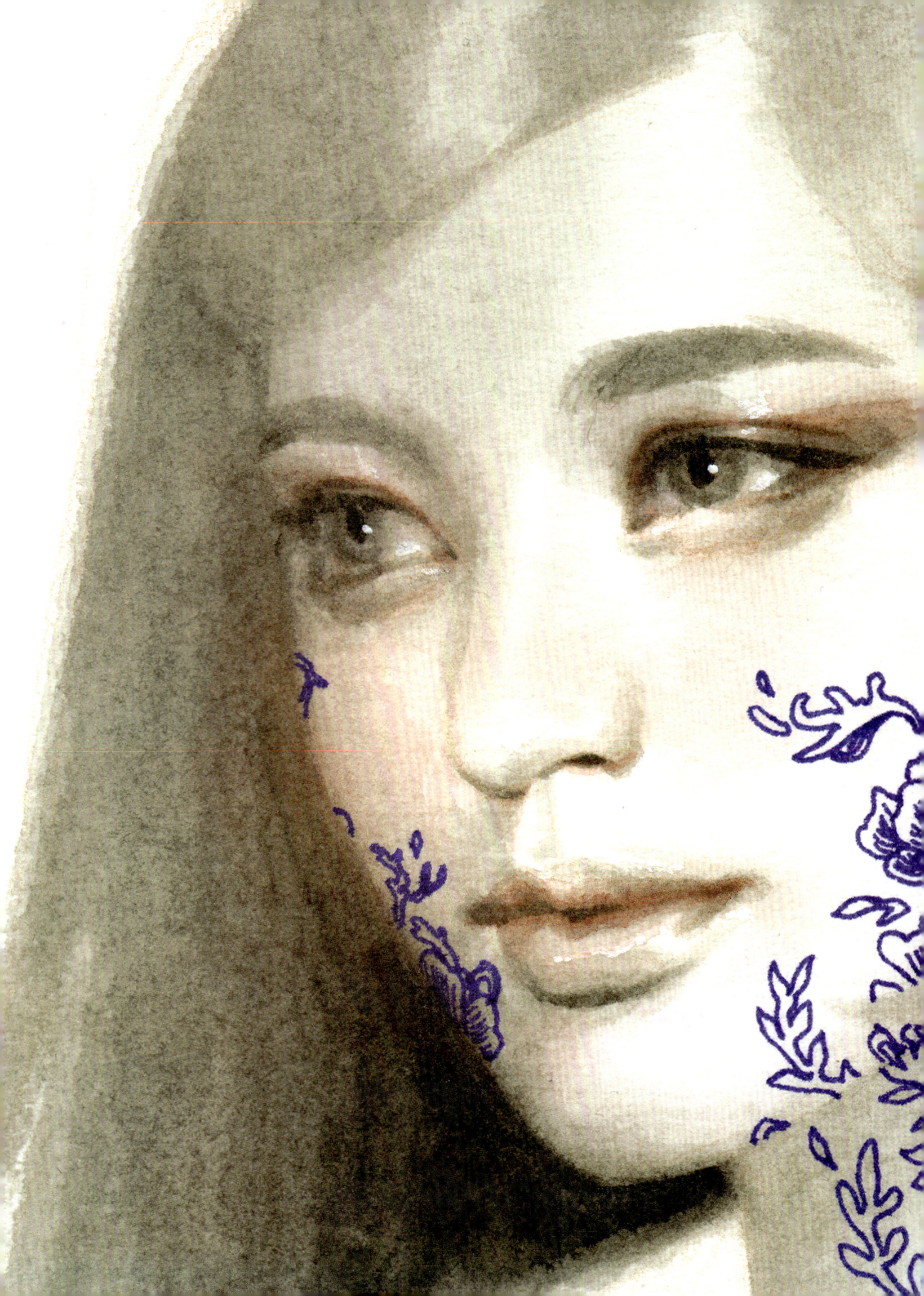

WET MEDIA

Works made with water-based paint are among the first studies that kickstarted my endeavor to try unfamiliar media. The focused experiment in this section documents my exploration into watercolor, ink, acrylic and gouache on different types of paper.

Each painting is an opportunity to acquaint myself with a medium's unique characteristics and behavior. In the following sections, I dedicate time to uncover new application techniques, such as drybrush and glazing. I learn best through the process of trial and error. Because of this, a technique is practiced on a minimum of ten iterations before I feel confident enough to bring it into my polished illustration work. The studies are also tested on a multitude of cotton-based papers with varying weight to further understand the interaction between water and fiber. Every subsequent piece completed is a move closer to technical mastery.

STUDY NO. 1
acrylic & colored pencil, 5" x 7", 2014

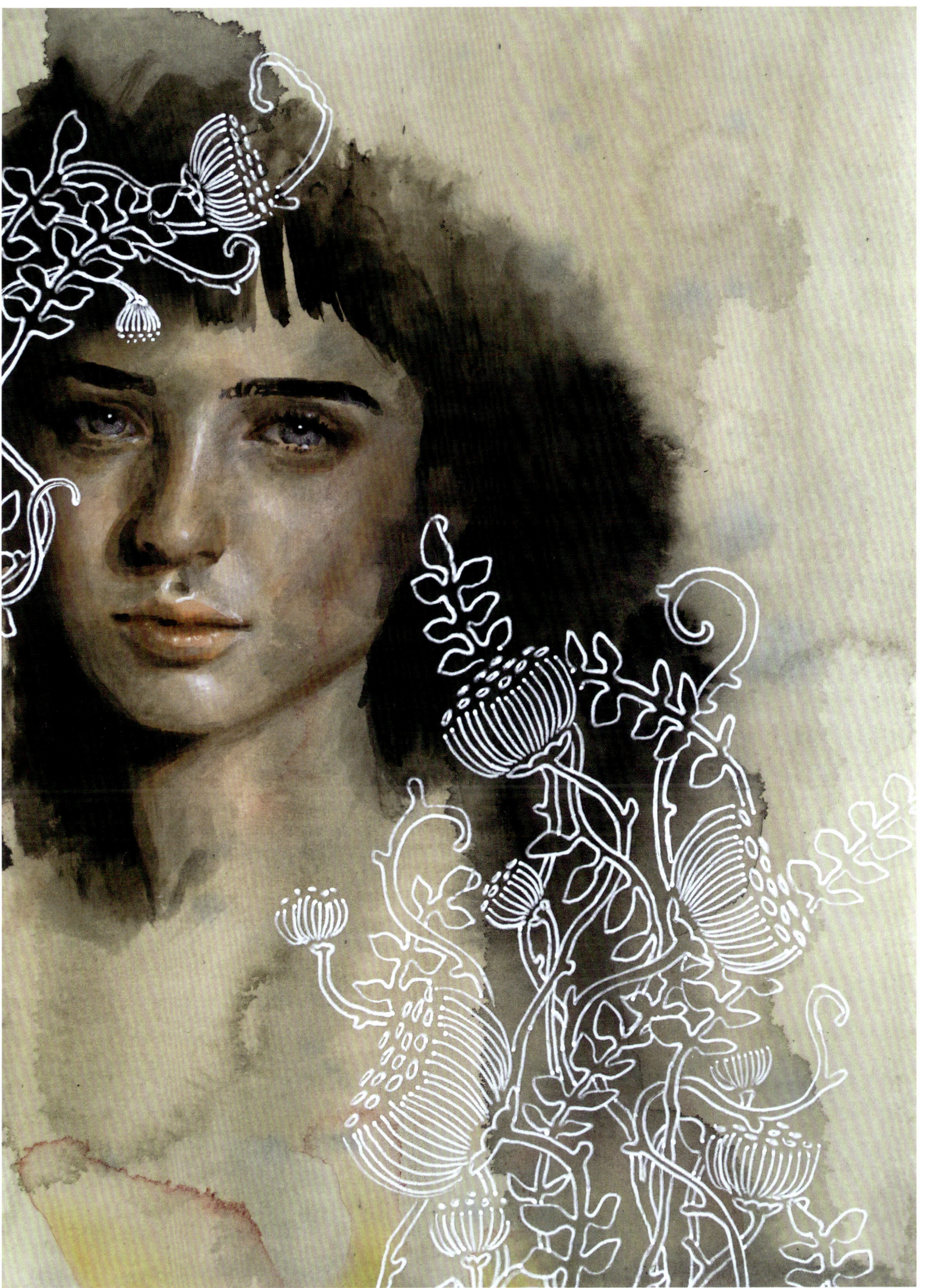

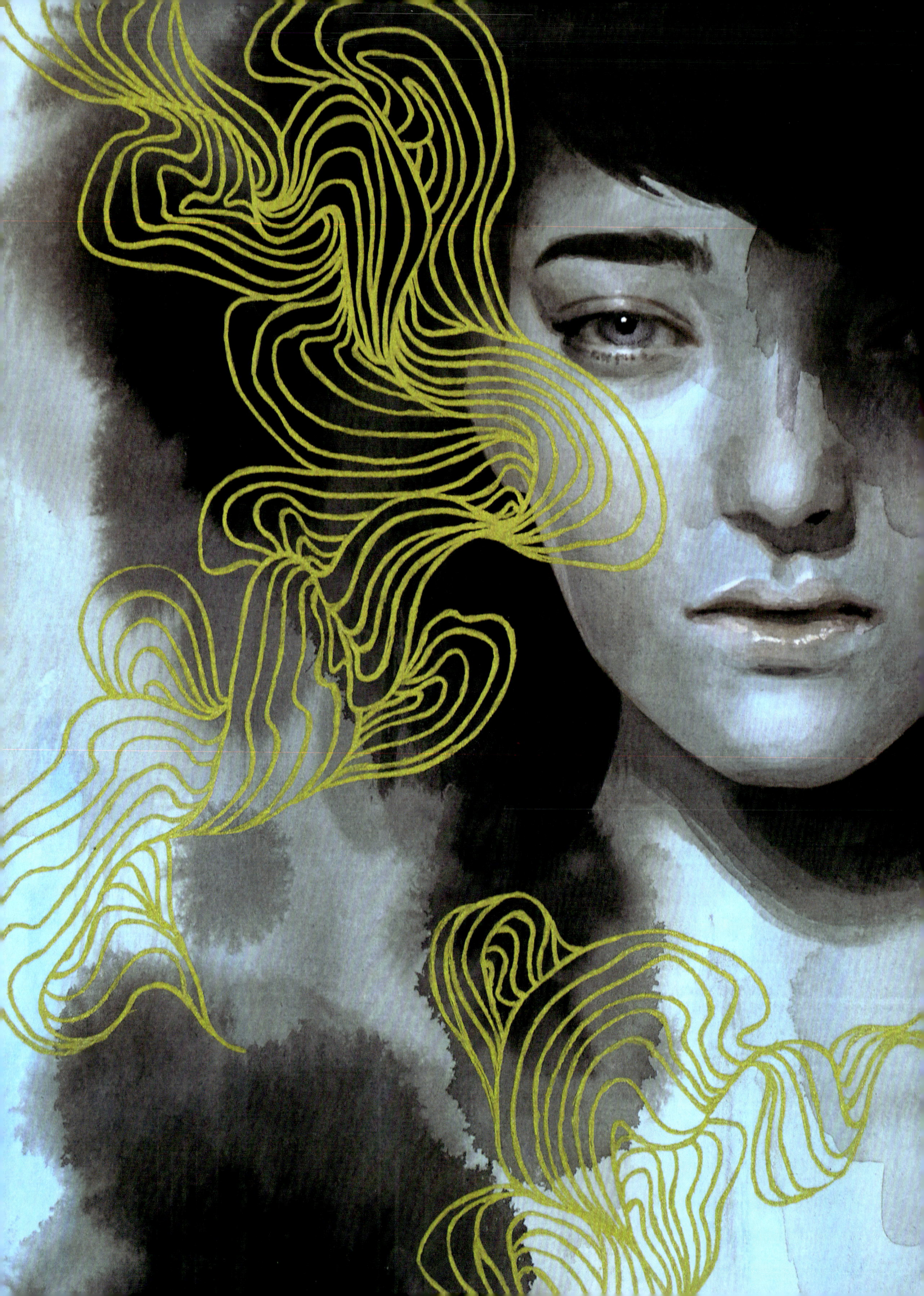

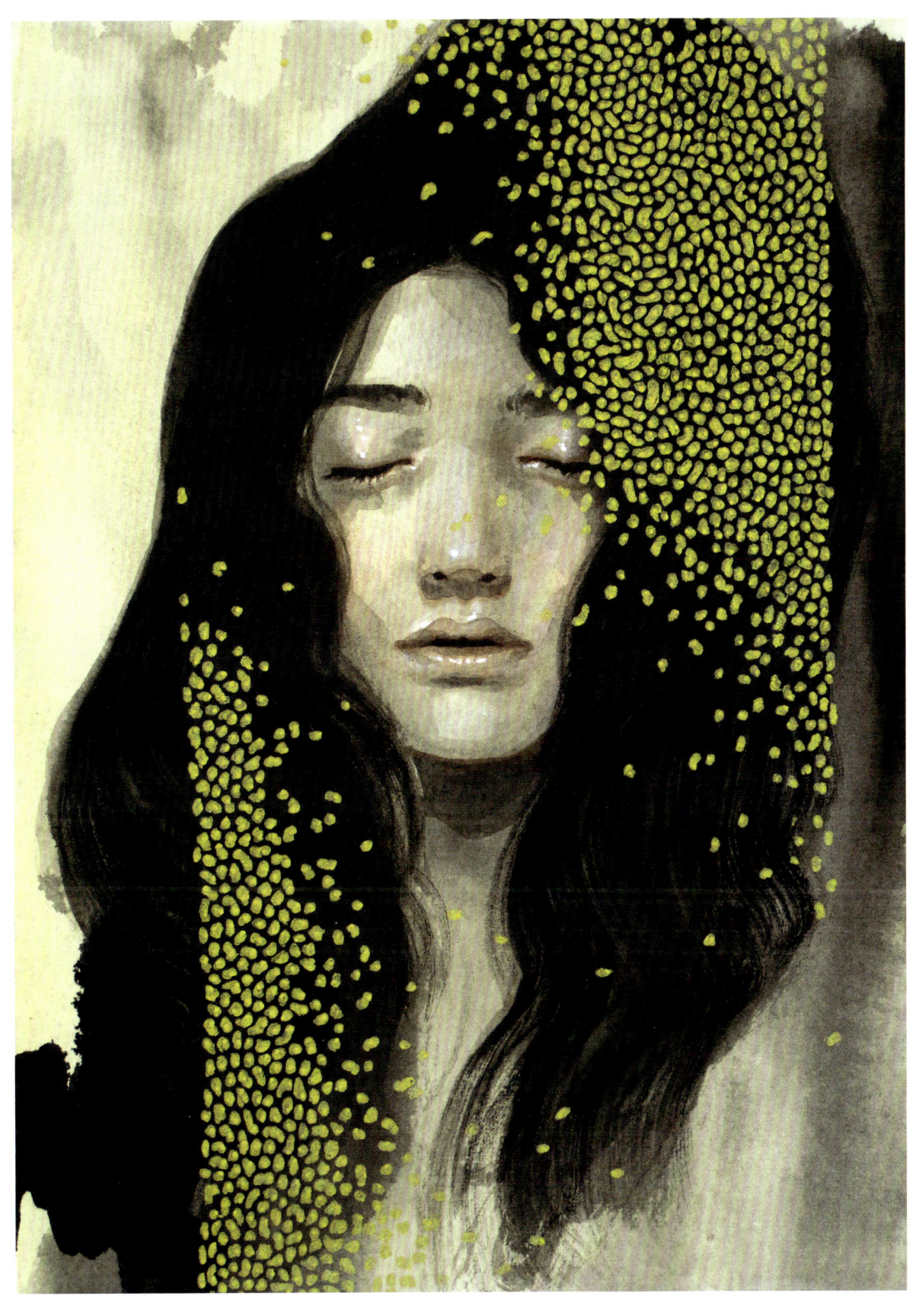

left
STUDY NO. 2
acrylic & colored pencil, 5" × 7", 2014

above
STUDY NO. 3
acrylic & colored pencil, 5" × 7", 2014

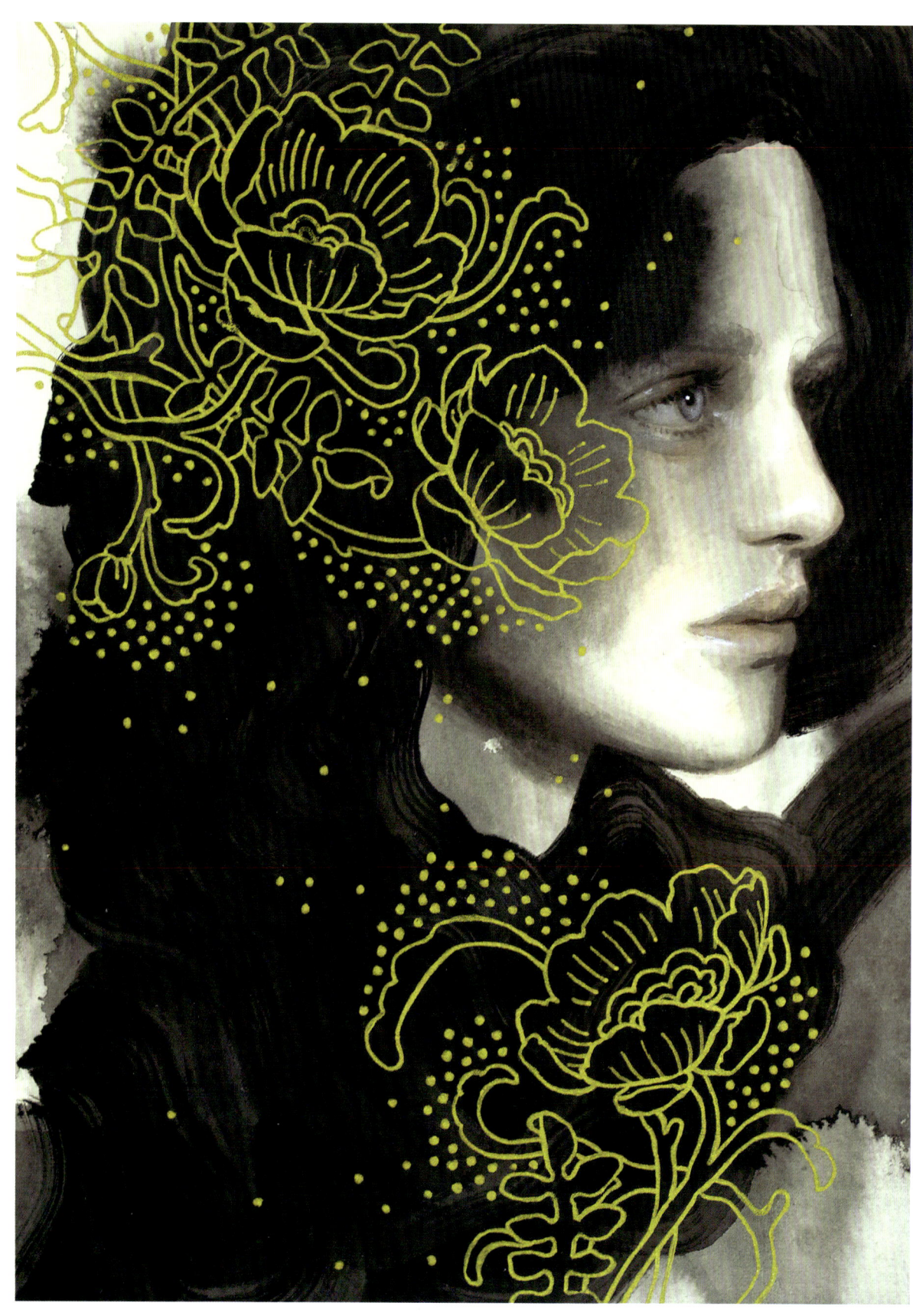

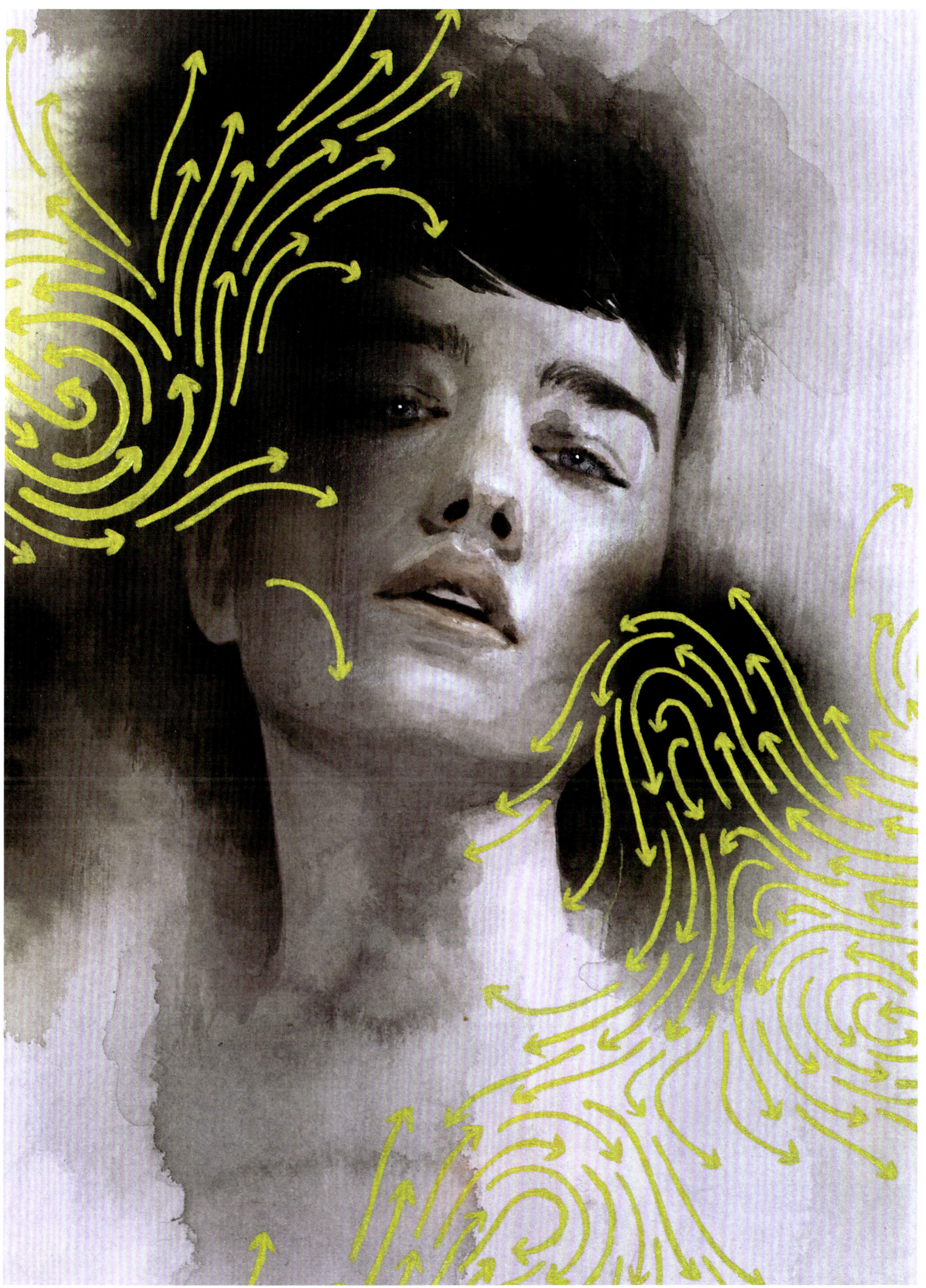

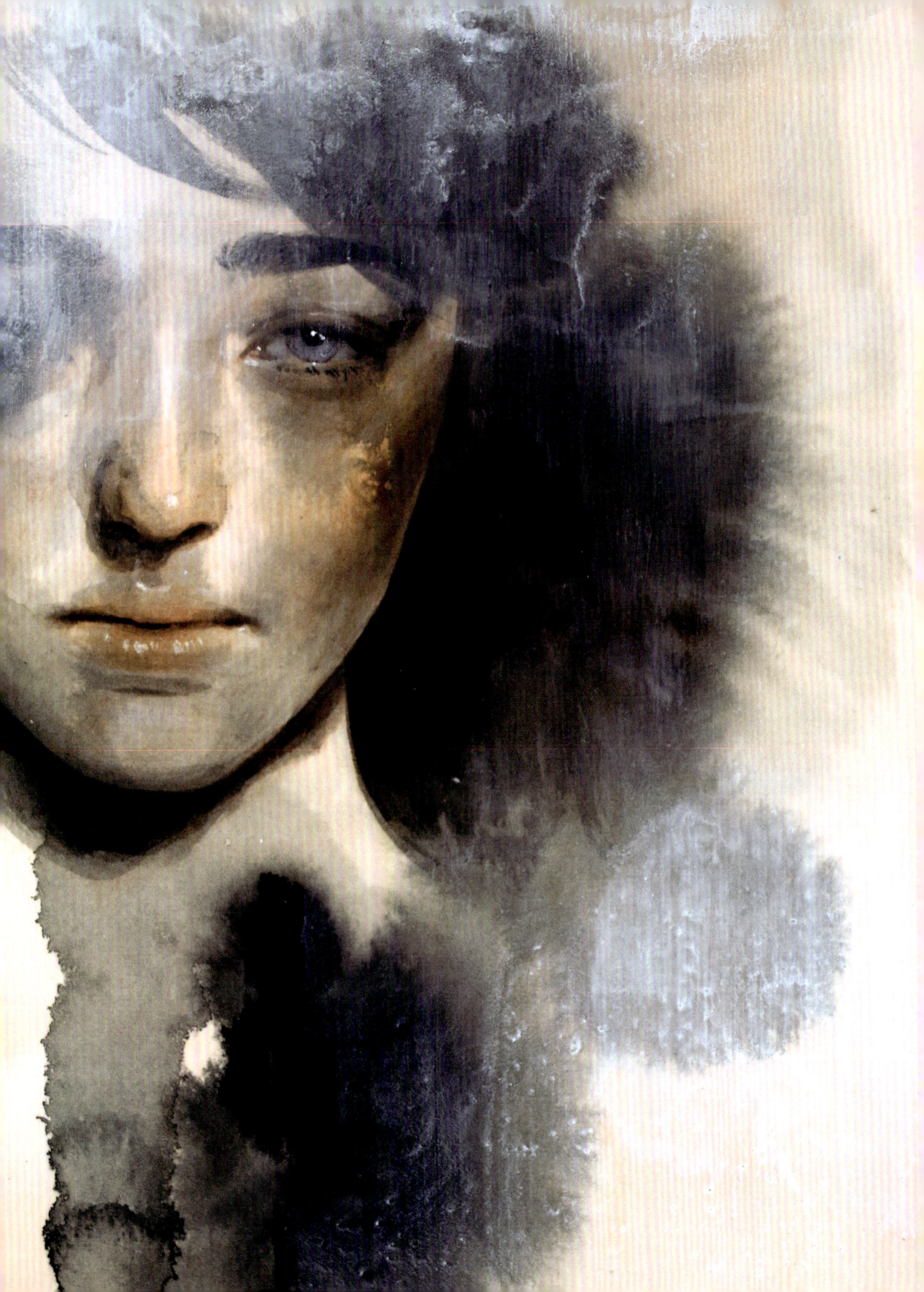

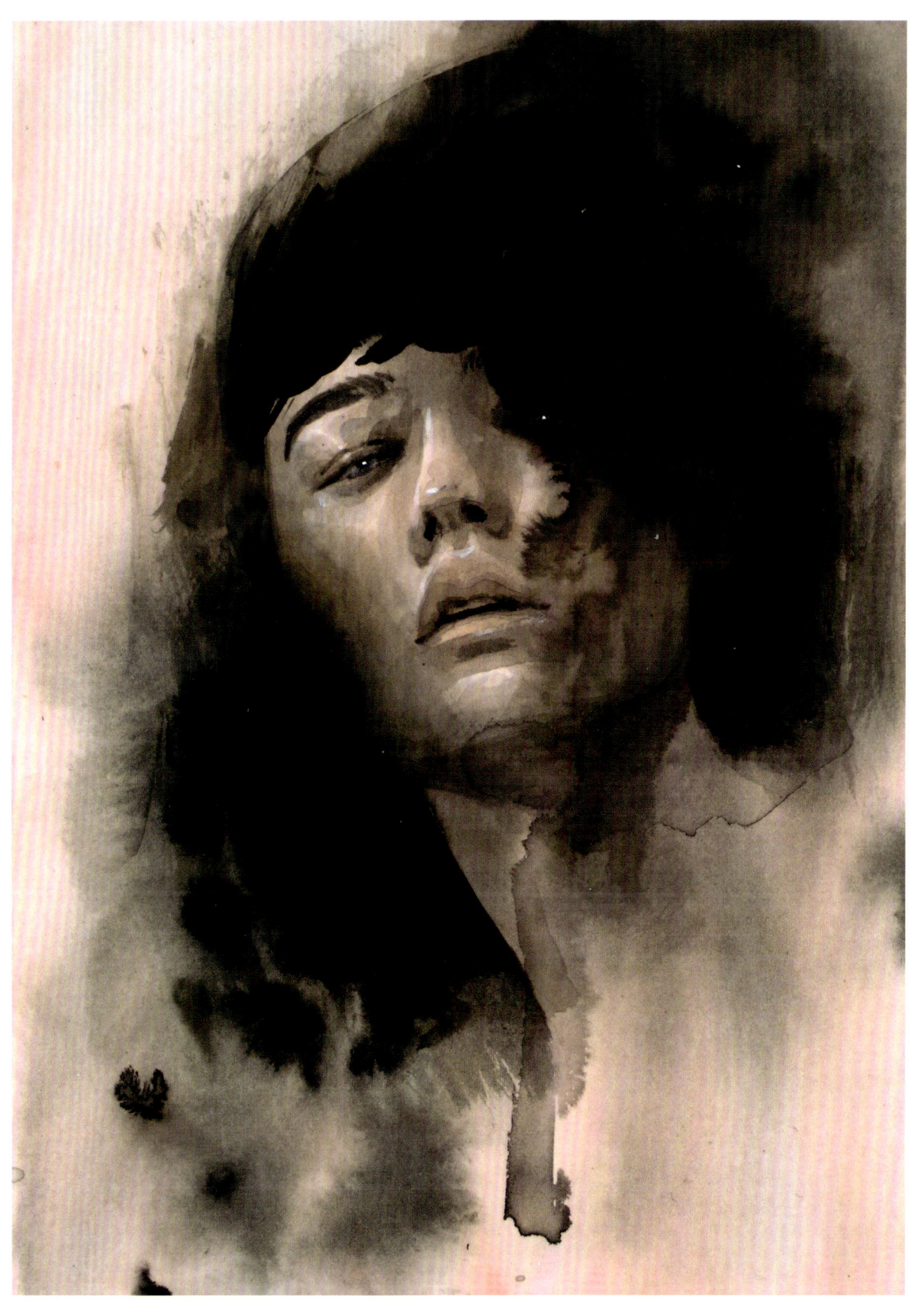

left
STUDY NO. 6
acrylic & colored pencil, 5″ × 7″, 2014

above
STUDY NO. 7
acrylic & colored pencil, 5″ × 7″, 2014

17

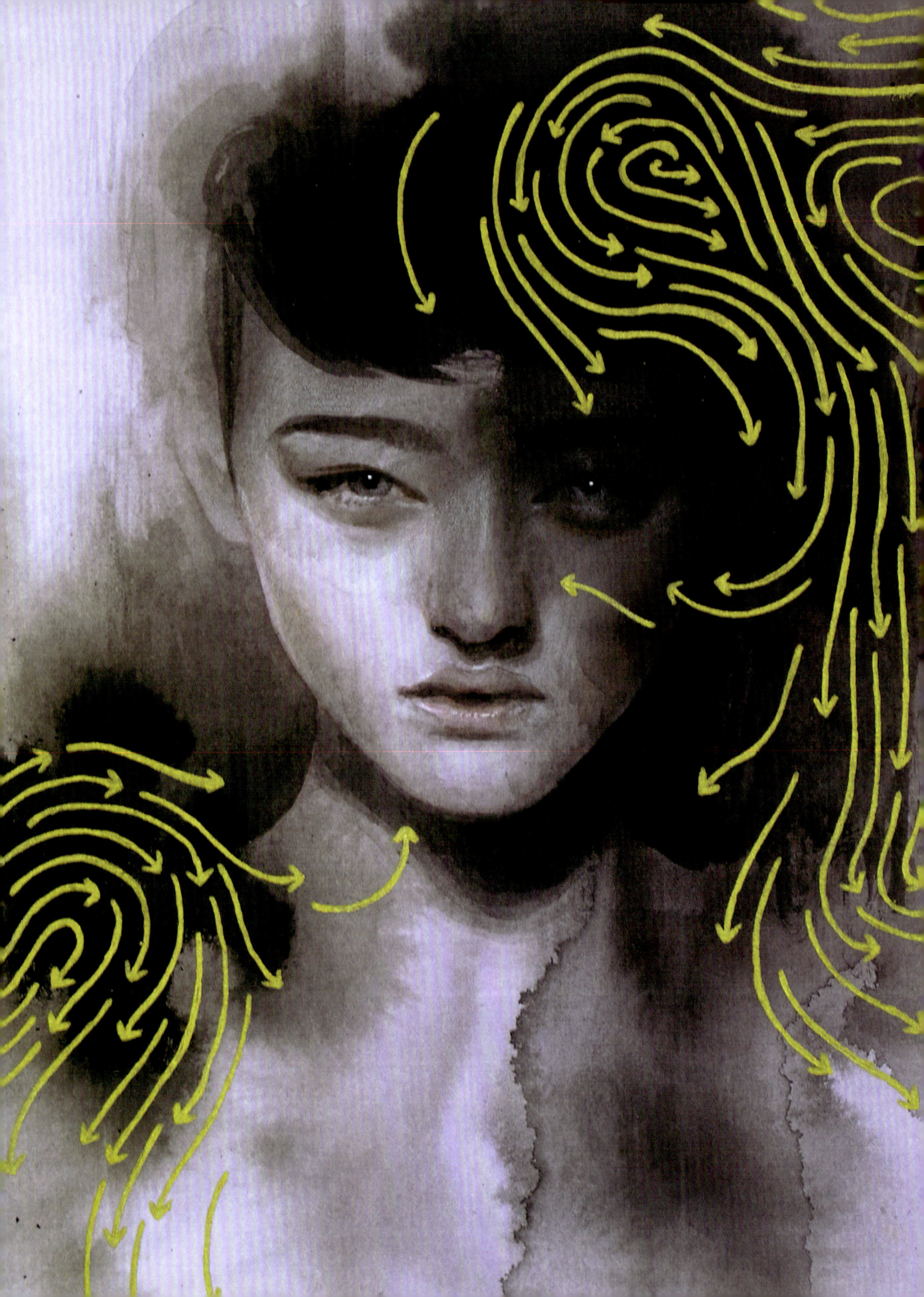

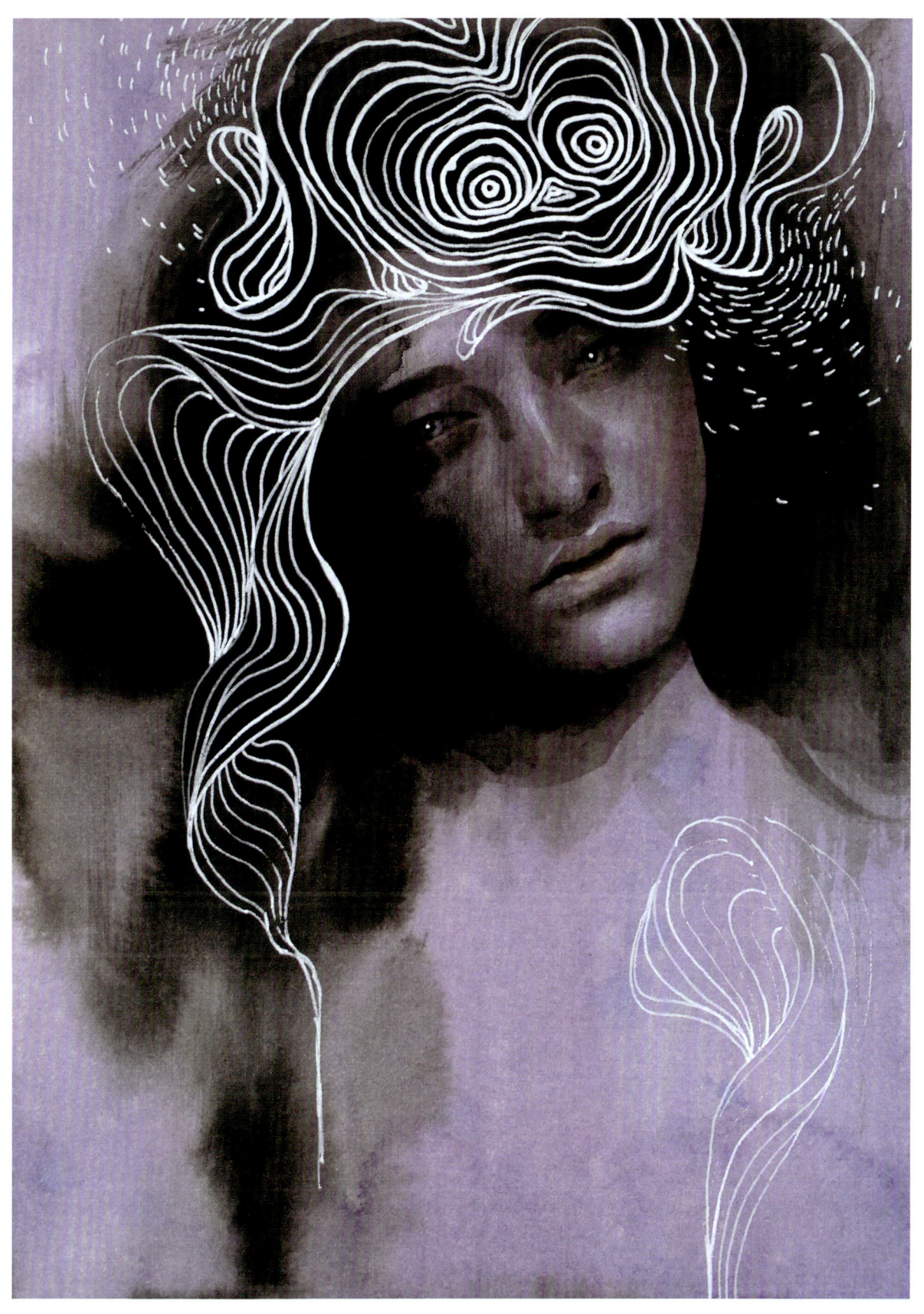

left
STUDY NO. 8
acrylic & colored pencil, 5" × 7", 2014

above
STUDY NO. 9
acrylic & colored pencil, 5" × 7", 2014

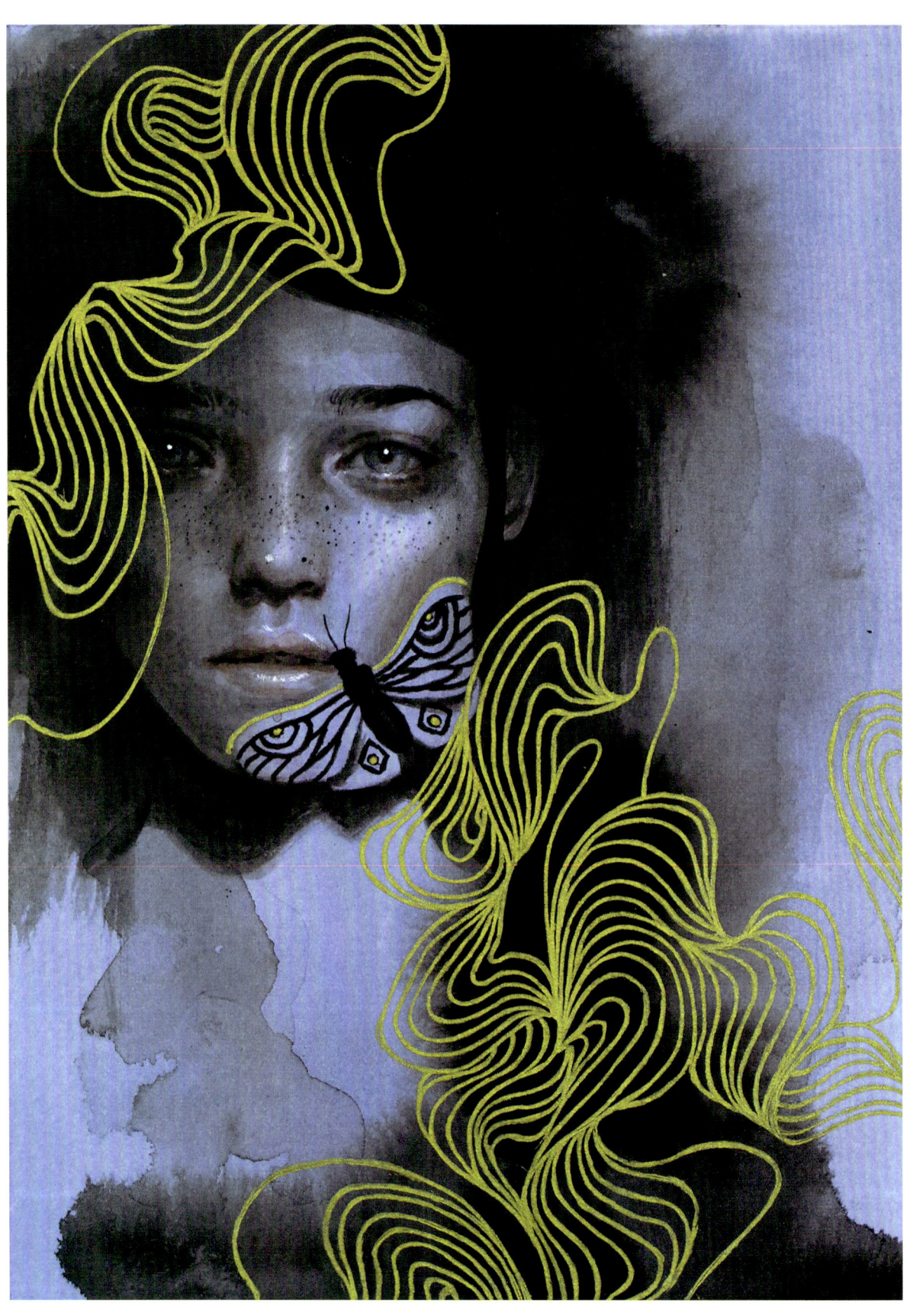

above
STUDY NO. 10
acrylic & colored pencil, 5" × 7", 2014

right
STUDY NO. 12
acrylic & colored pencil, 5" × 7", 2014

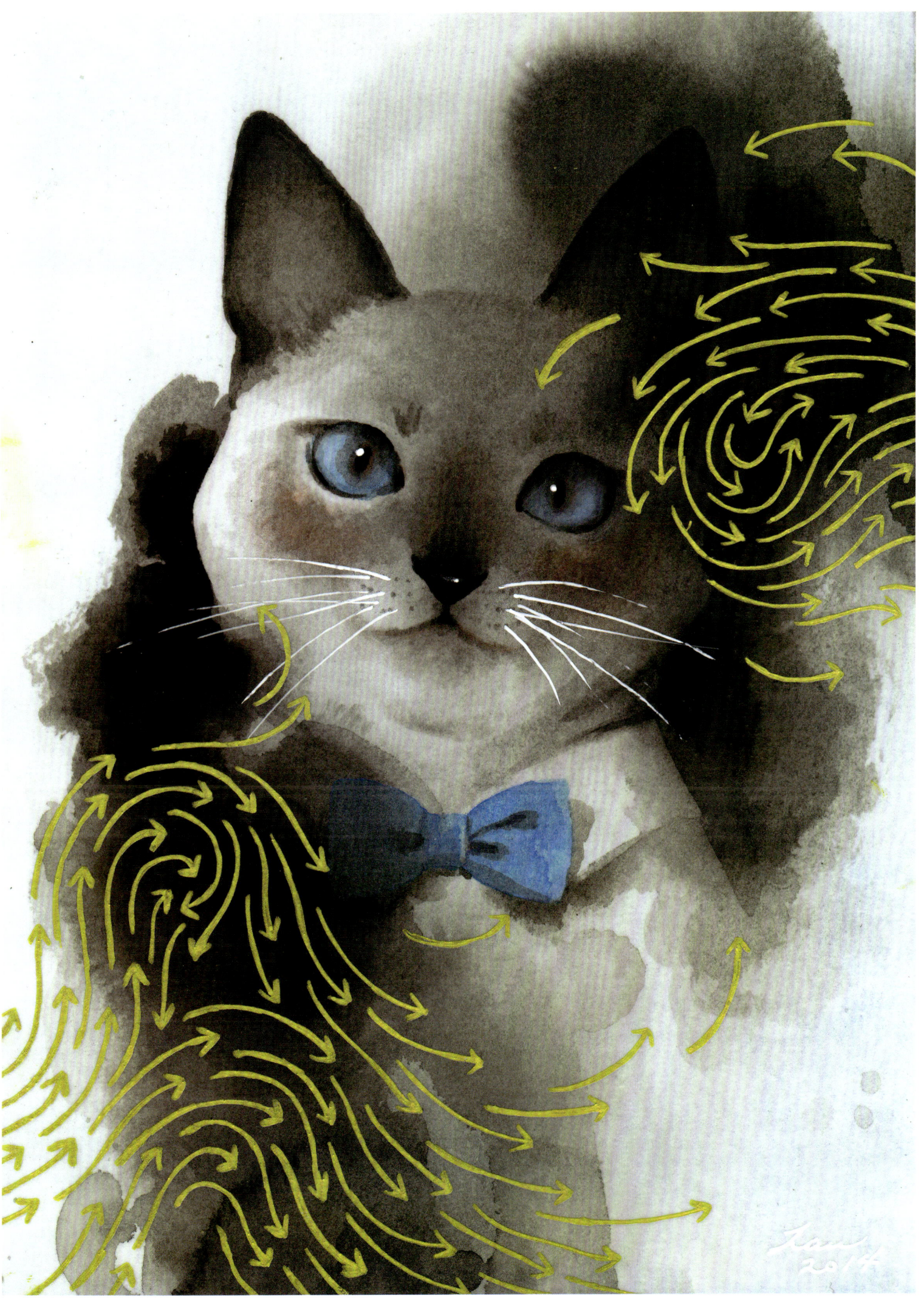

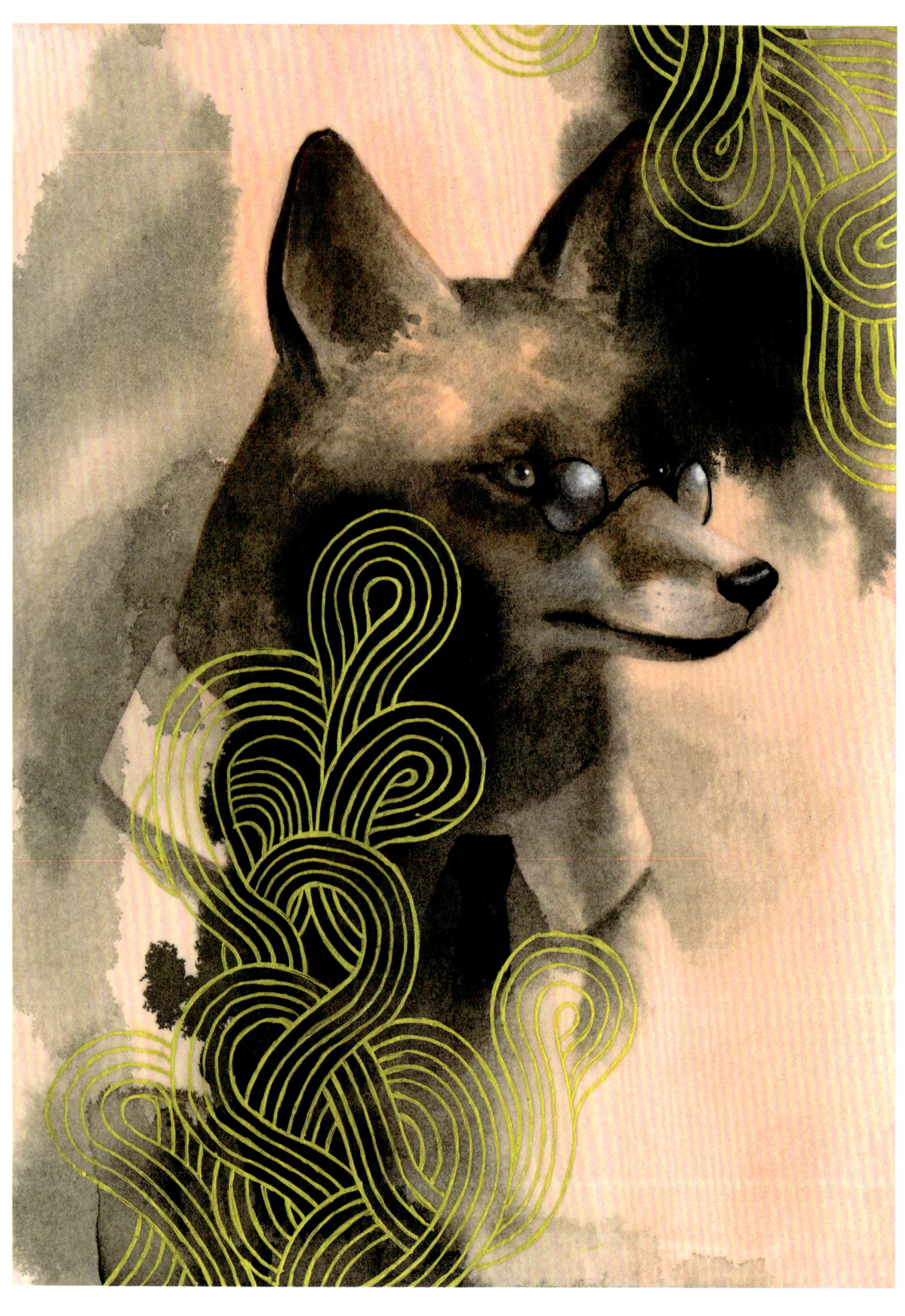

STUDY NO. 13
acrylic & colored pencil, 5″ × 7″, 2014

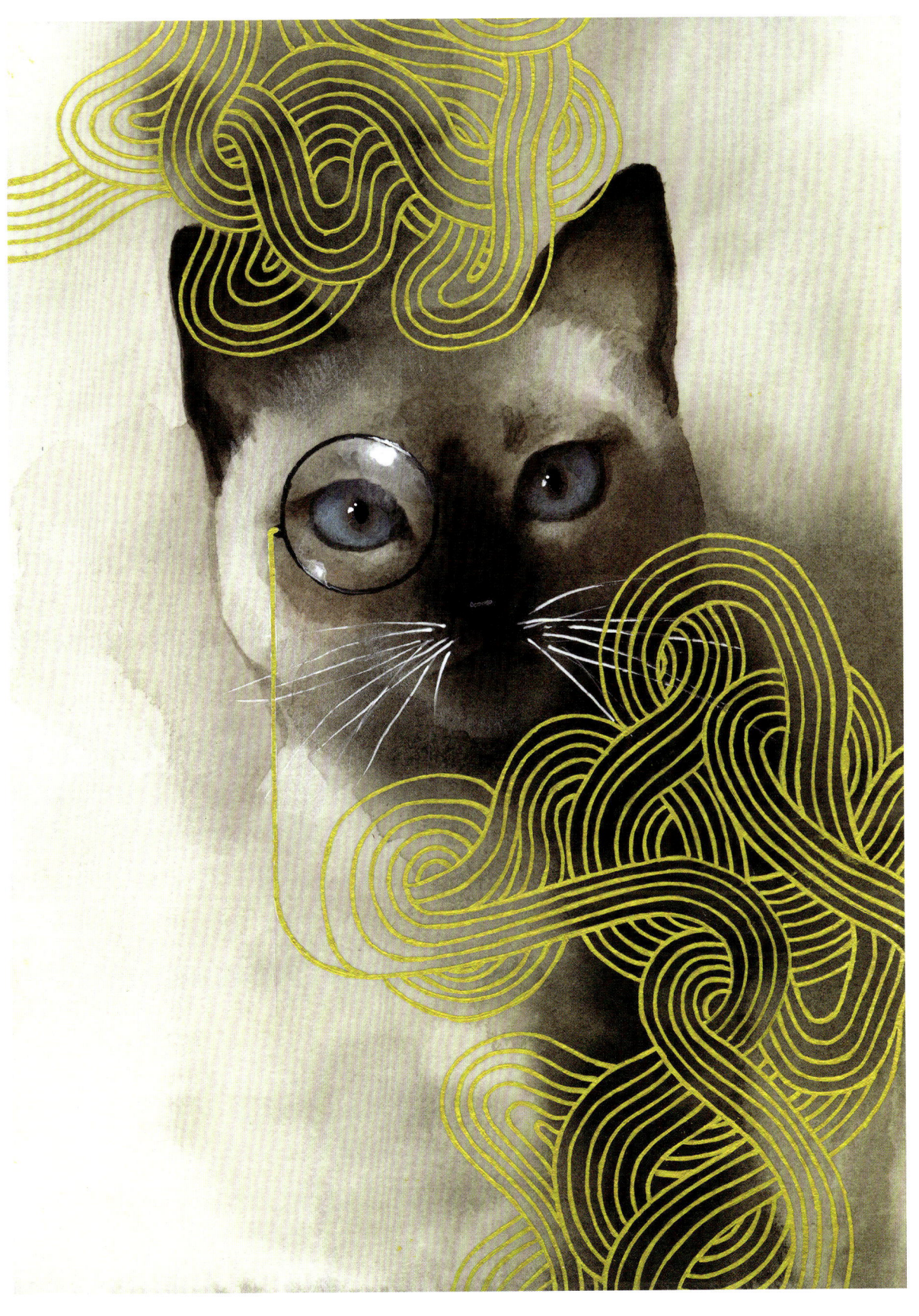

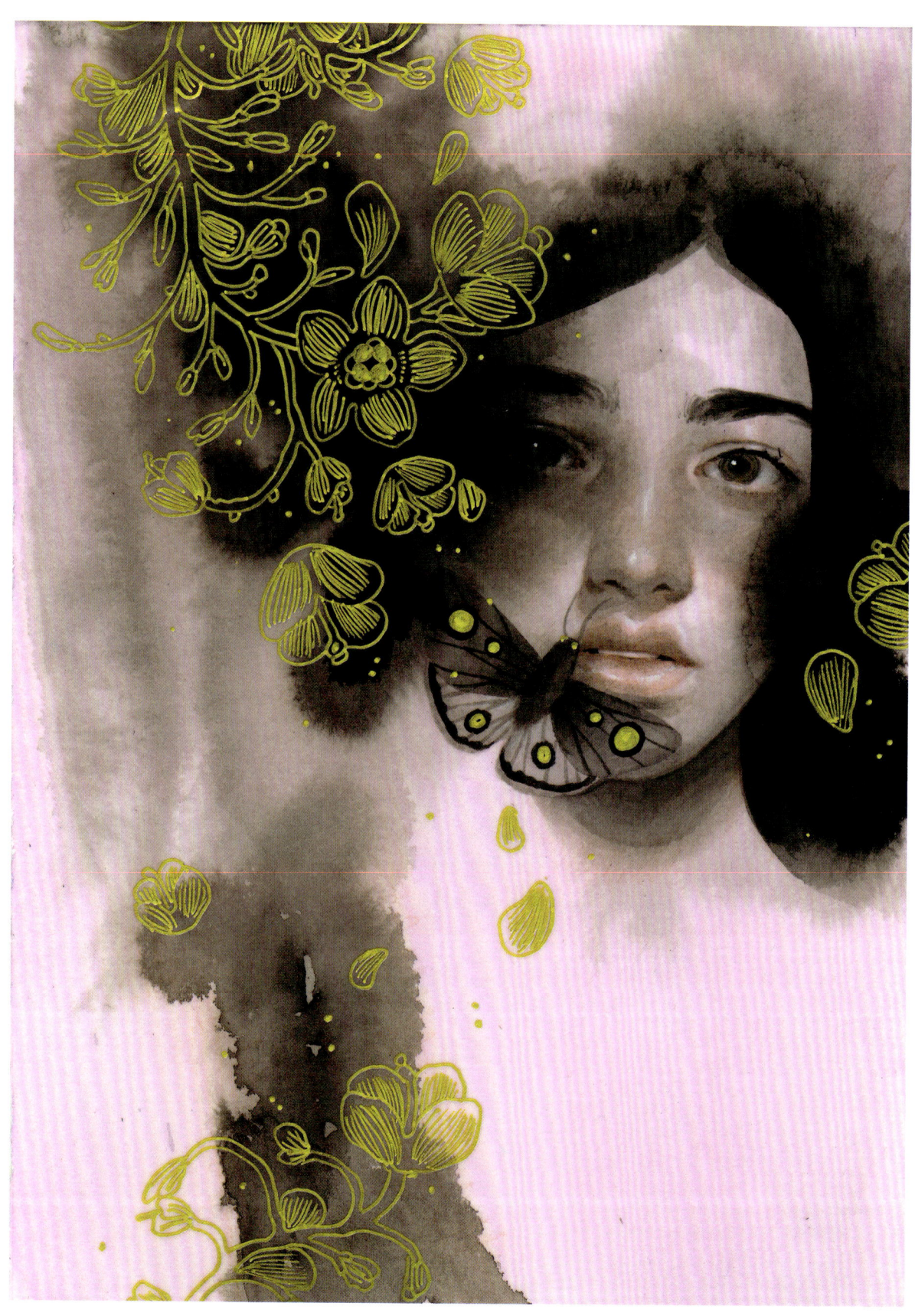

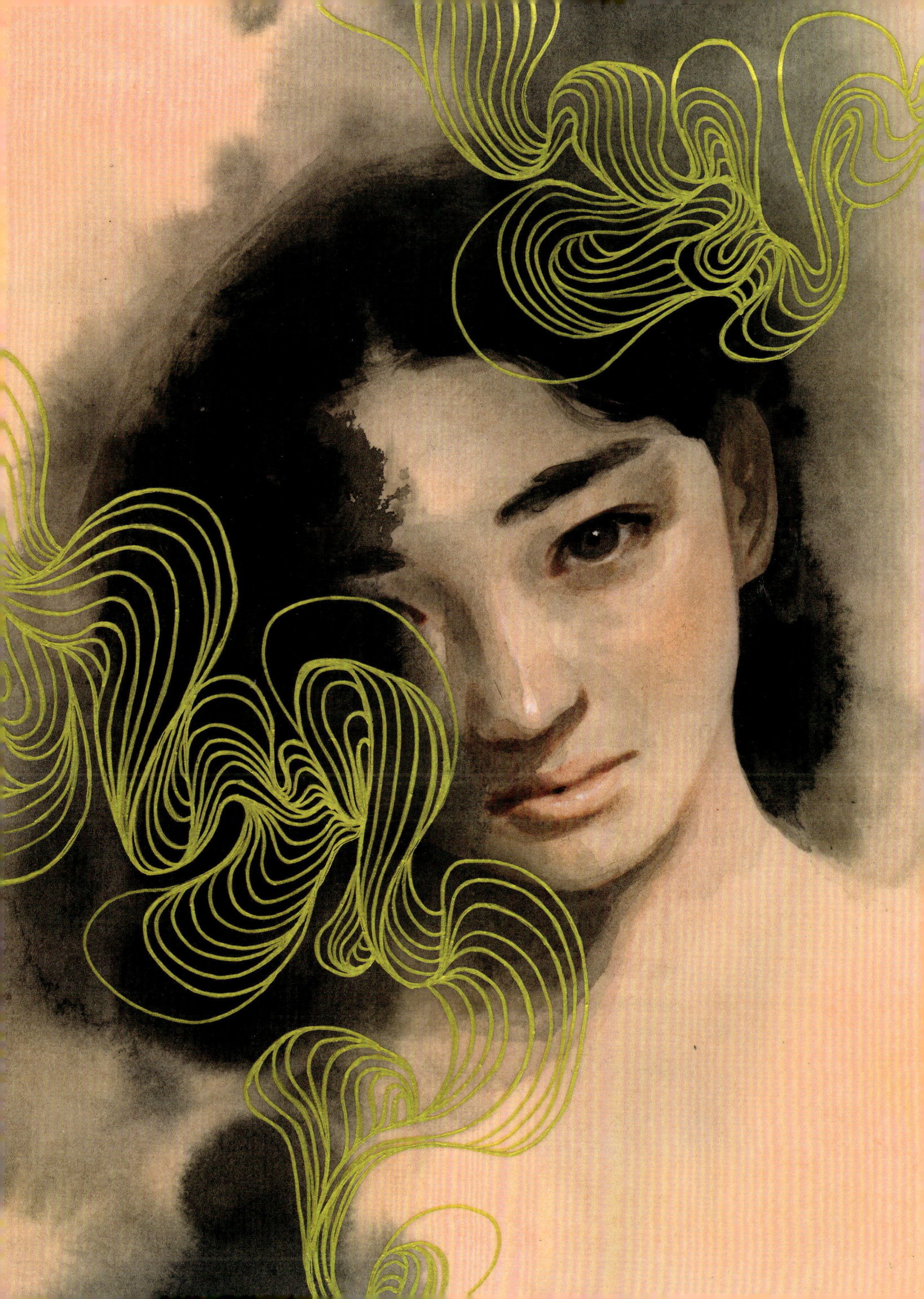

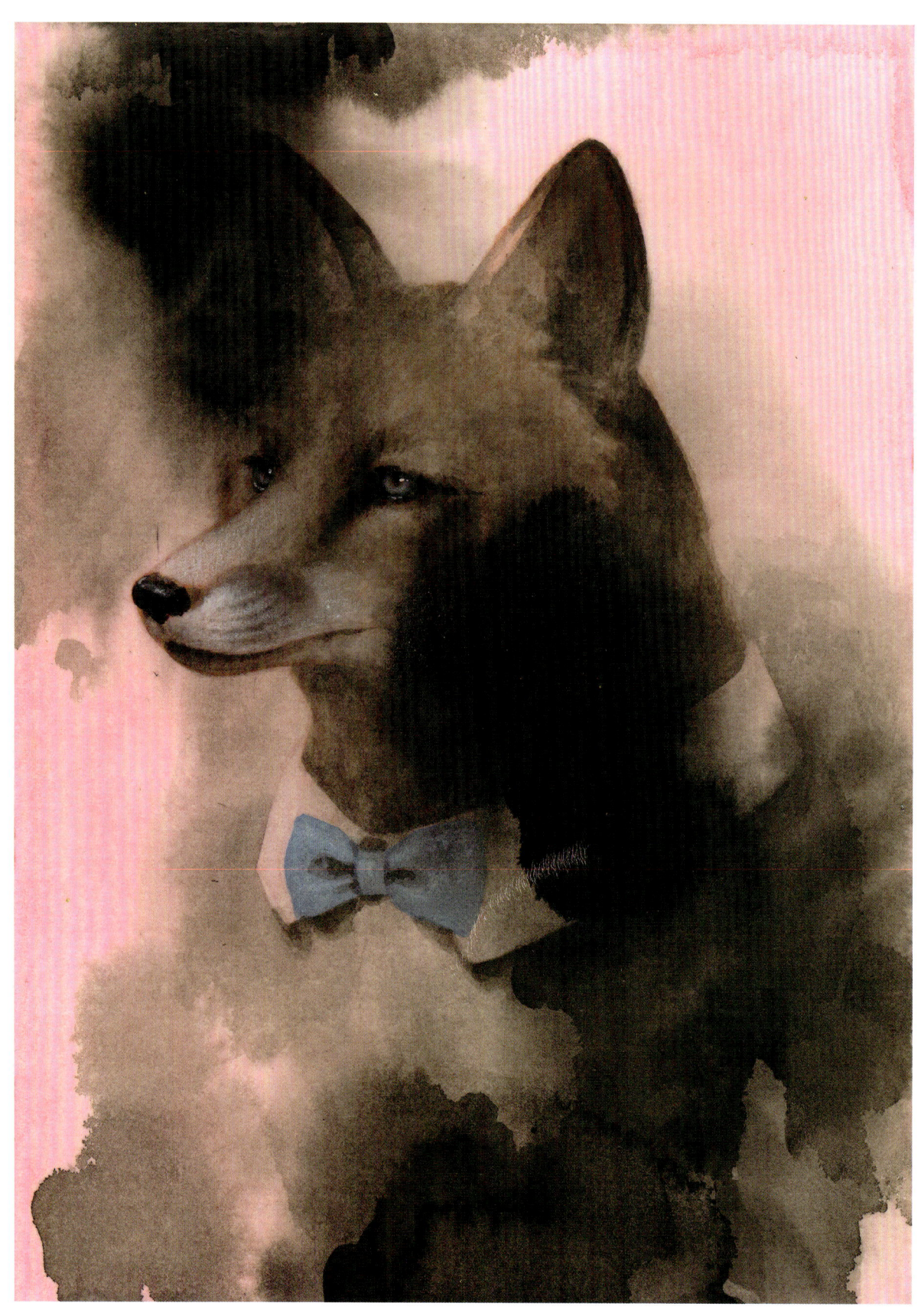

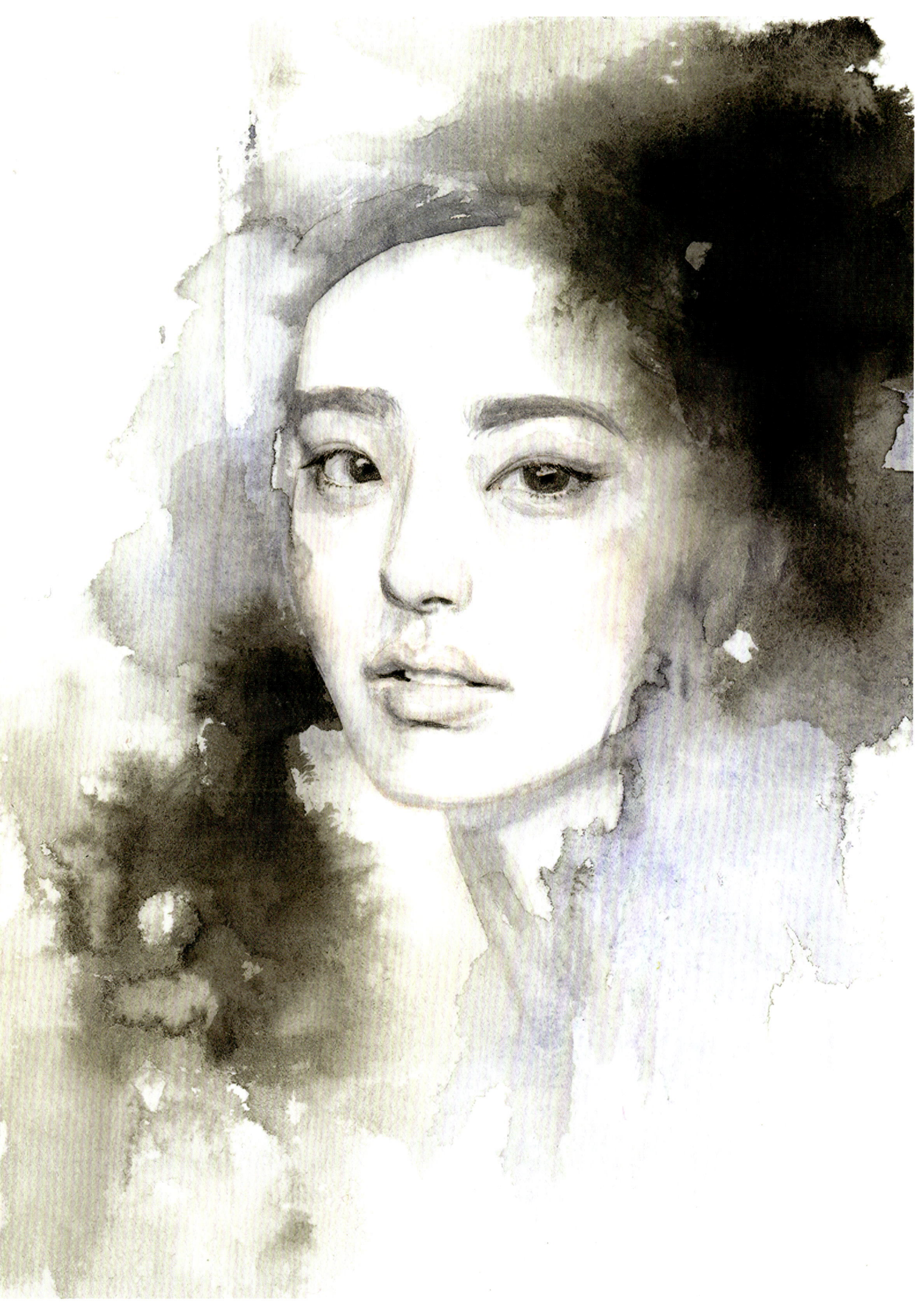

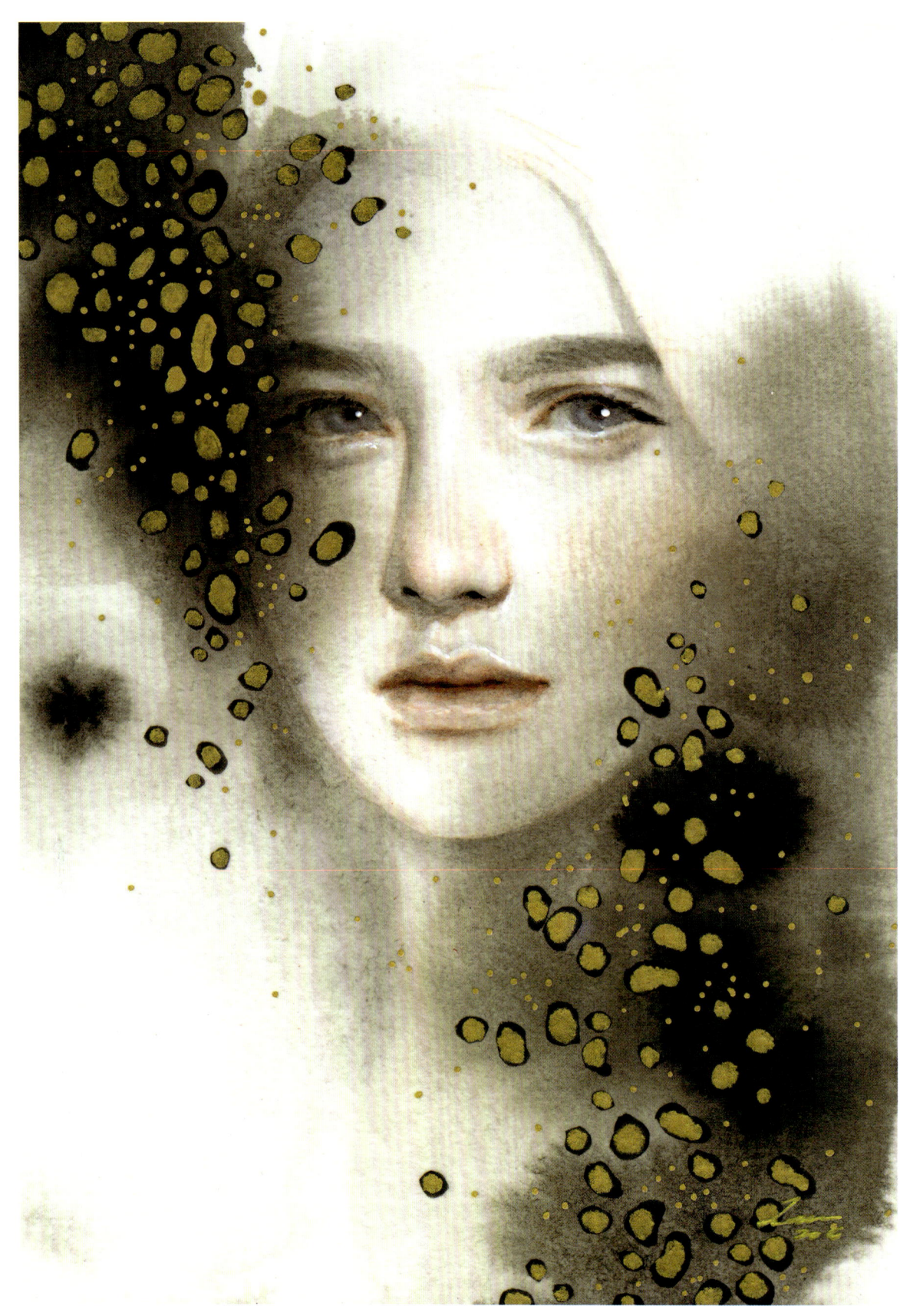

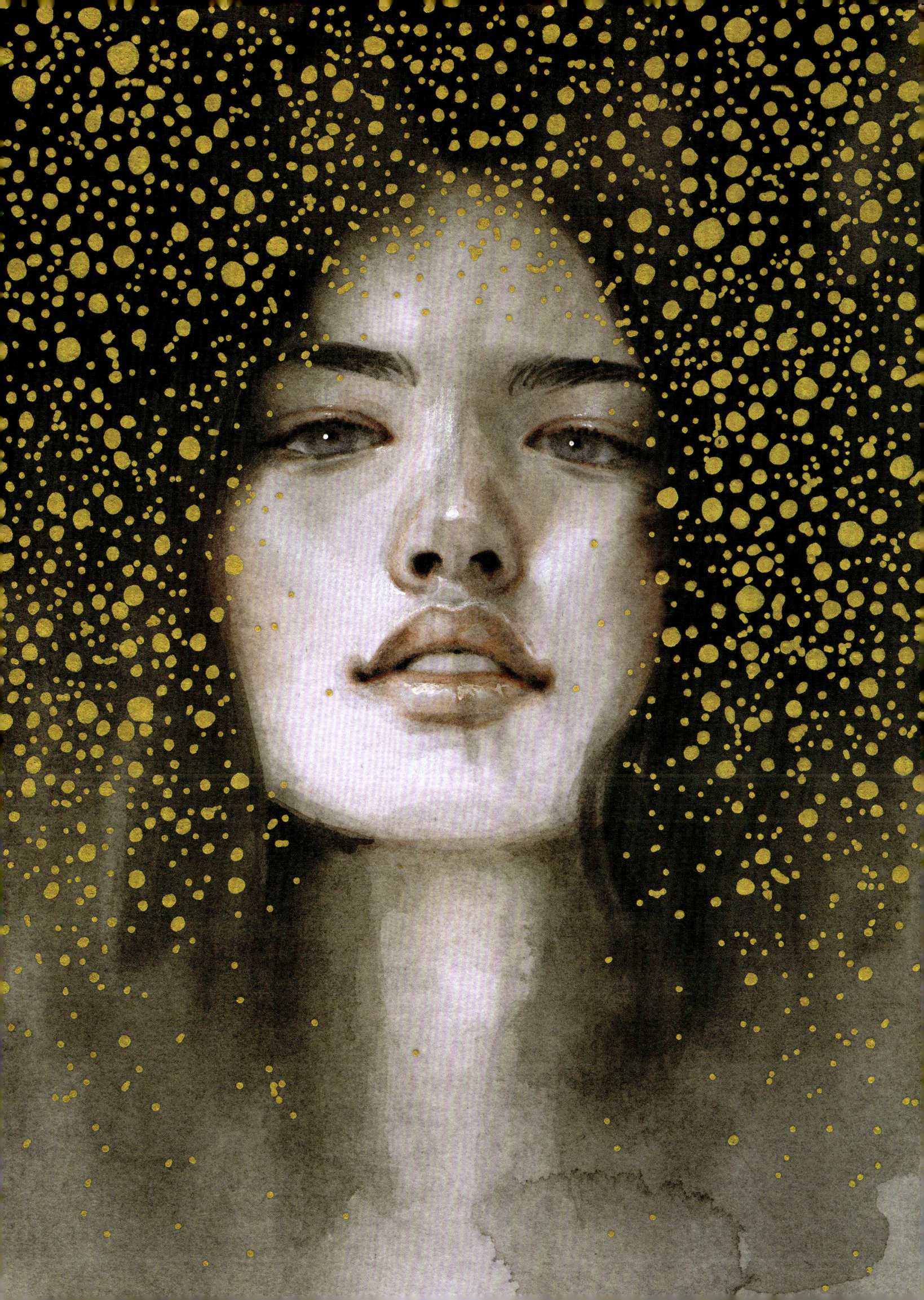

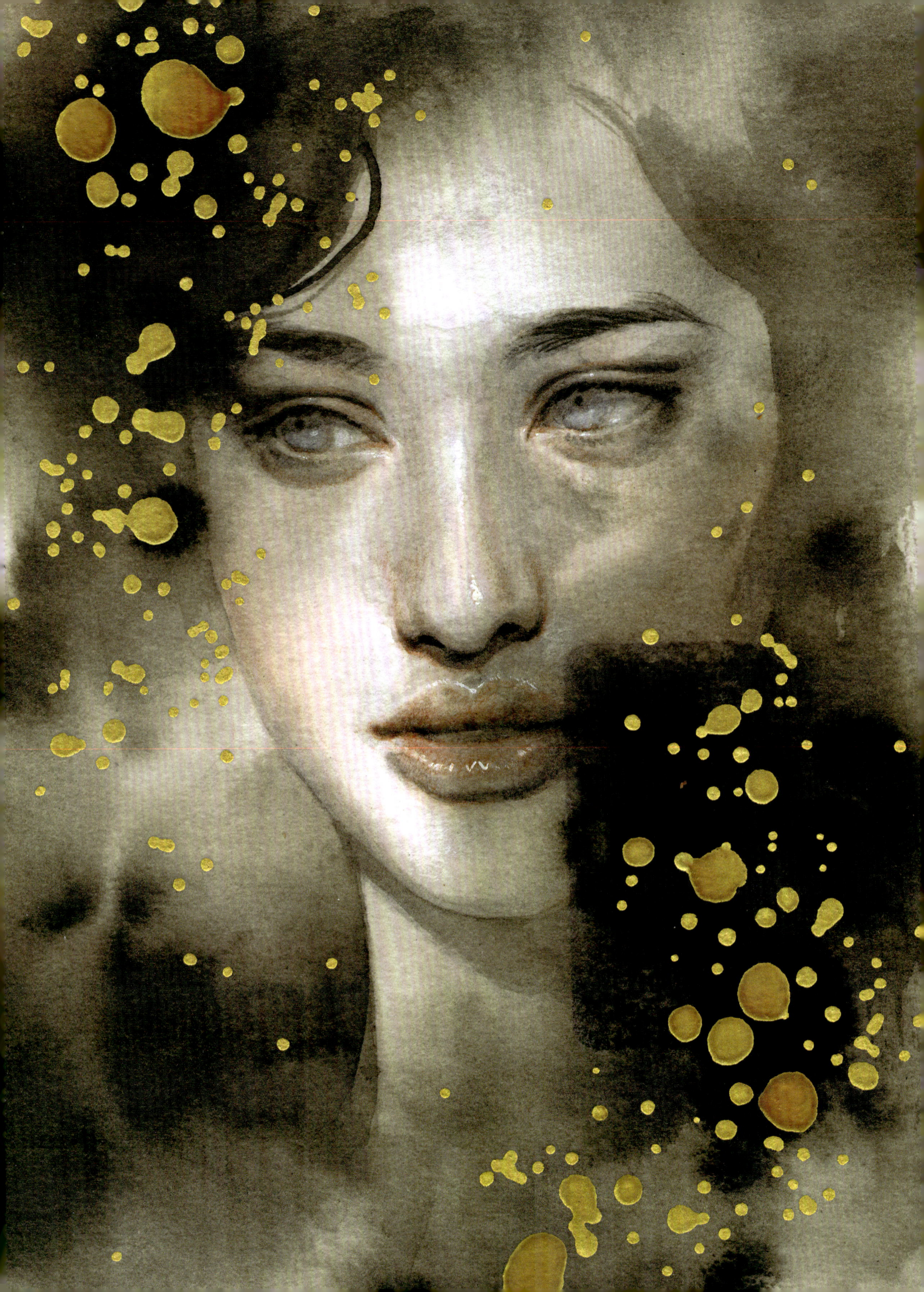

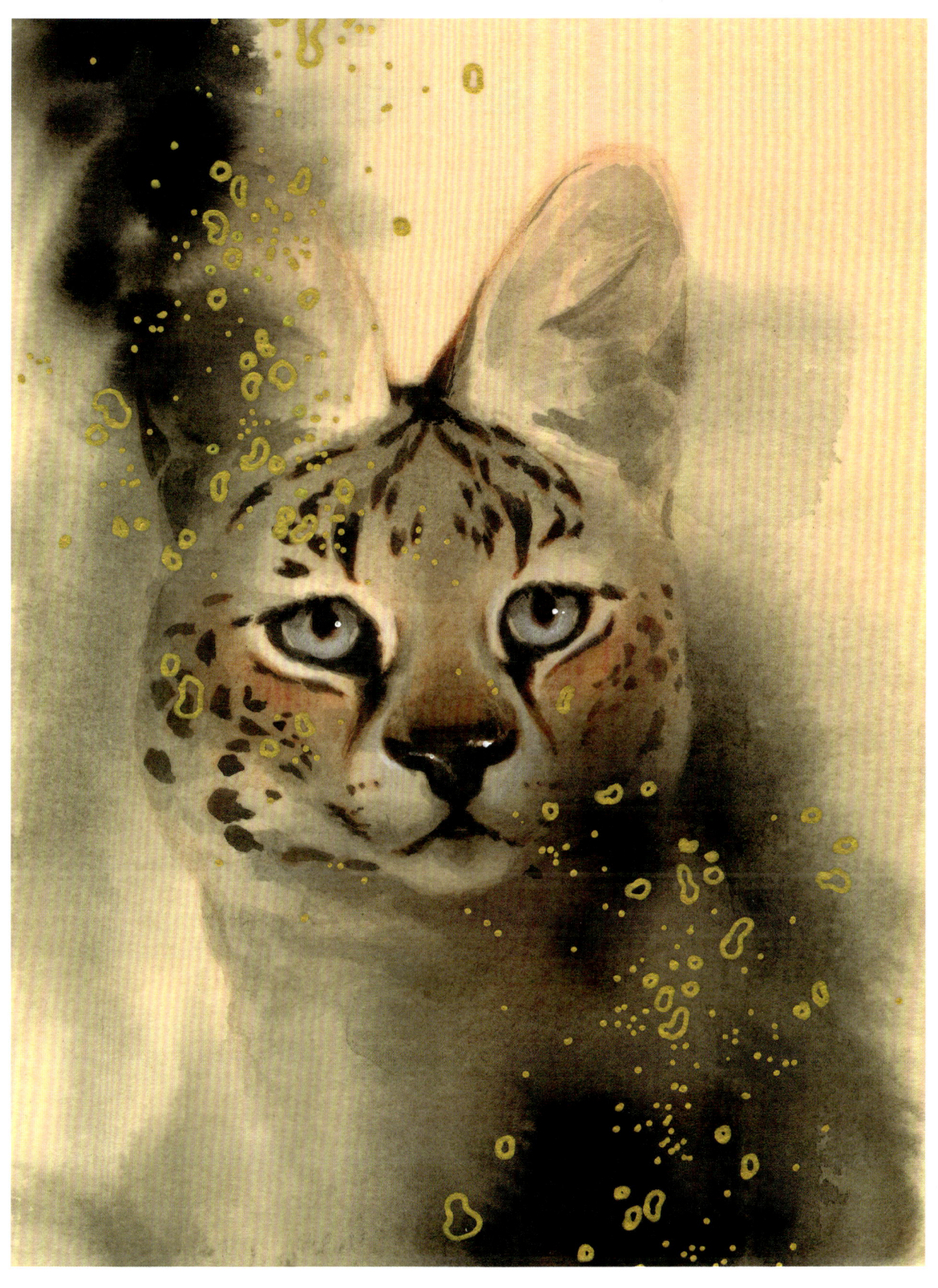

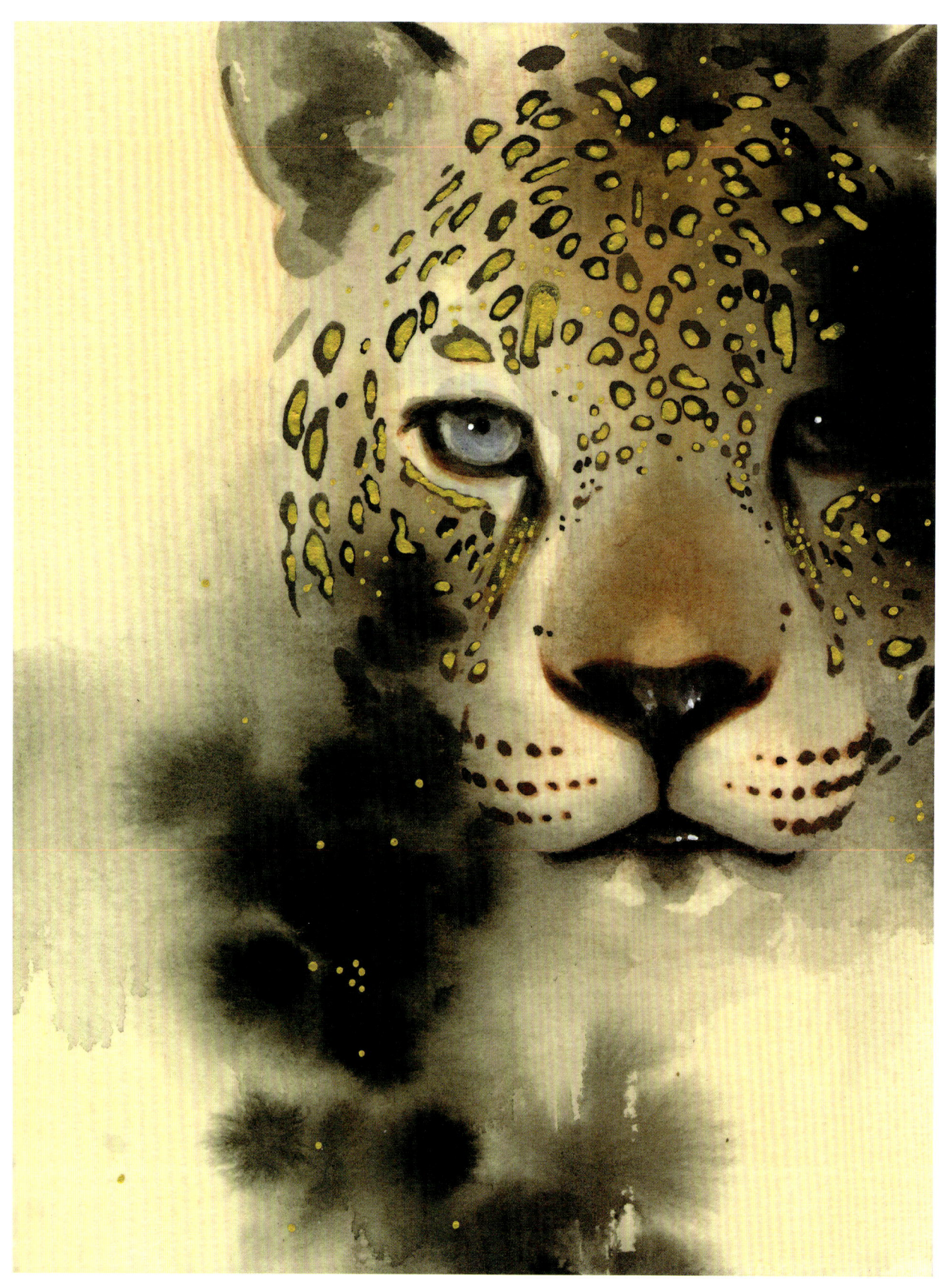

above
STUDY NO. 47
acrylic & colored pencil, 5" x 7", 2016

right
STUDY NO. 48
acrylic & colored pencil, 5" x 7", 2016

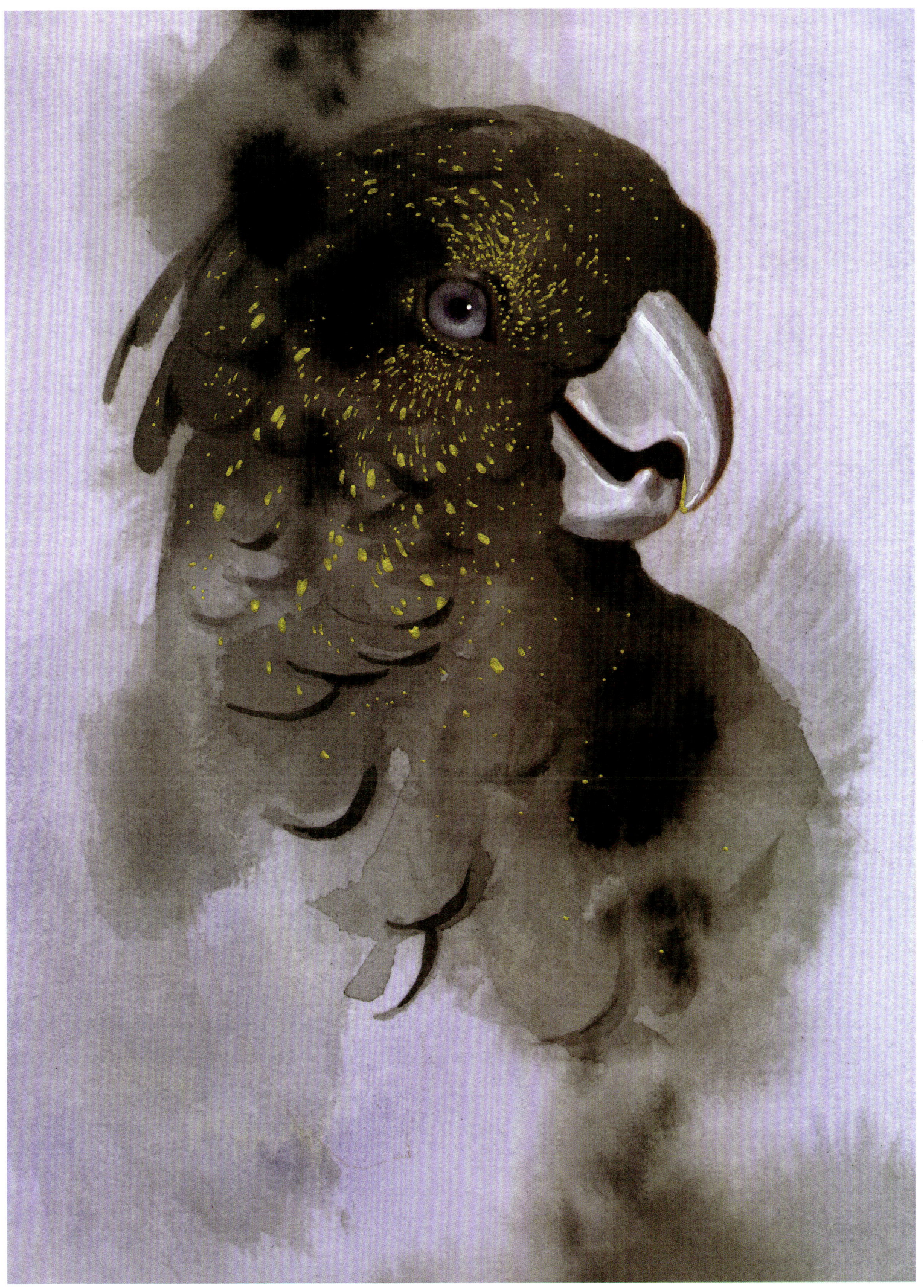

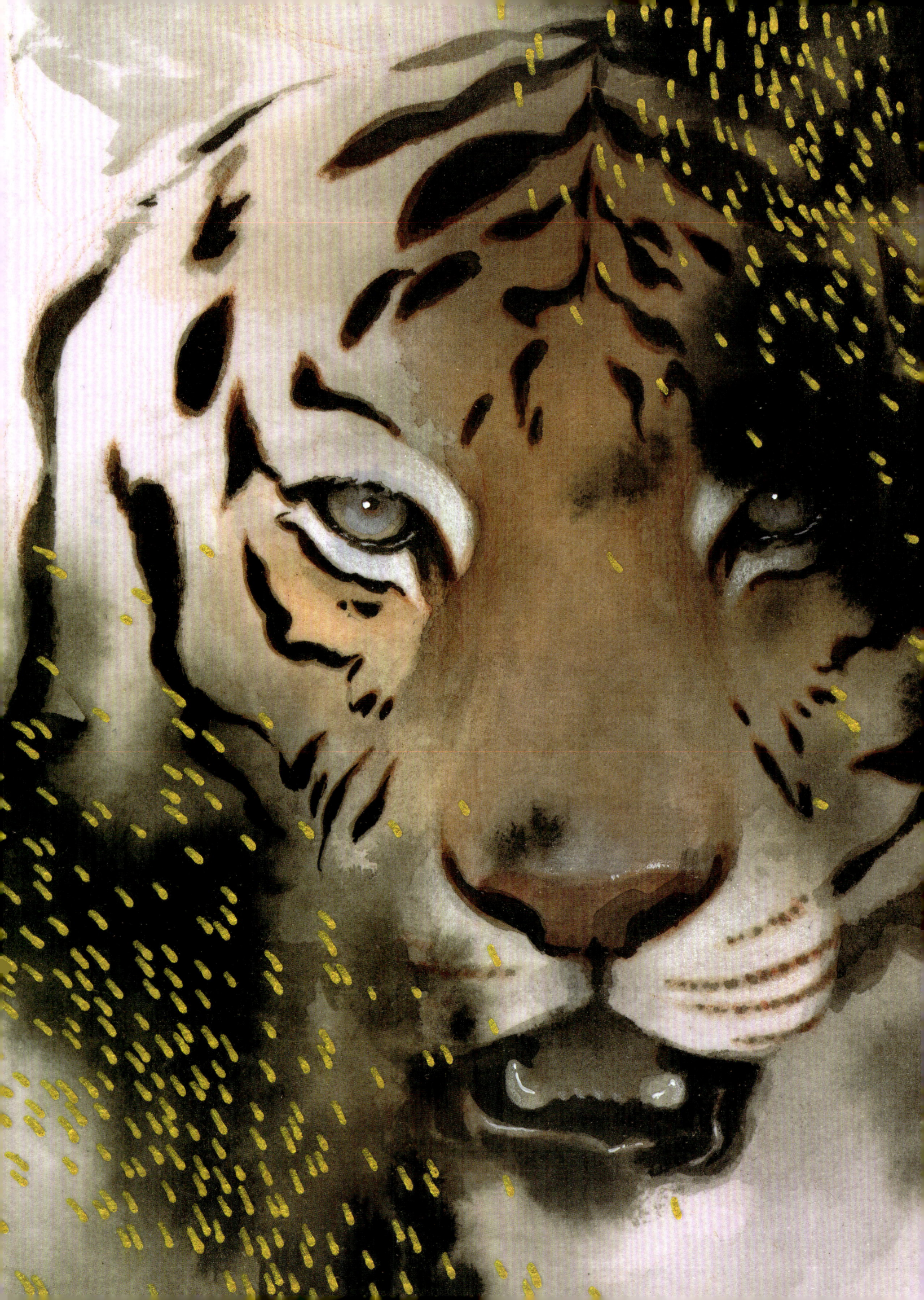

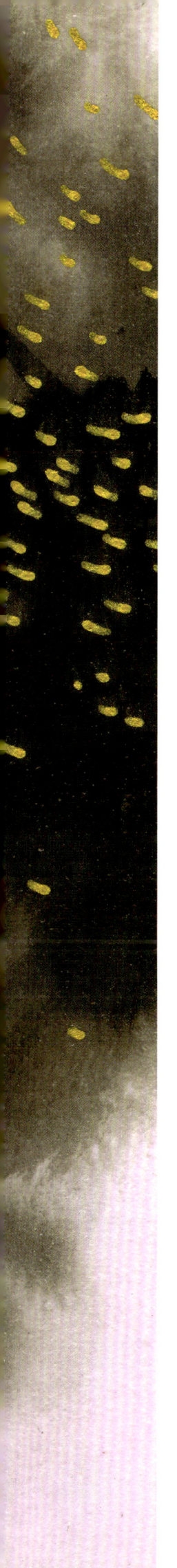

STUDY NO. 49
acrylic & colored pencil, 5" × 7", 2016

35

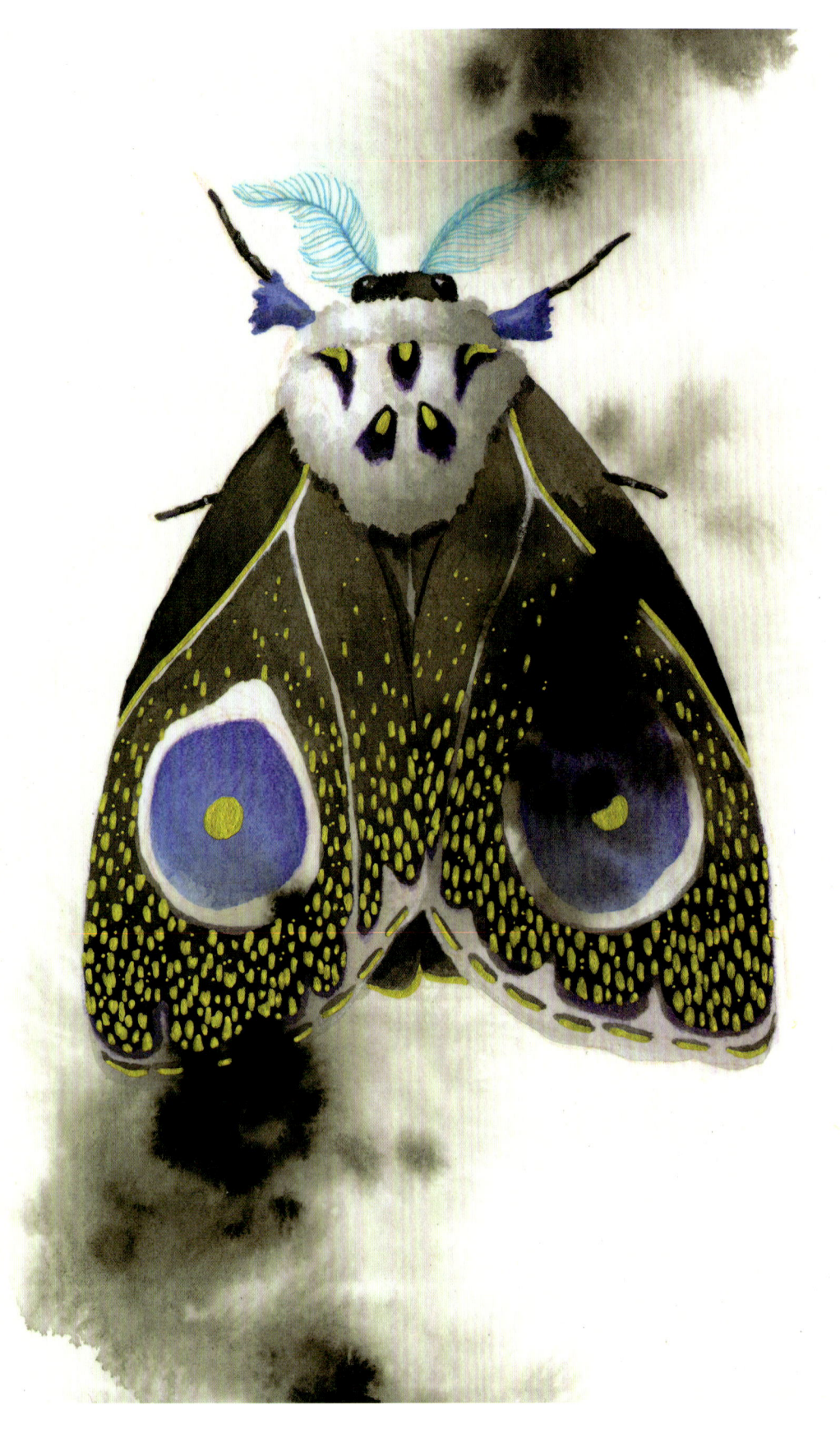

above
STUDY NO. 50
acrylic & colored pencil, 5″ × 7″, 2016

right
STUDY NO. 51
acrylic & colored pencil, 5″ × 7″, 2016

36

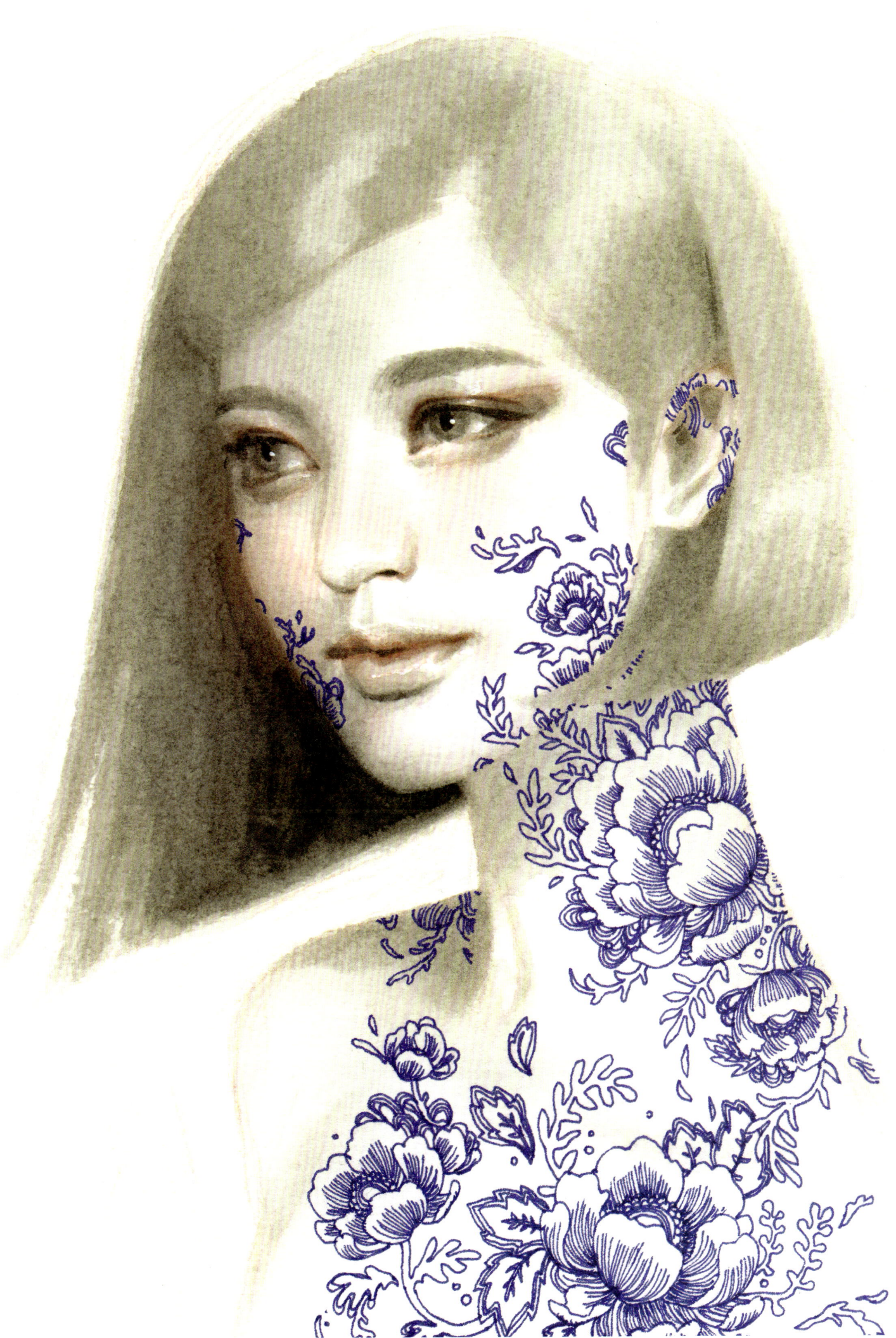

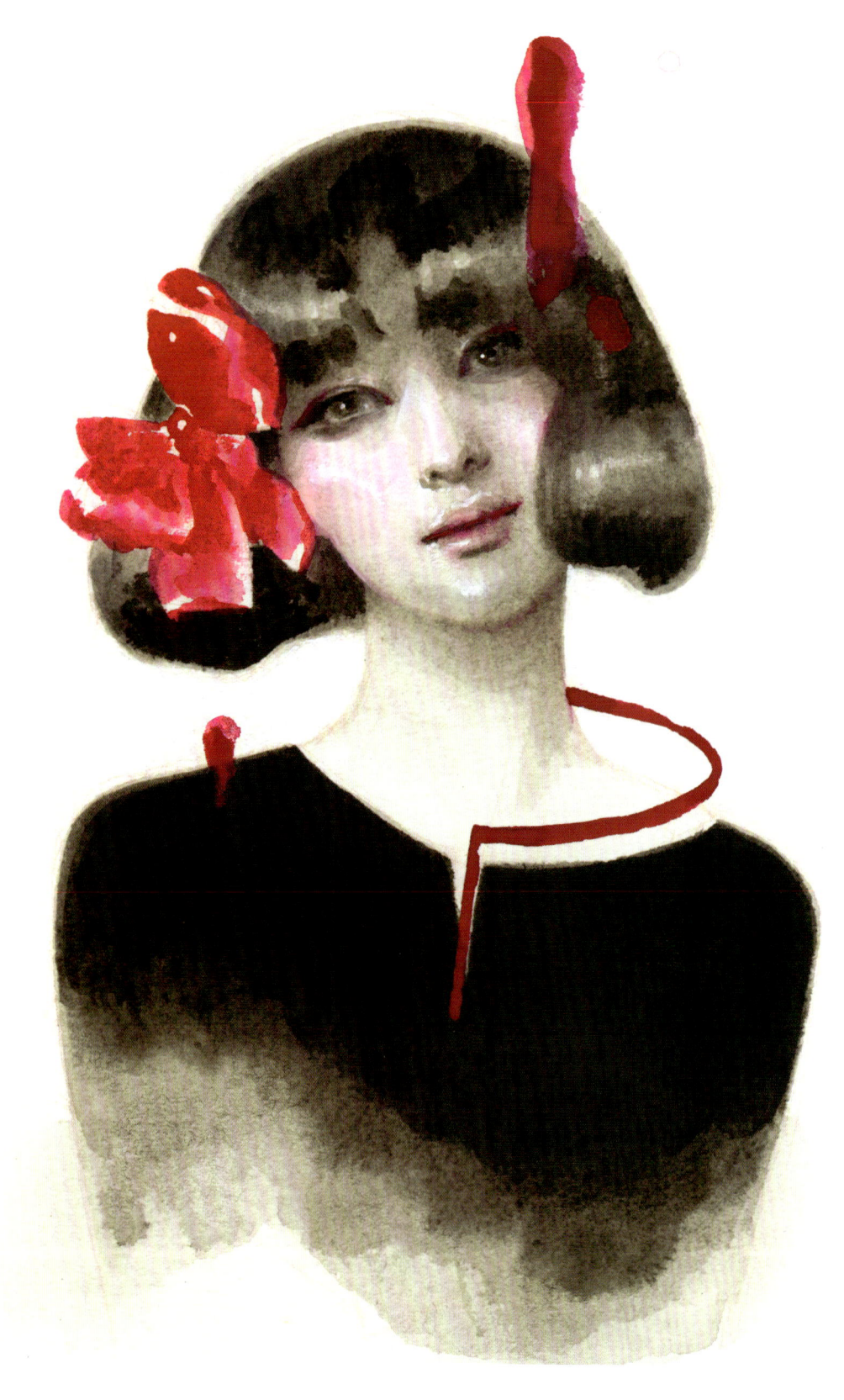

STUDY NO. 53
ink & gouache, 5.5" x 8.5", 2017

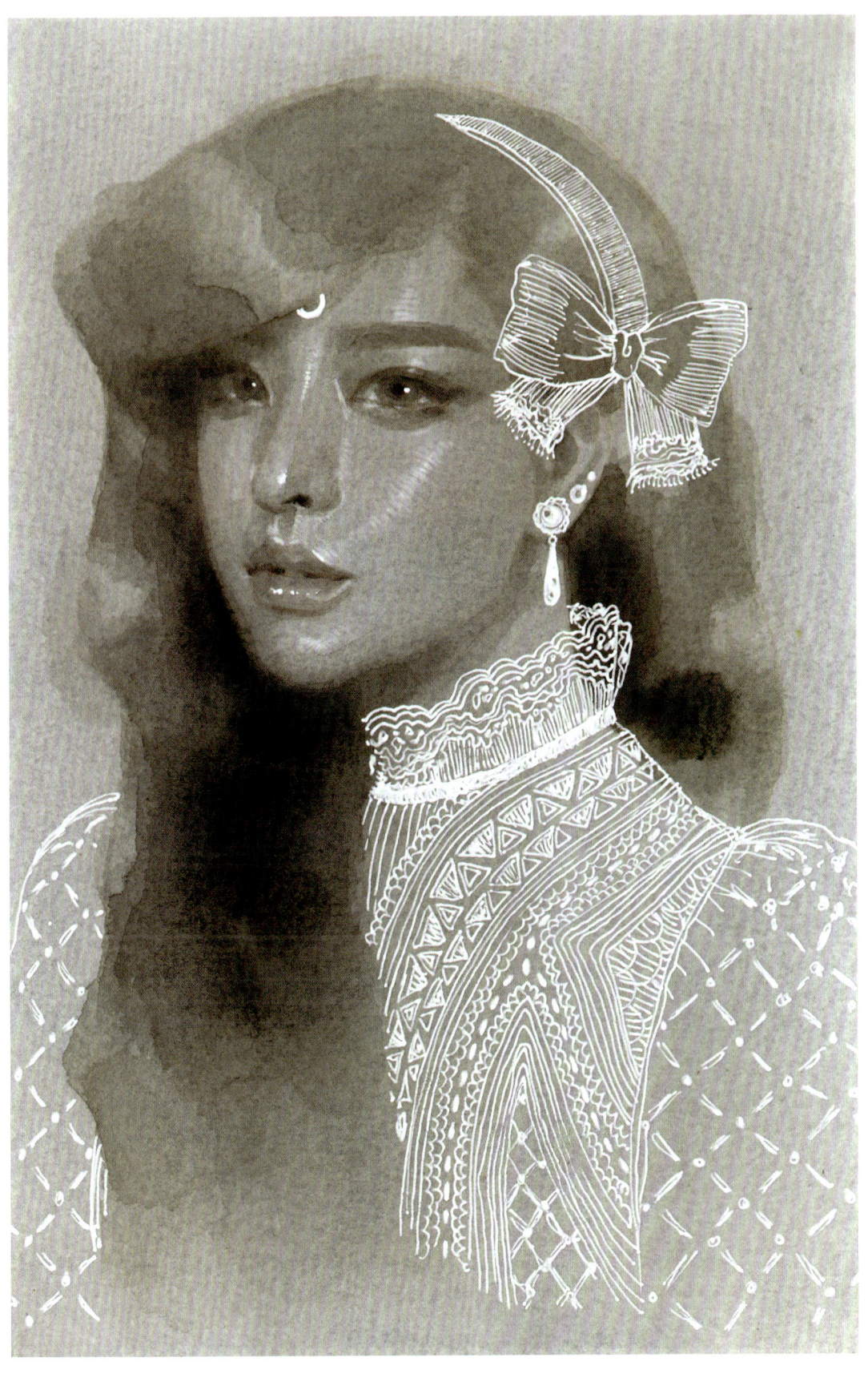

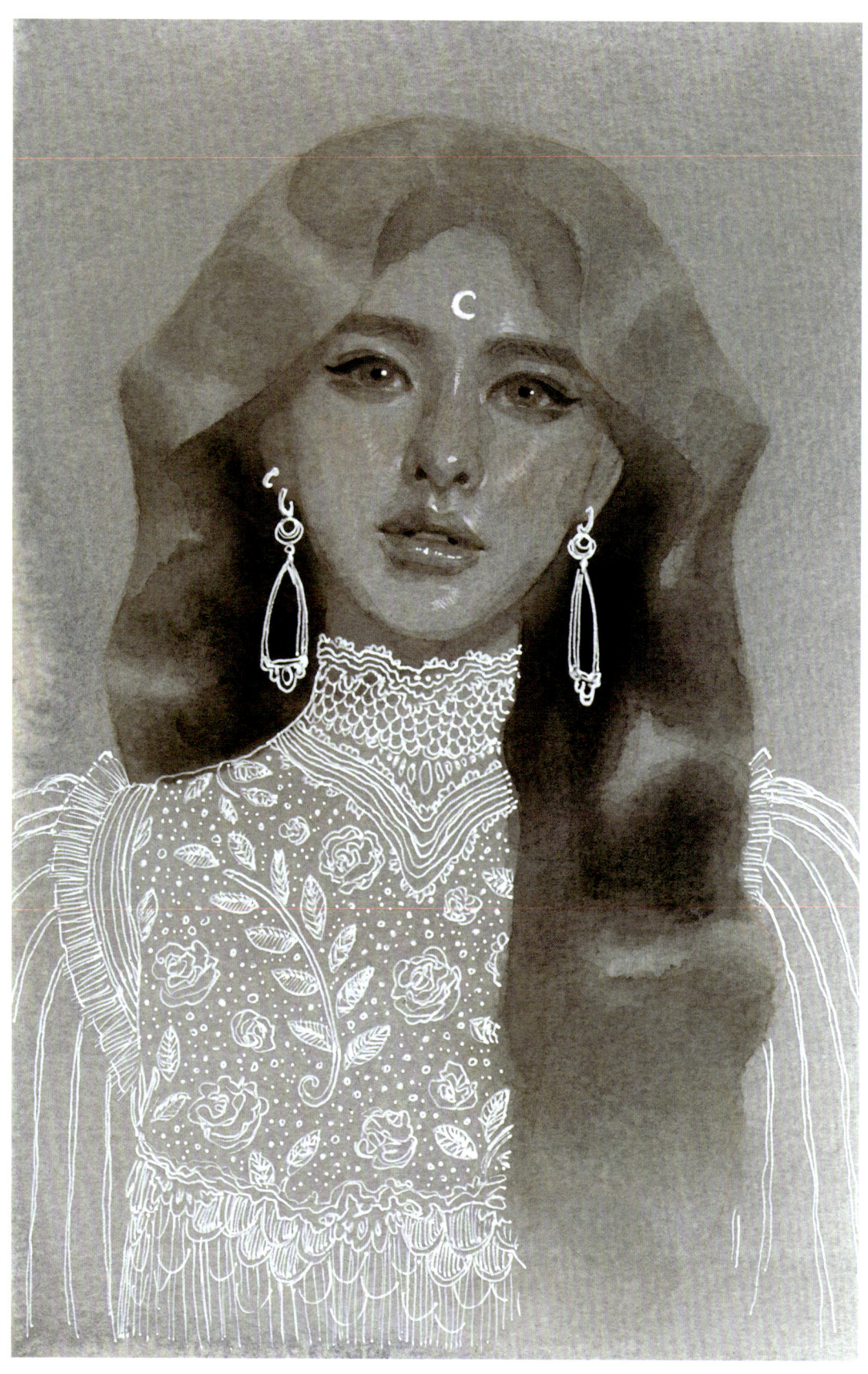

above
STUDY NO. 55
ink & colored pencil, 5.5" x 8.5", 2017

right
STUDY NO. 56
ink & colored pencil, 5.5" x 8.5", 2017

40

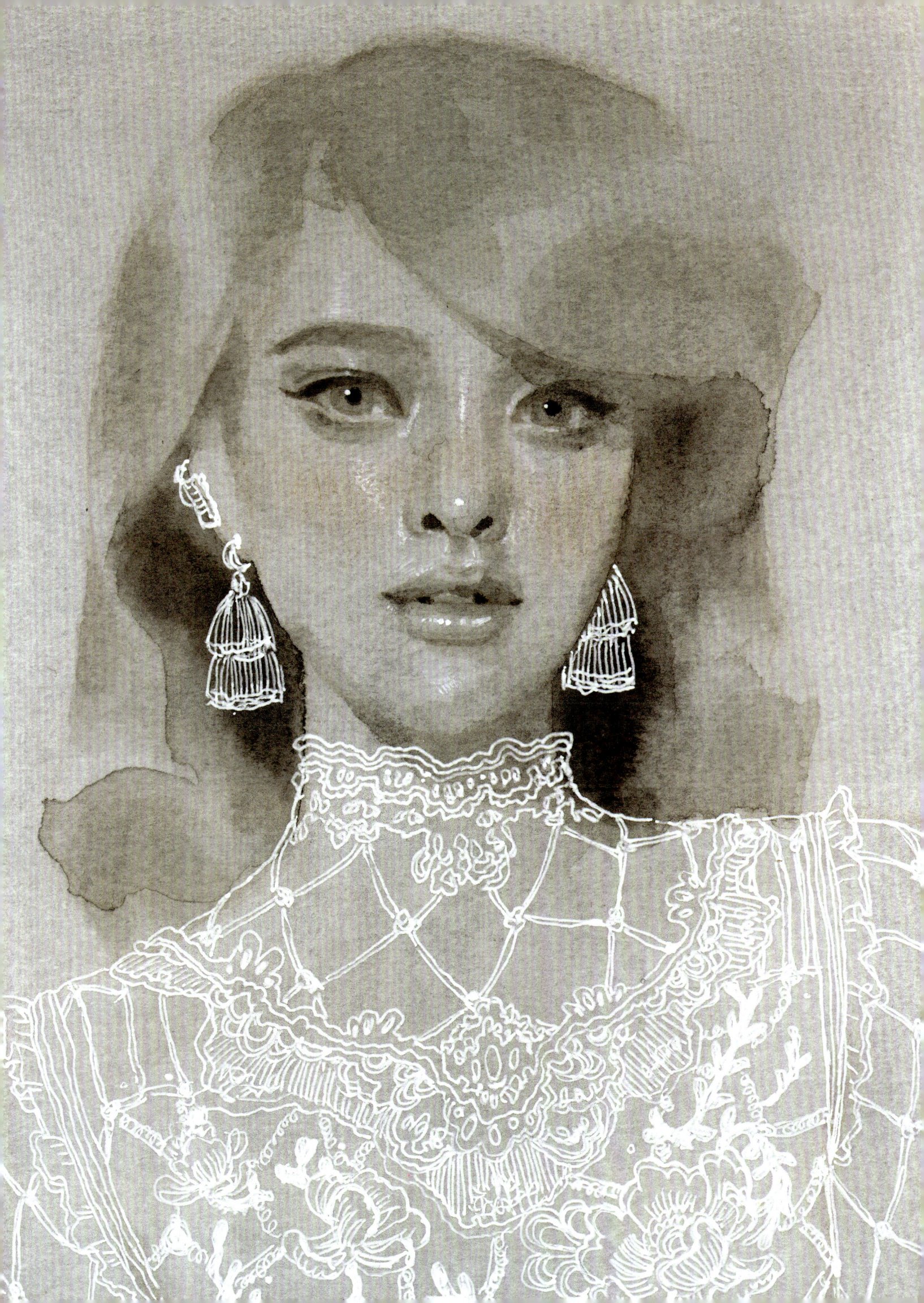

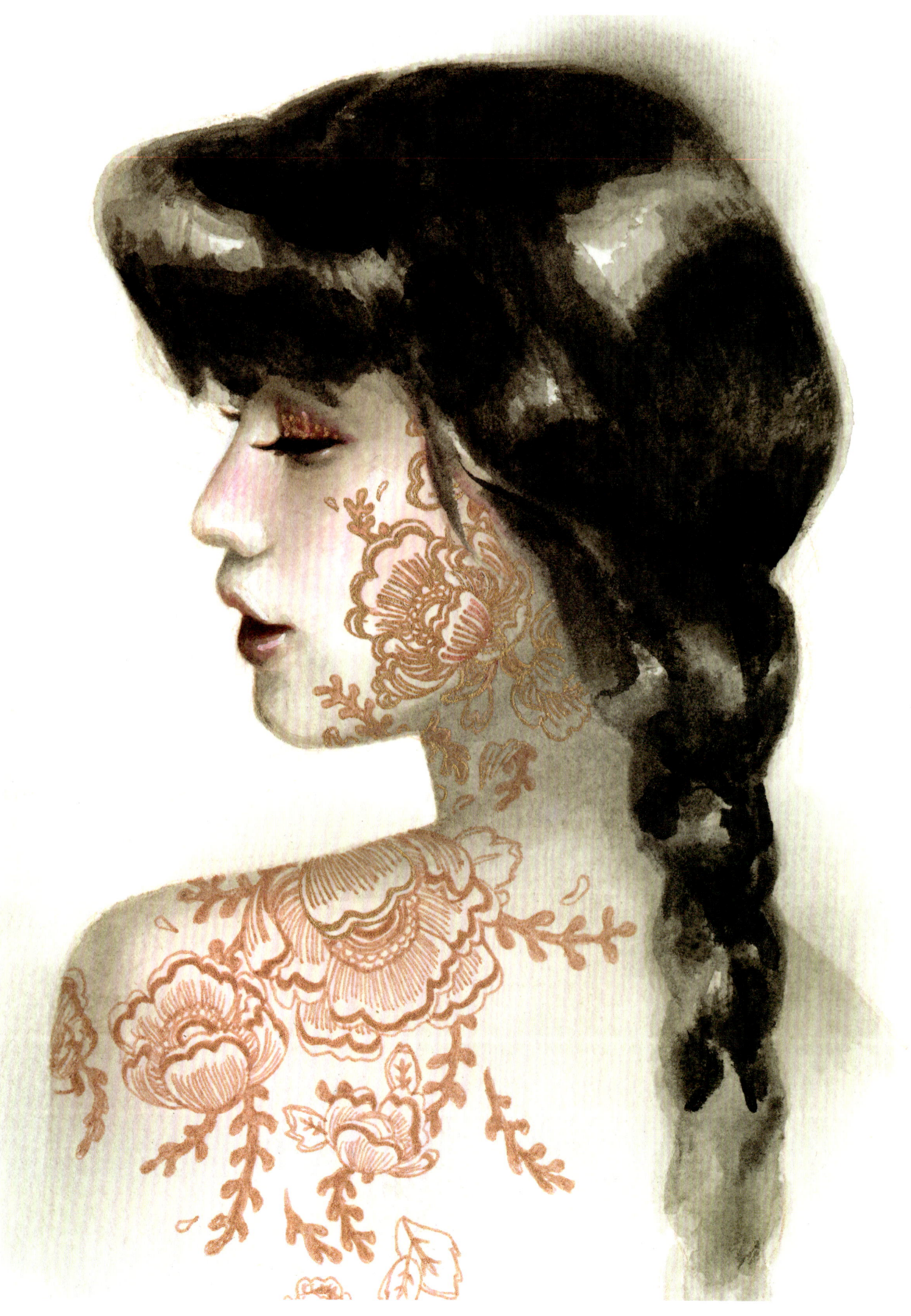

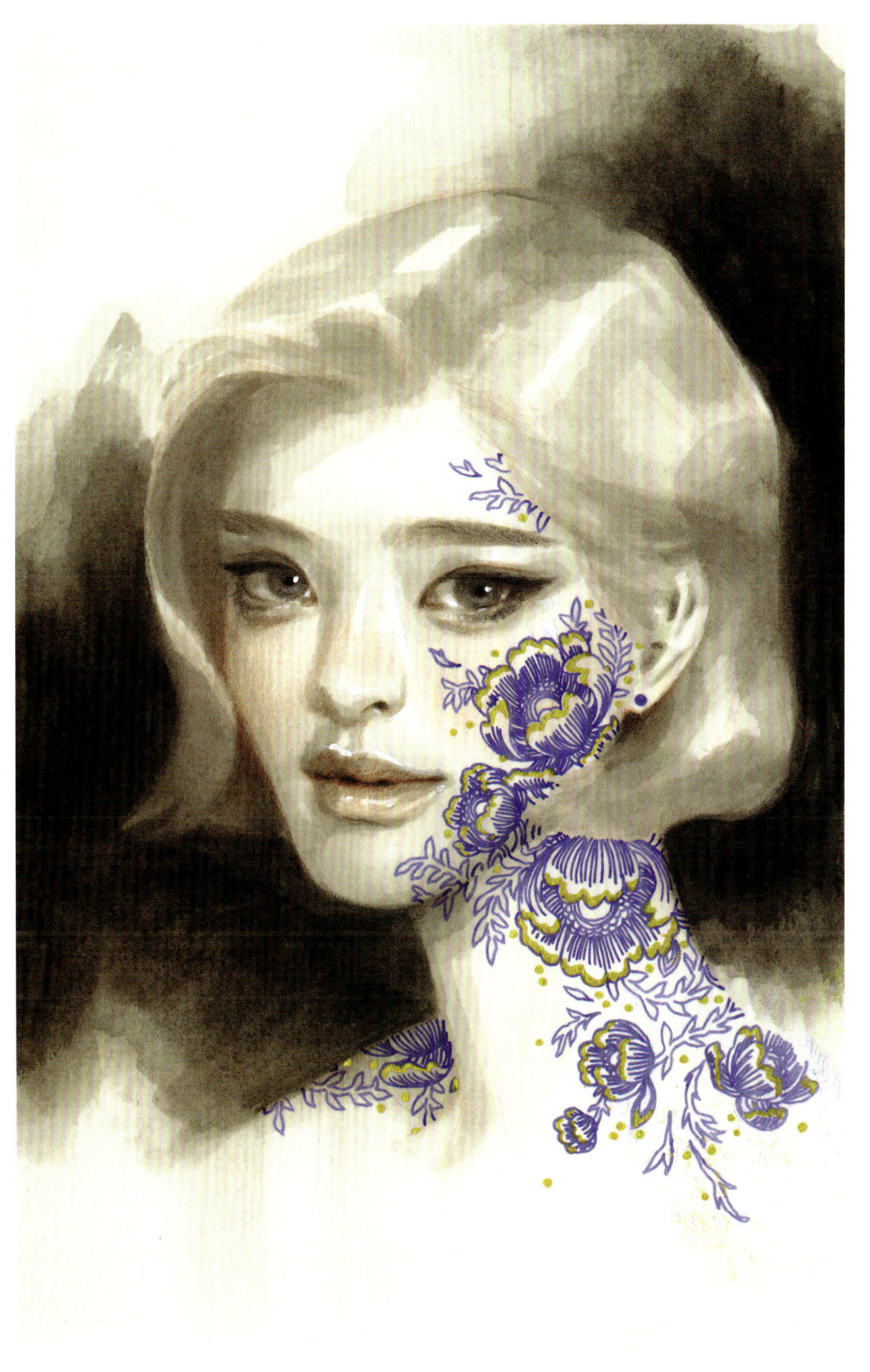

left
STUDY NO. 57
ink & colored pencil, 5.5" x 8.5", 2017

above
STUDY NO. 58
ink & colored pencil, 5.5" x 8.5", 2017

43

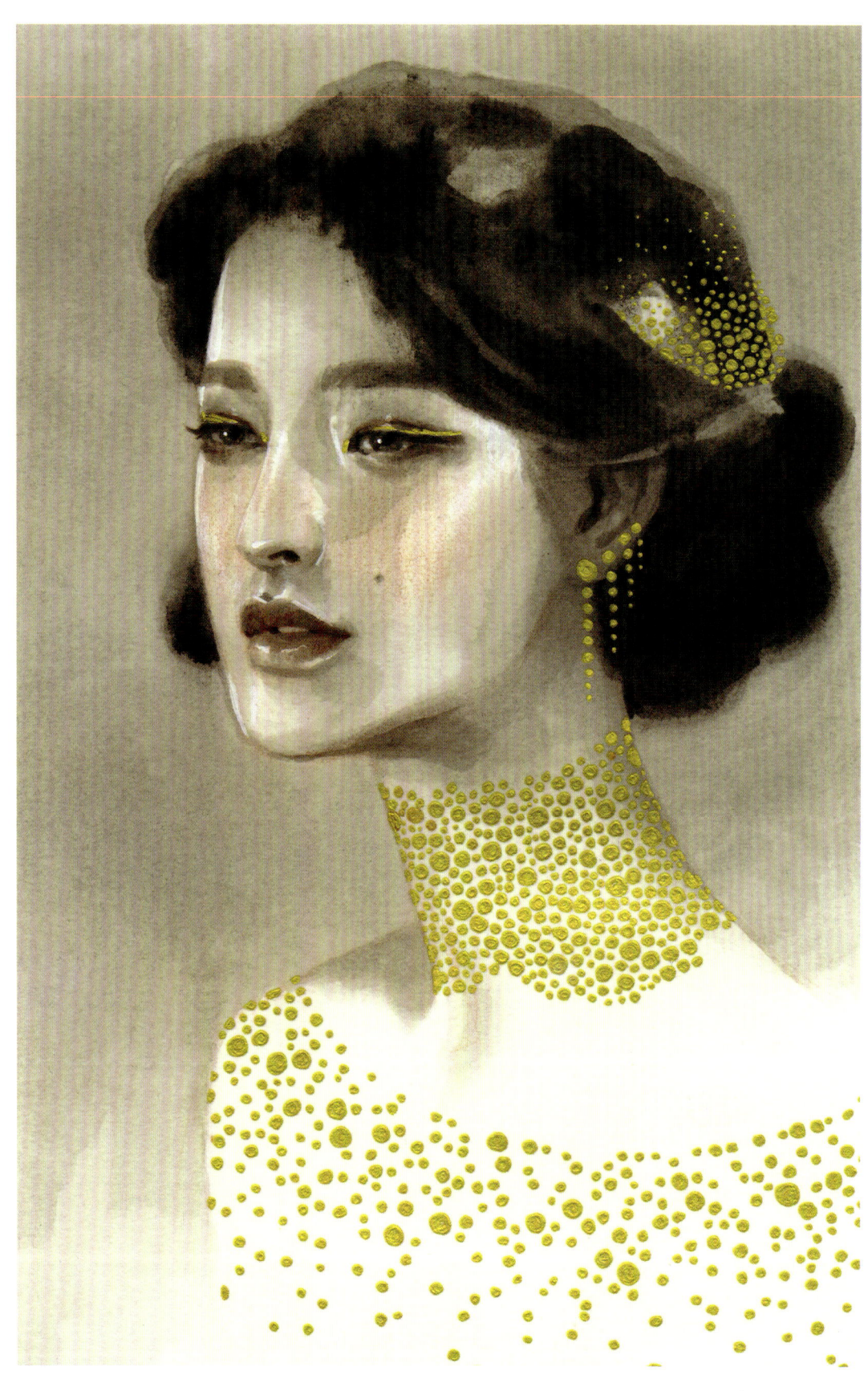

above
STUDY NO. 60
ink & colored pencil, 5.5" x 8.5", 2017

right
STUDY NO. 61
ink & colored pencil, 5.5" x 8.5", 2017

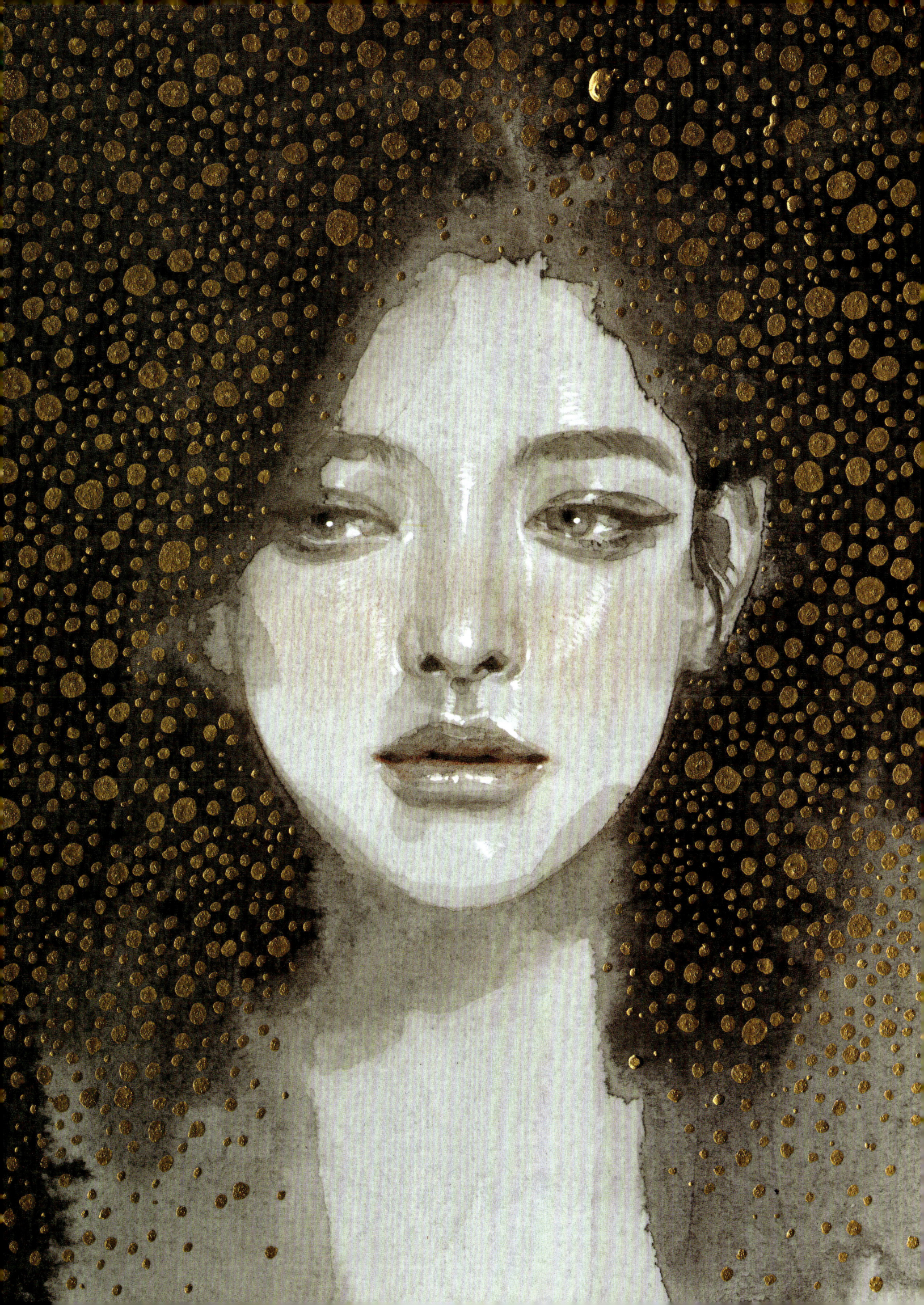

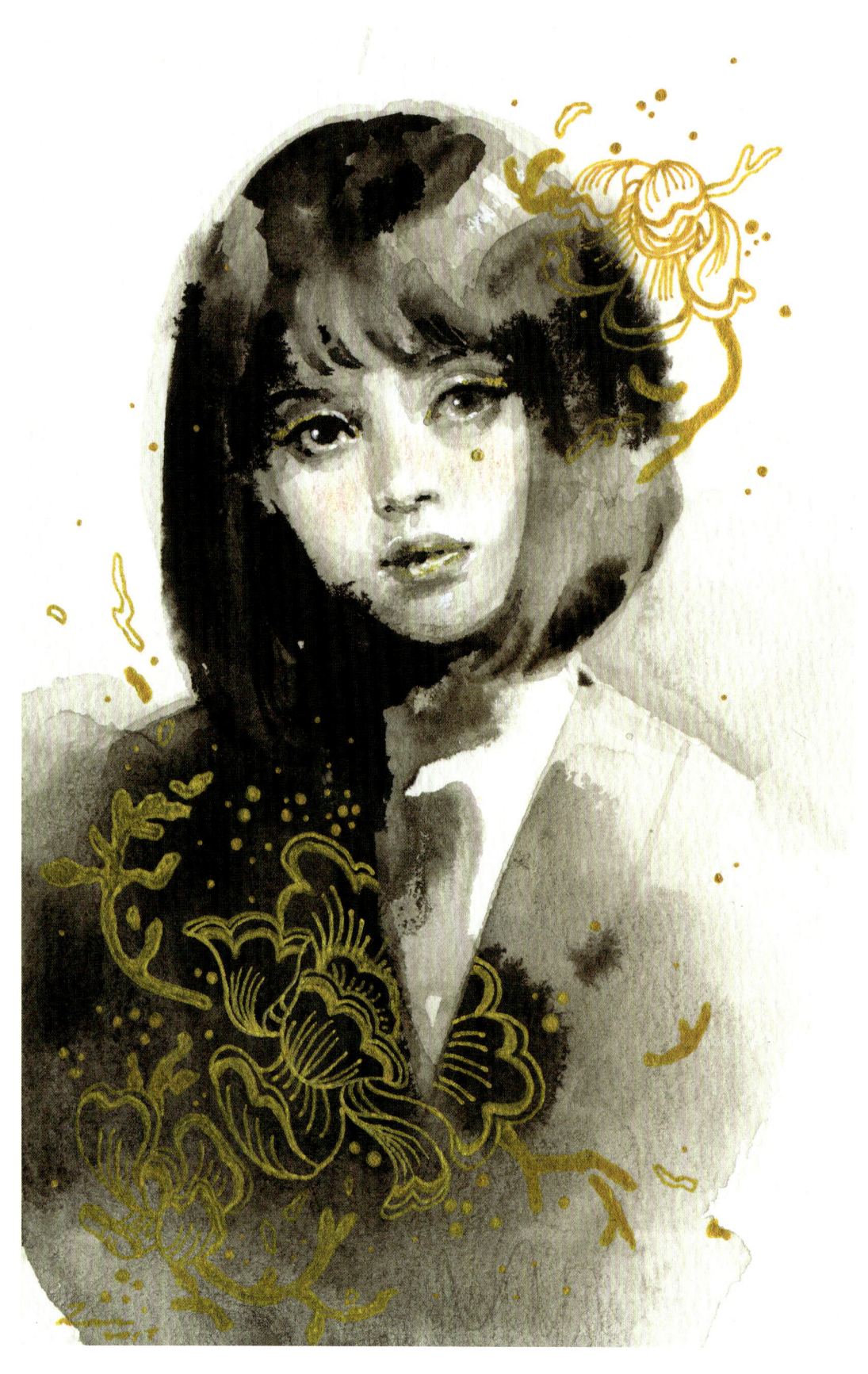

STUDY NO. 64
ink & colored pencil, 5.5" x 8.5", 2017

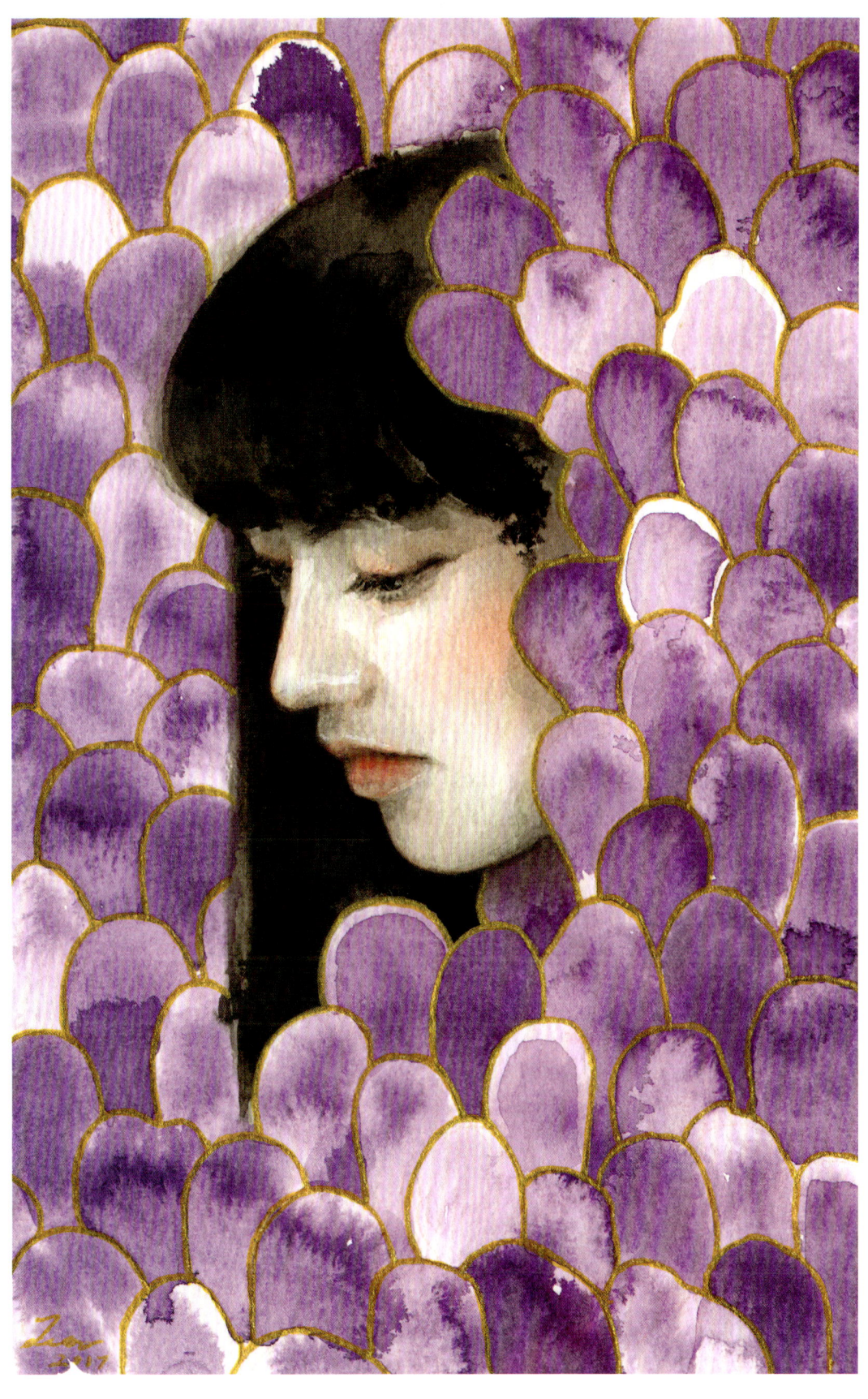

STUDY NO. 65
ink & colored pencil, 5.5″ x 8.5″, 2017

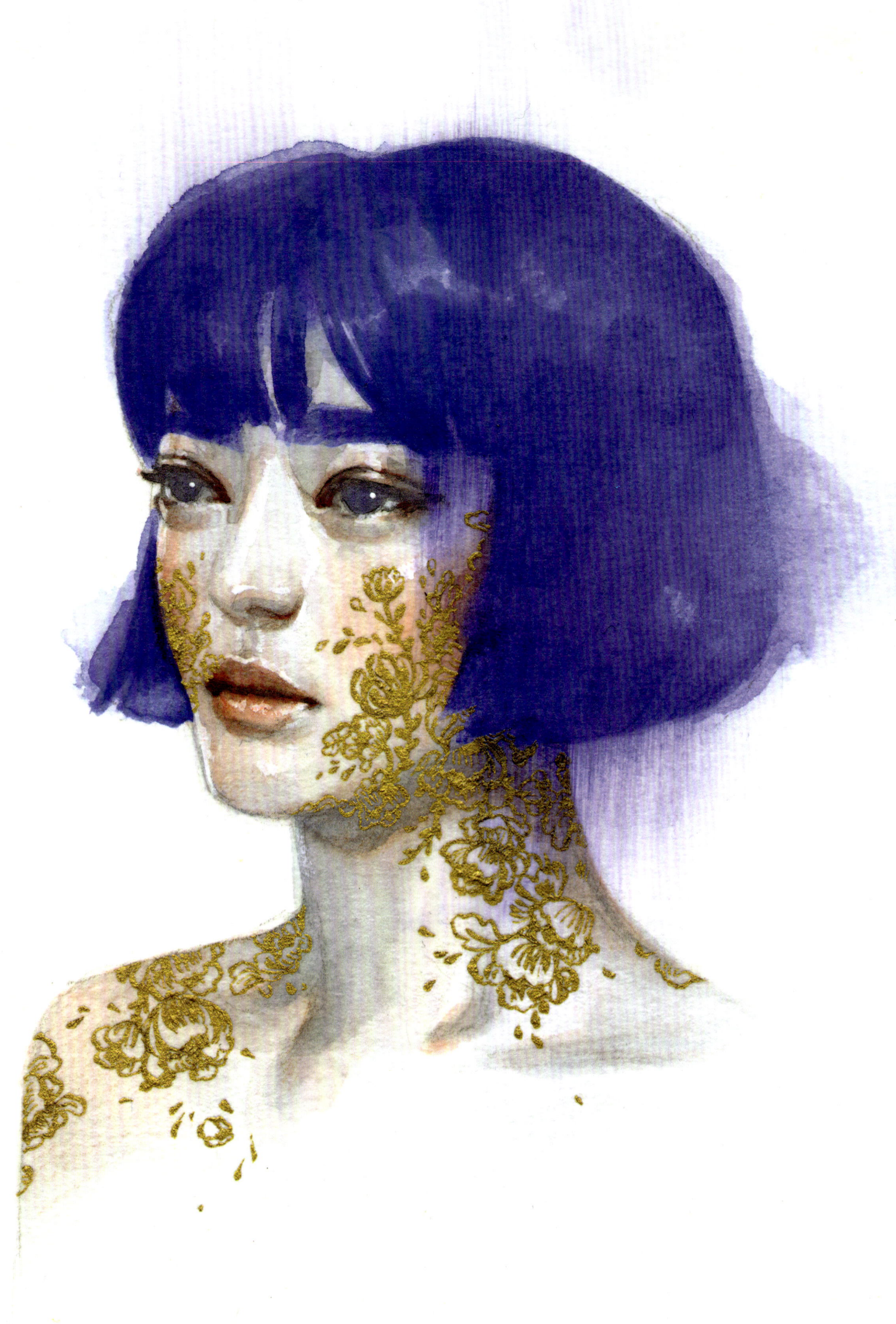

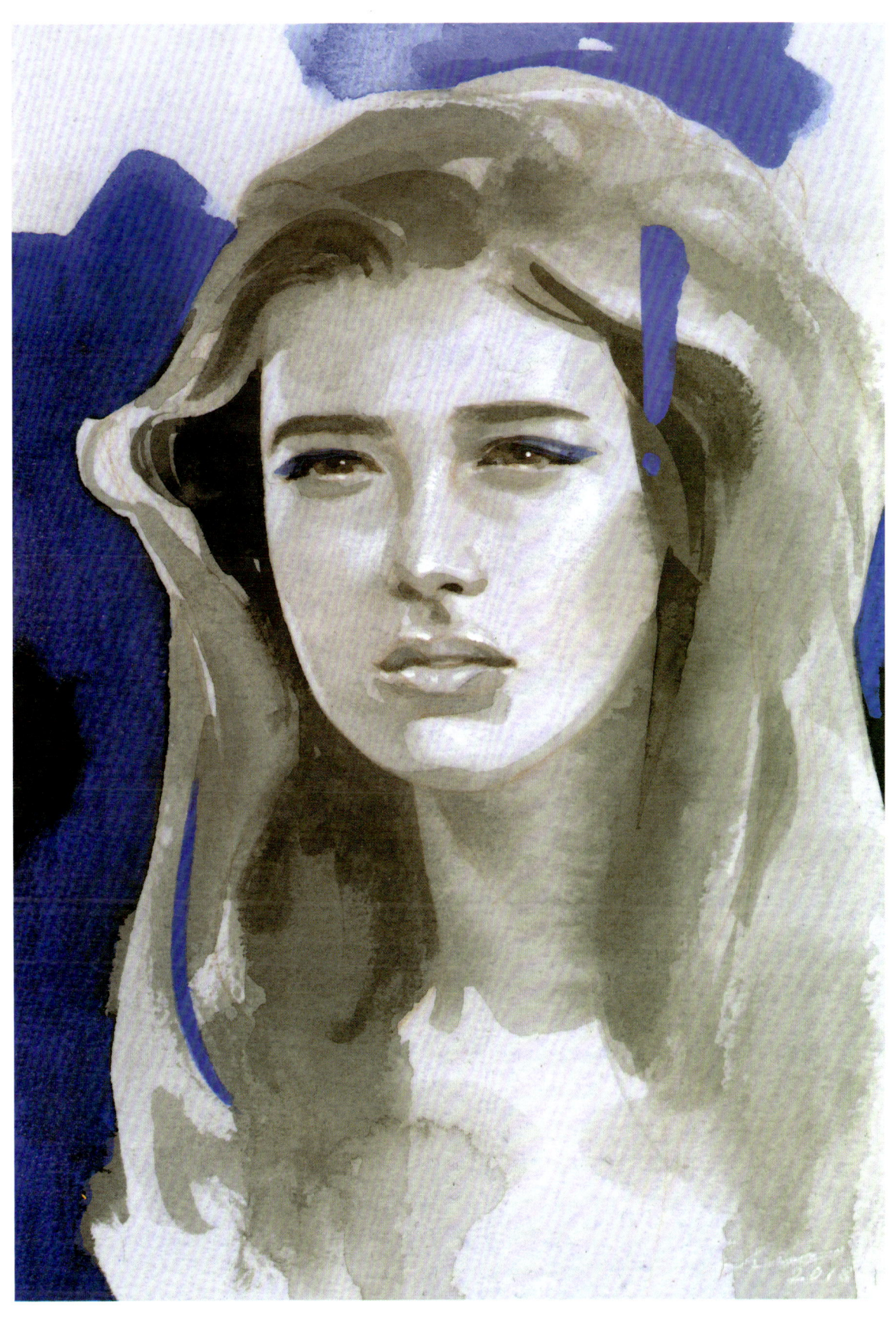

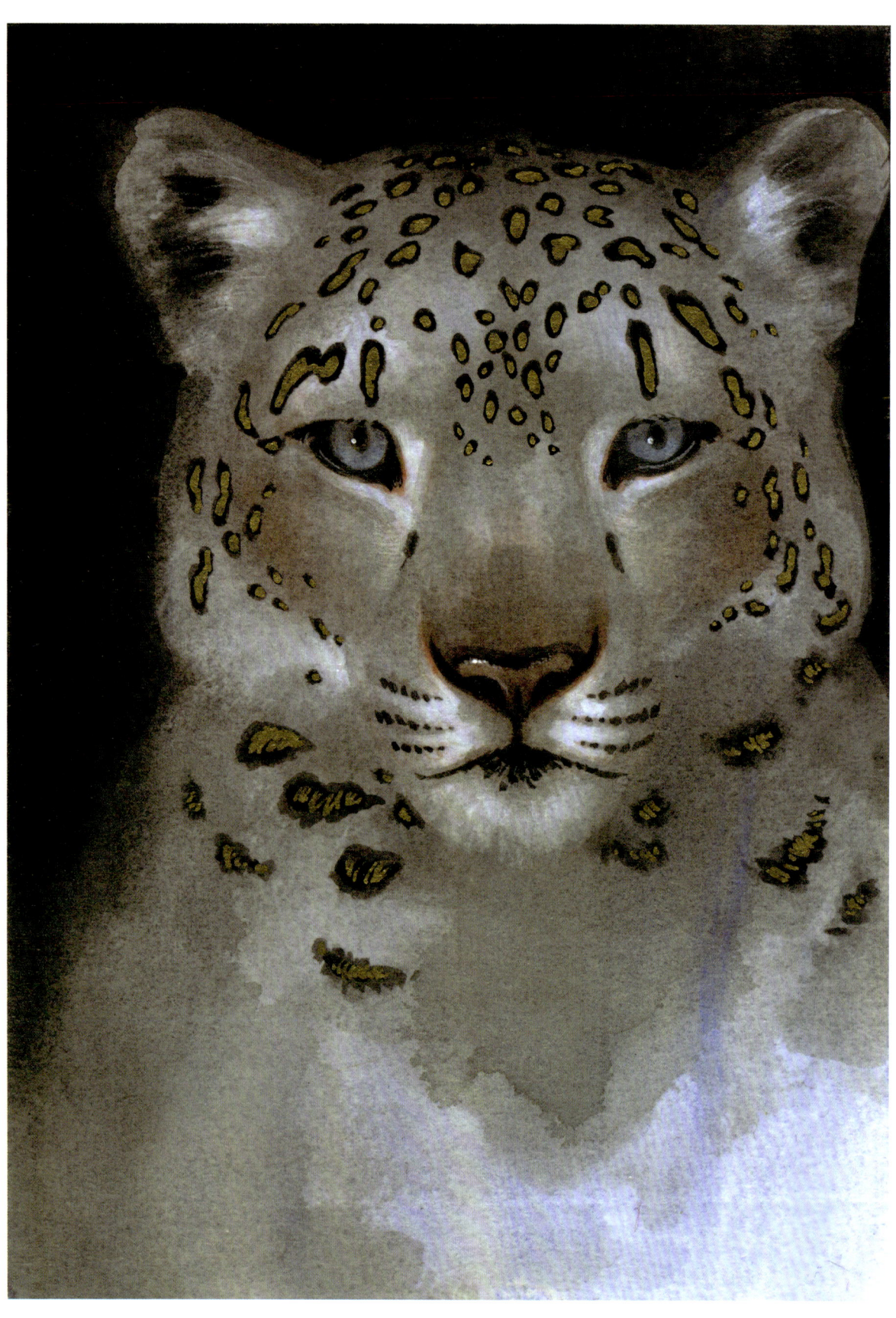

above
STUDY NO. 76
ink & colored pencil, 5" × 7", 2018

right
STUDY NO. 77
ink & colored pencil, 5" × 7", 2018

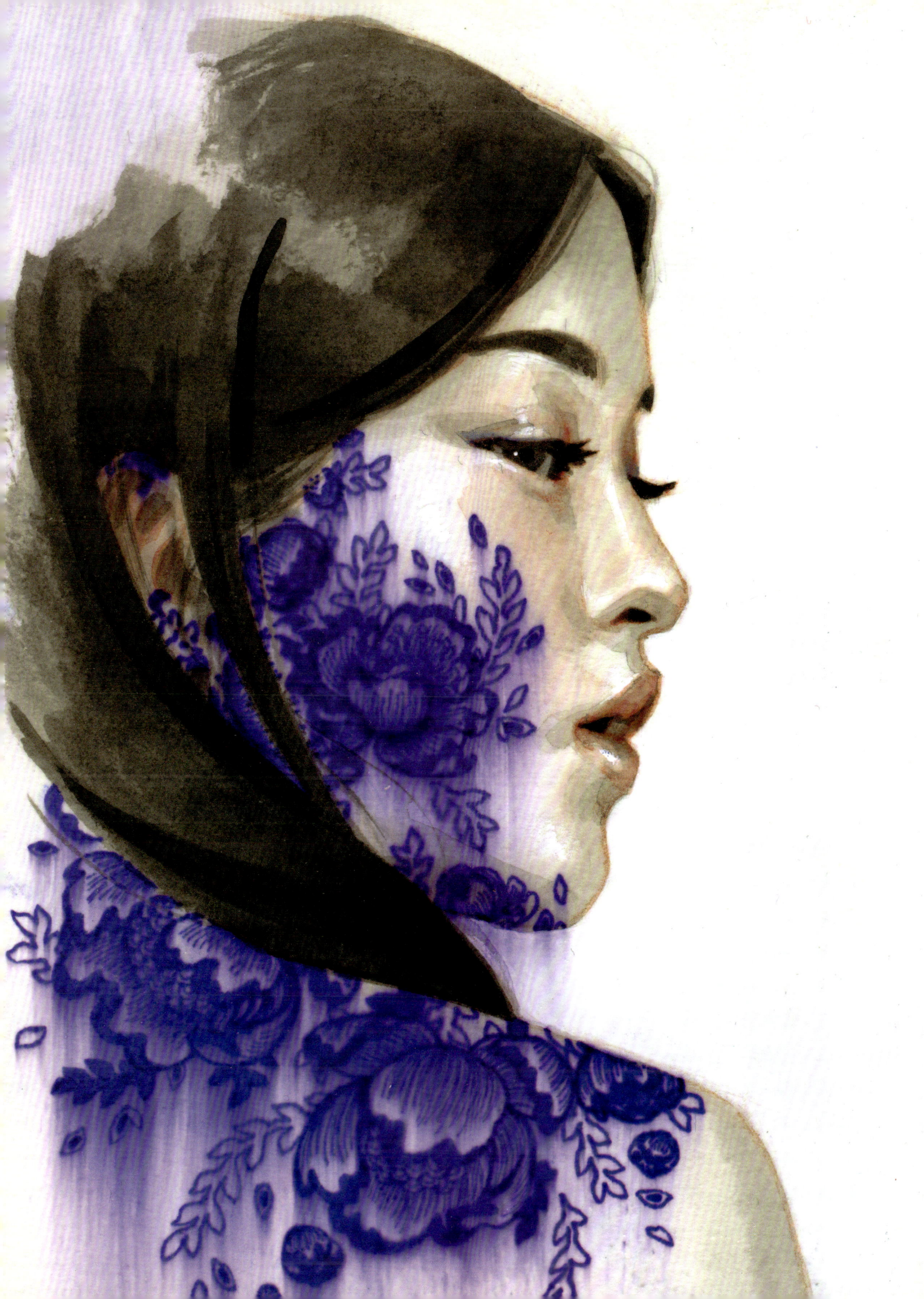

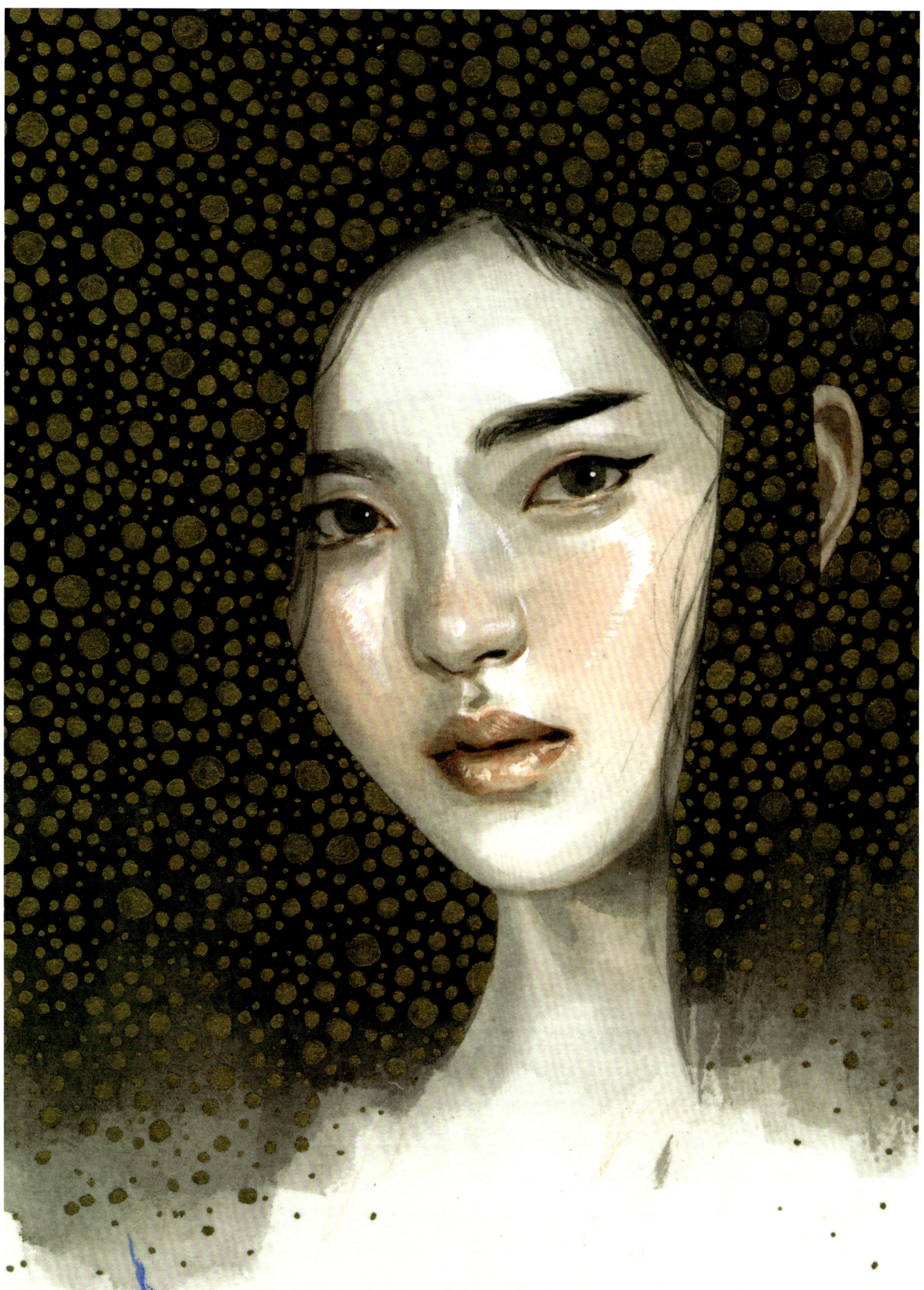

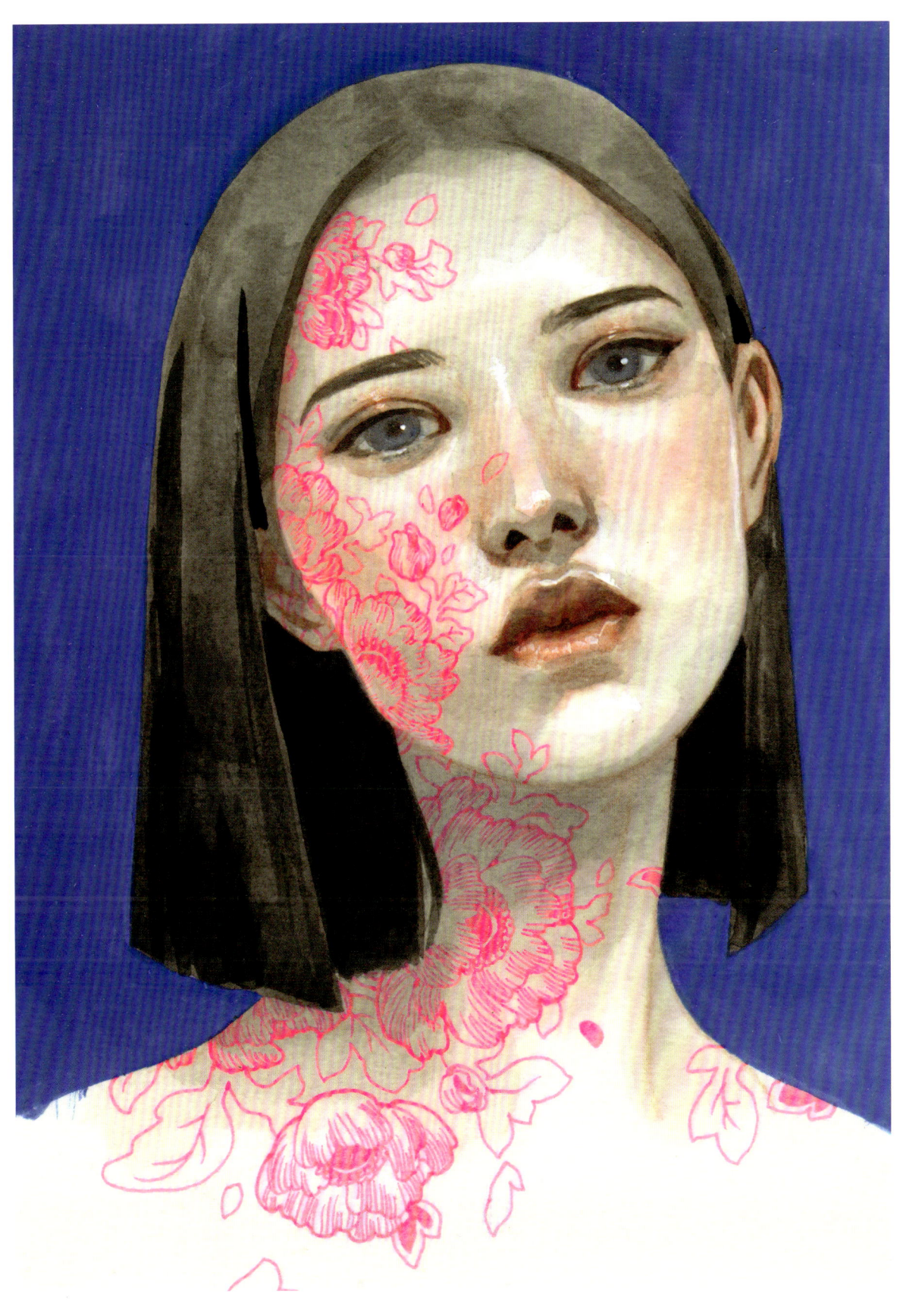

left
STUDY NO. 78
ink & colored pencil, 5" × 7", 2018

above
STUDY NO. 79
ink & acrylic, 5" × 7", 2018

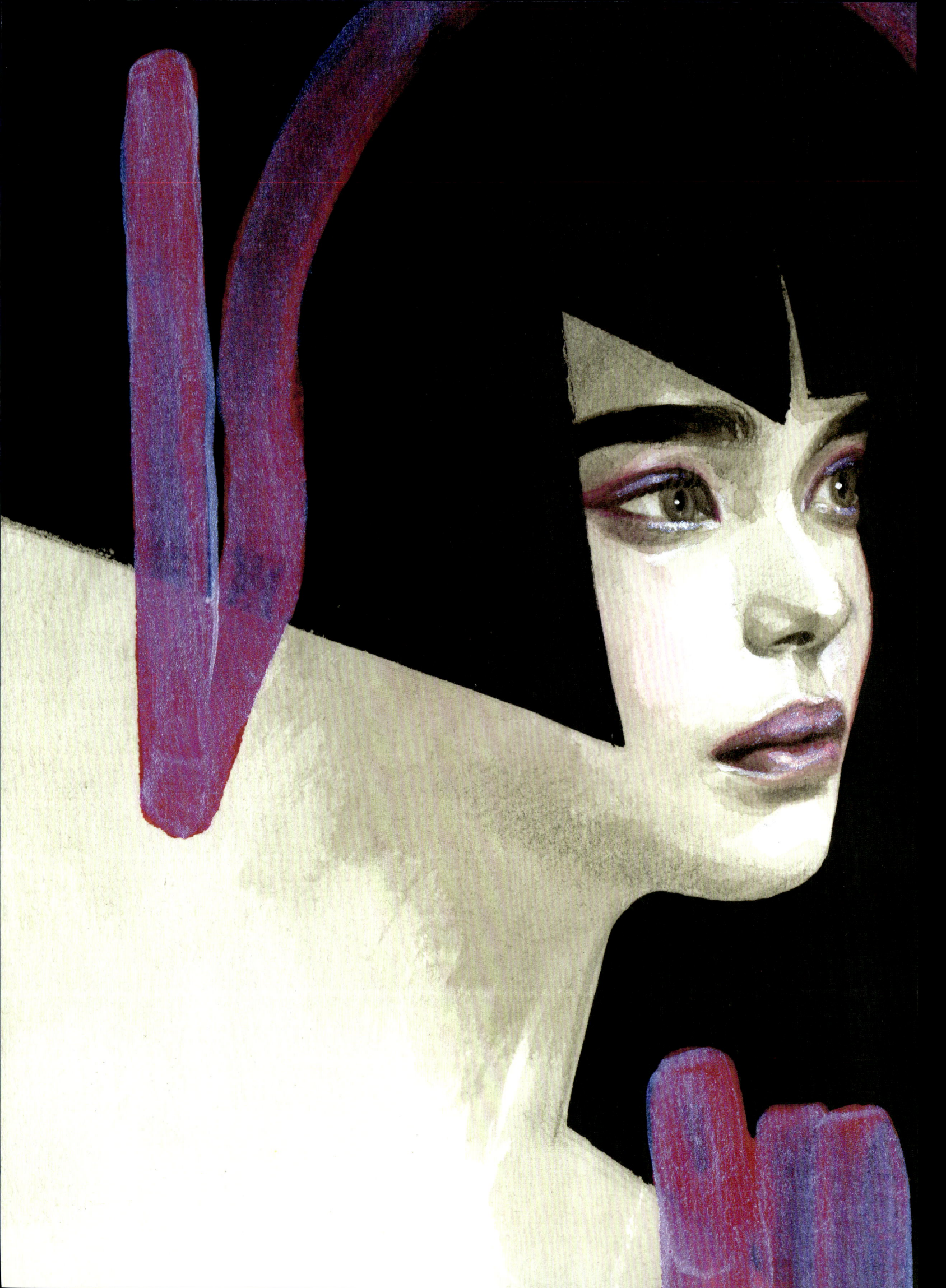

STUDY NO. 86
acrylic & colored pencil, 6" × 9", 2019

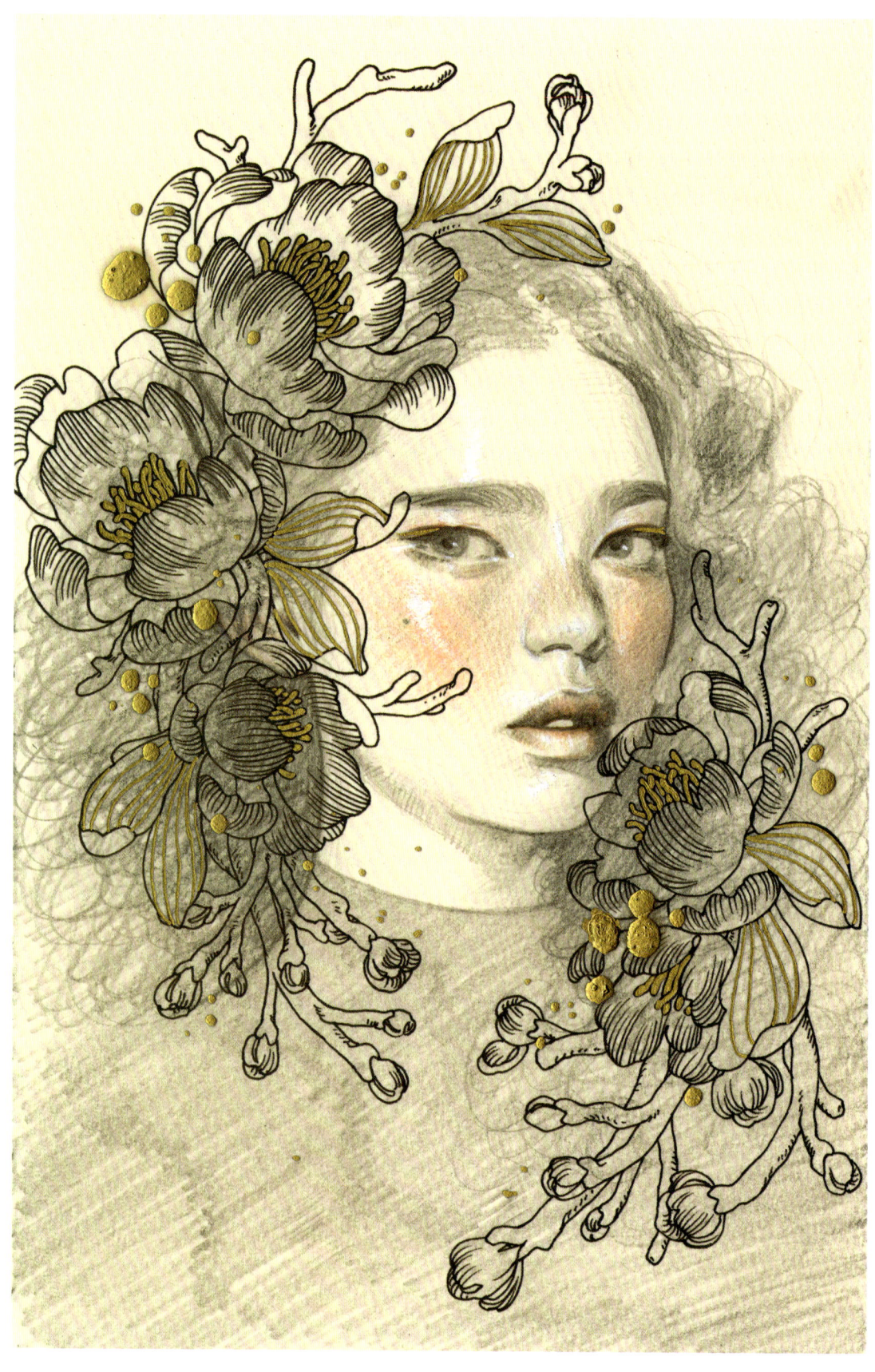

above
STUDY NO. 89
ink, colored pencil & graphite, 6″ × 9″, 2020

right
STUDY NO. 90
gouache & ink, 6″ × 9″, 2020

56

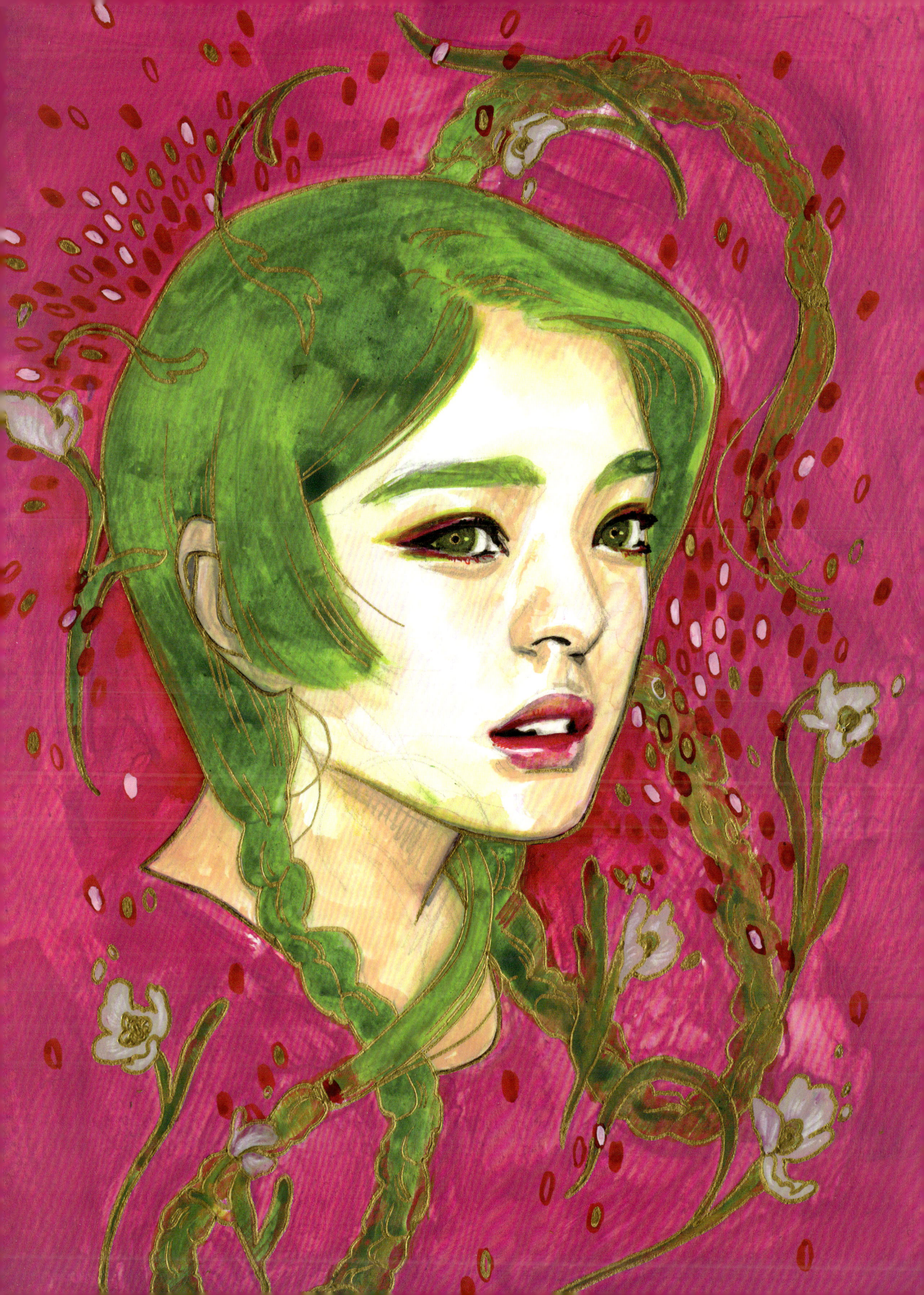

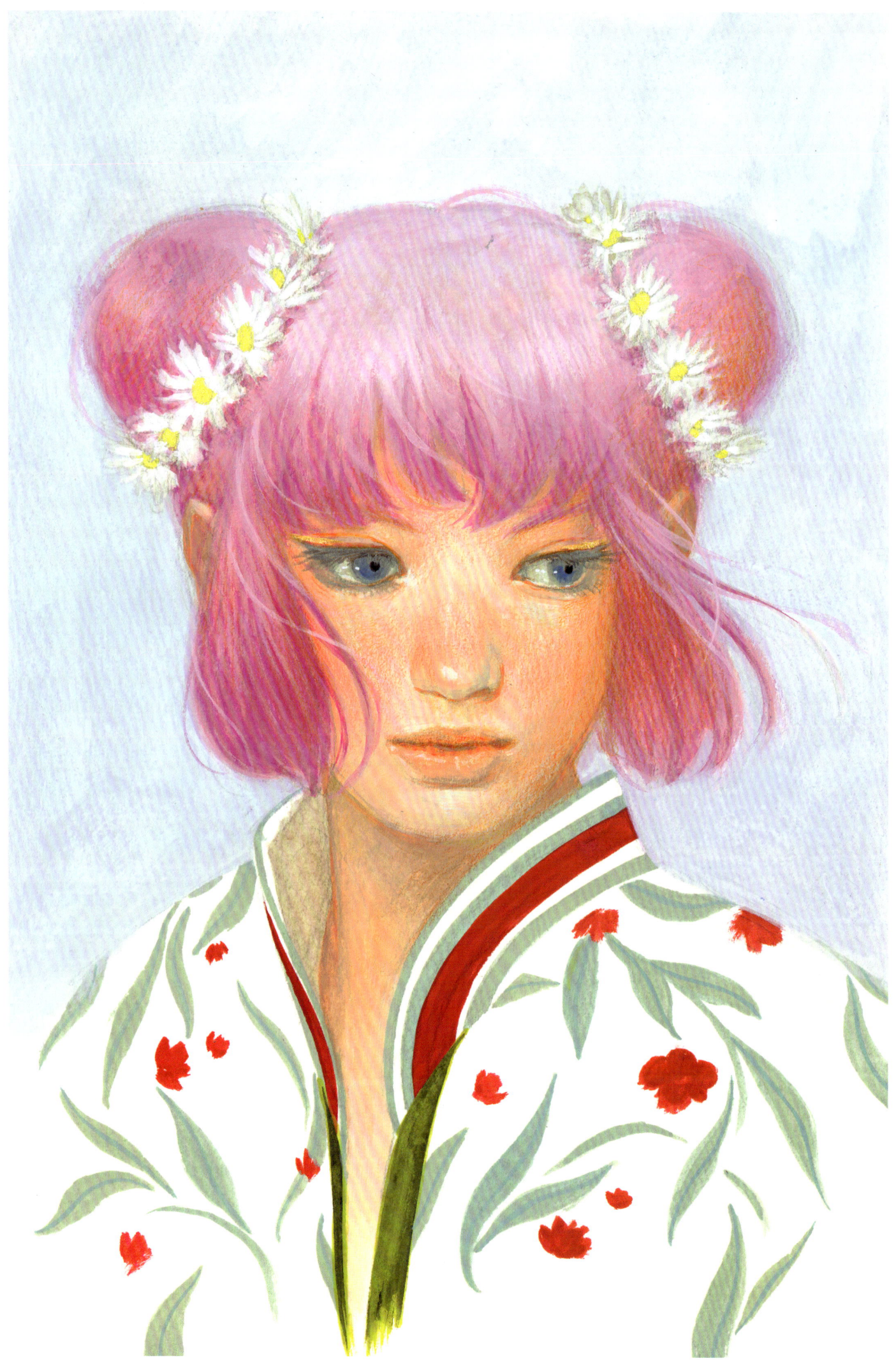

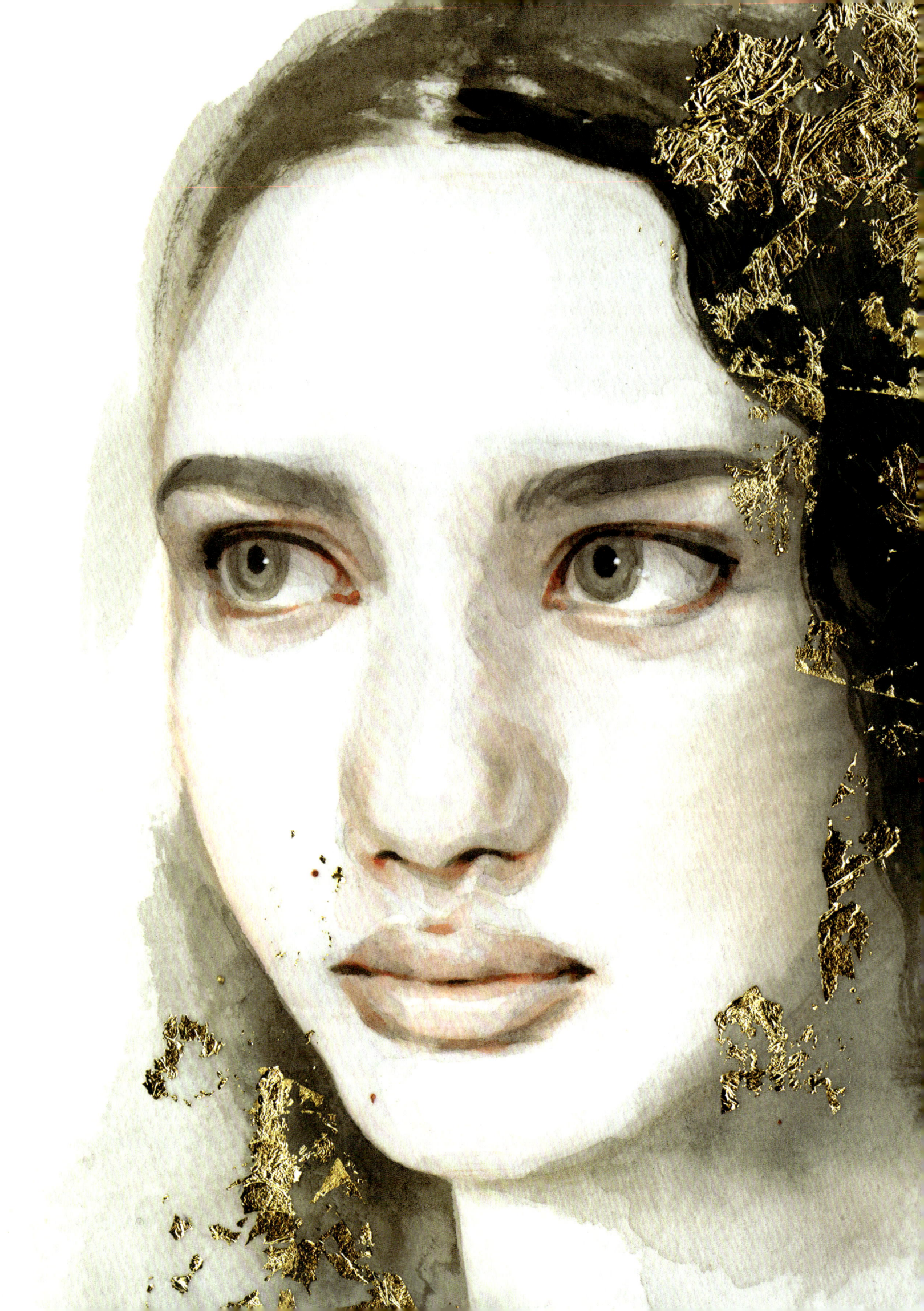

METAL LEAF

EXPERIMENTS WITH GOLD LEAFING & SIZE

I'm deeply captivated by works of art embellished with gold leaf, particularly through the process of gilding. Gilding has a timeless allure that infuses dynamism to the composition through color and reflectivity. I first learned about it when researching Gustav Klimt's process while attending college. The desire to learn more escalated when I encountered paintings utilizing this method at the Metropolitan Museum of Art and the Neue Galerie in New York City. There is a dimensional quality that emerges when gold leaf is applied to a flat surface and reflects light. The radiant gleam from its color adds opulence to the artwork's overall texture.

This series illustrates my attempts to apply delicate, thin sheets of gold and silver leaf in a variety of sizes to adhere it onto paper. I utilize different gilding tools, such as a soft brush, artist tape and a burnisher. Working around a loosely painted figure, I arrange the metal in a way that will enrich the composition.

STUDY NO. 14
acrylic, colored pencil & gold leaf, 5″ × 7″, 2014

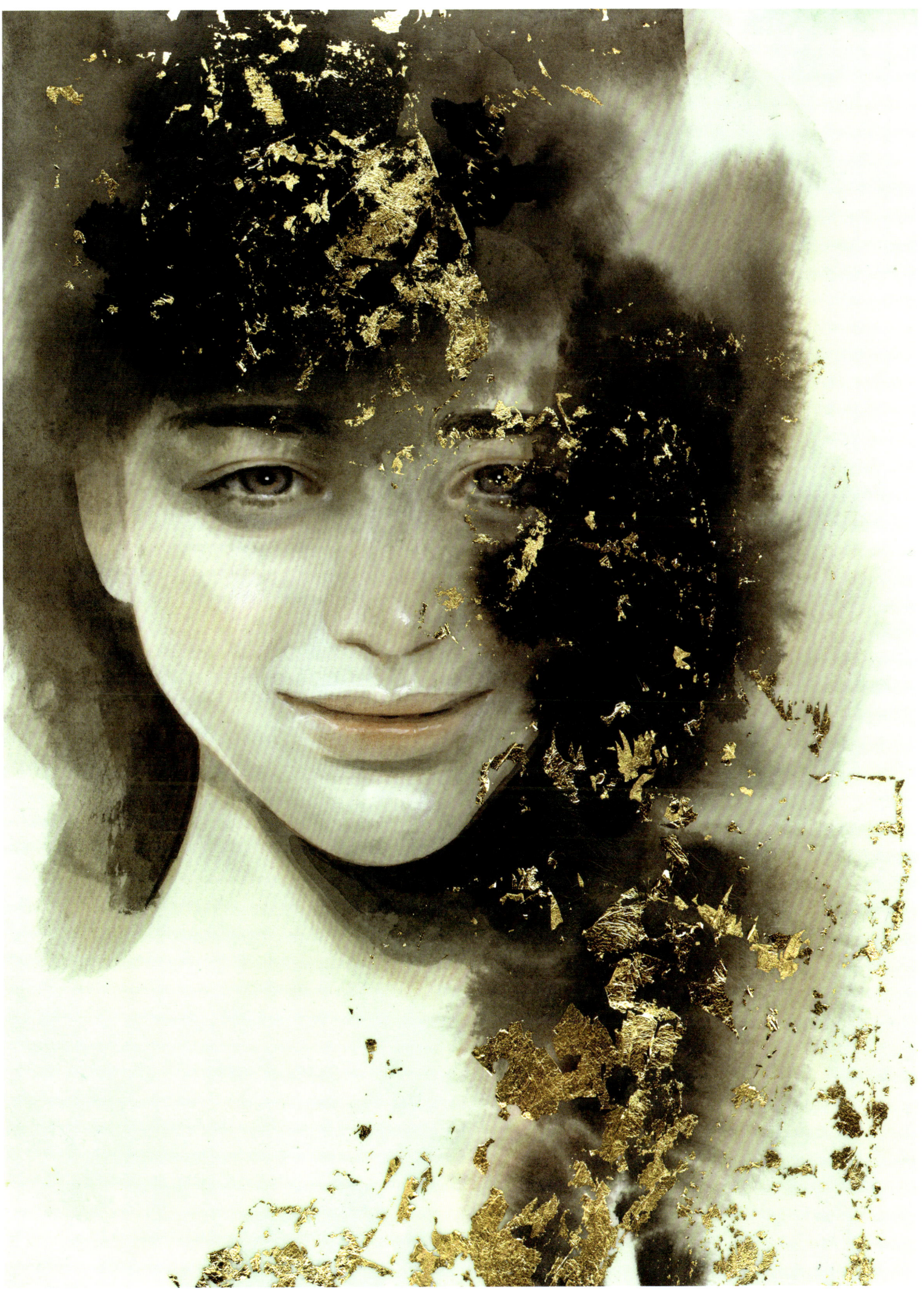

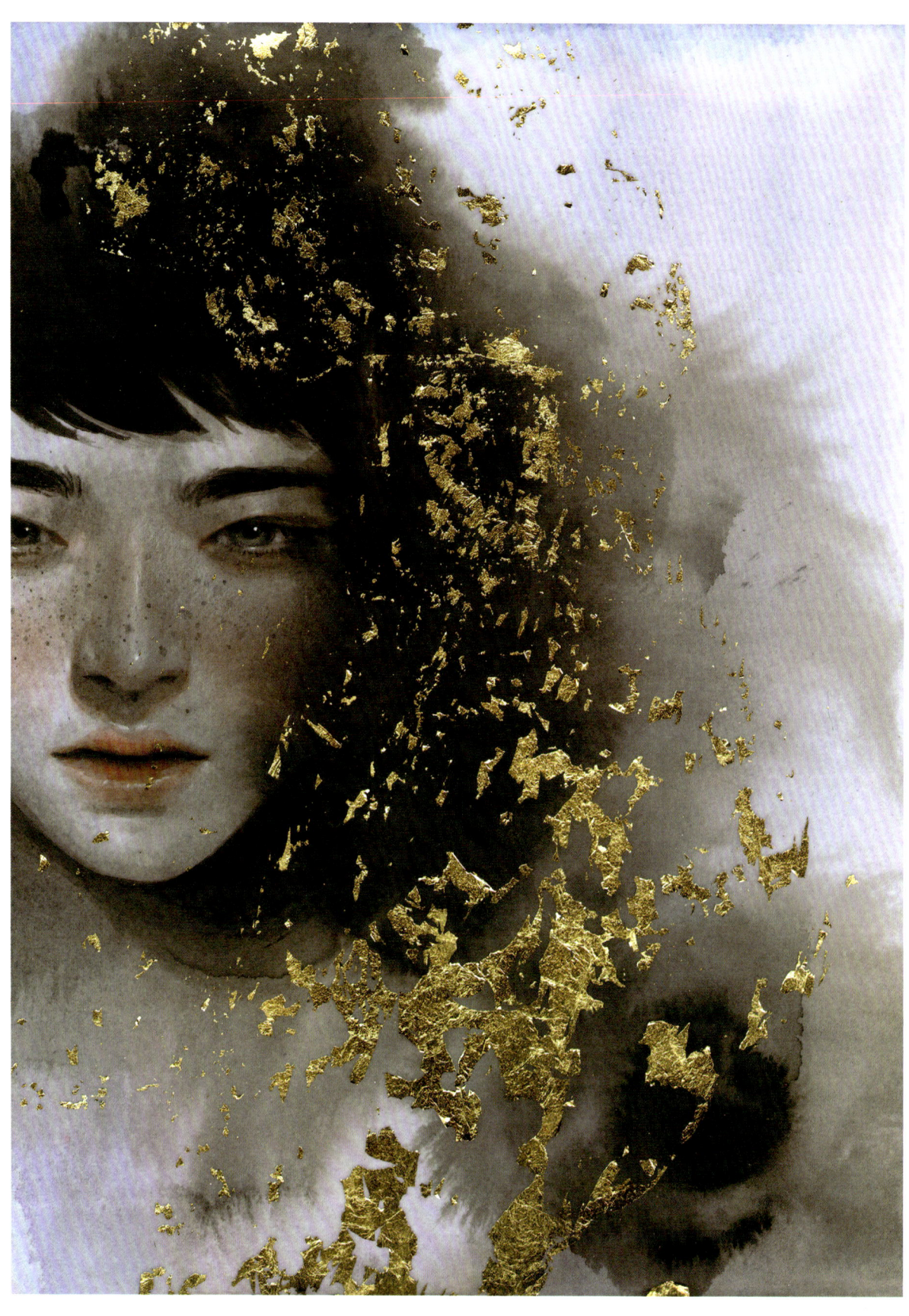

above
STUDY NO. 18
acrylic, colored pencil & gold leaf, 5" x 7", 2014

right
STUDY NO. 22
acrylic, colored pencil & gold leaf, 5" x 7", 2015

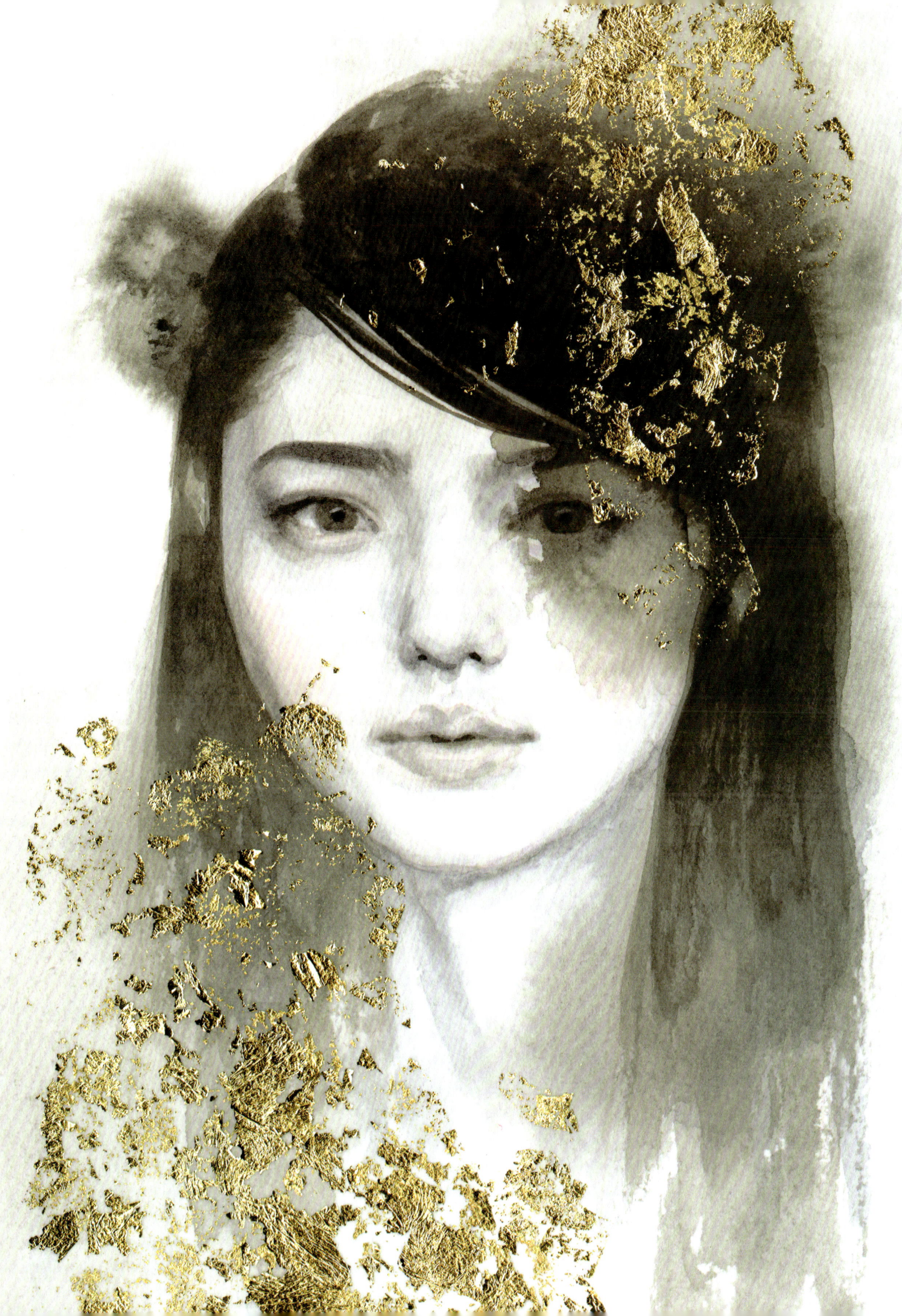

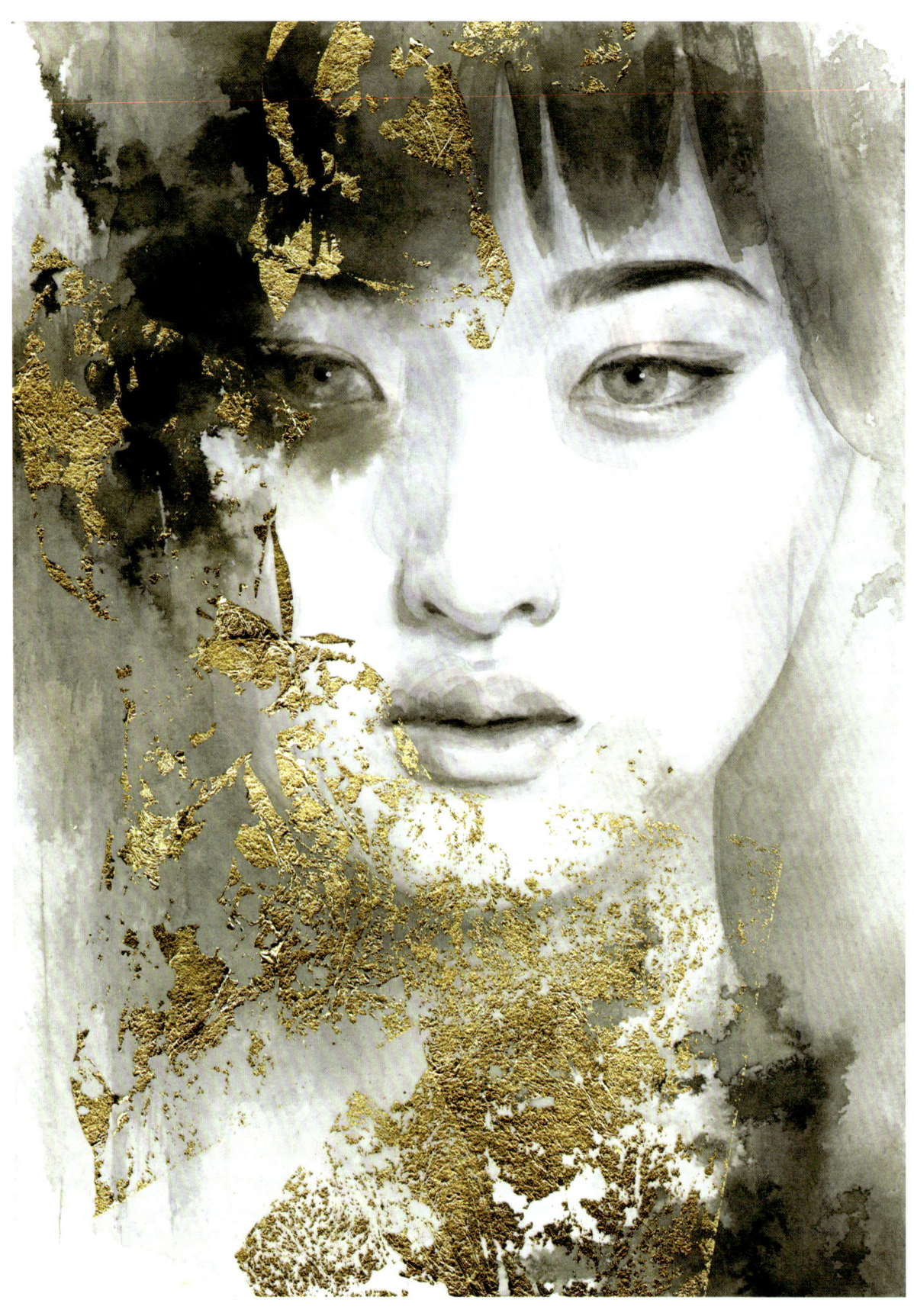

above
STUDY NO. 25
acrylic, colored pencil & gold leaf, 5" x 7", 2015

right
STUDY NO. 26
acrylic, colored pencil & gold leaf, 5" x 7", 2015

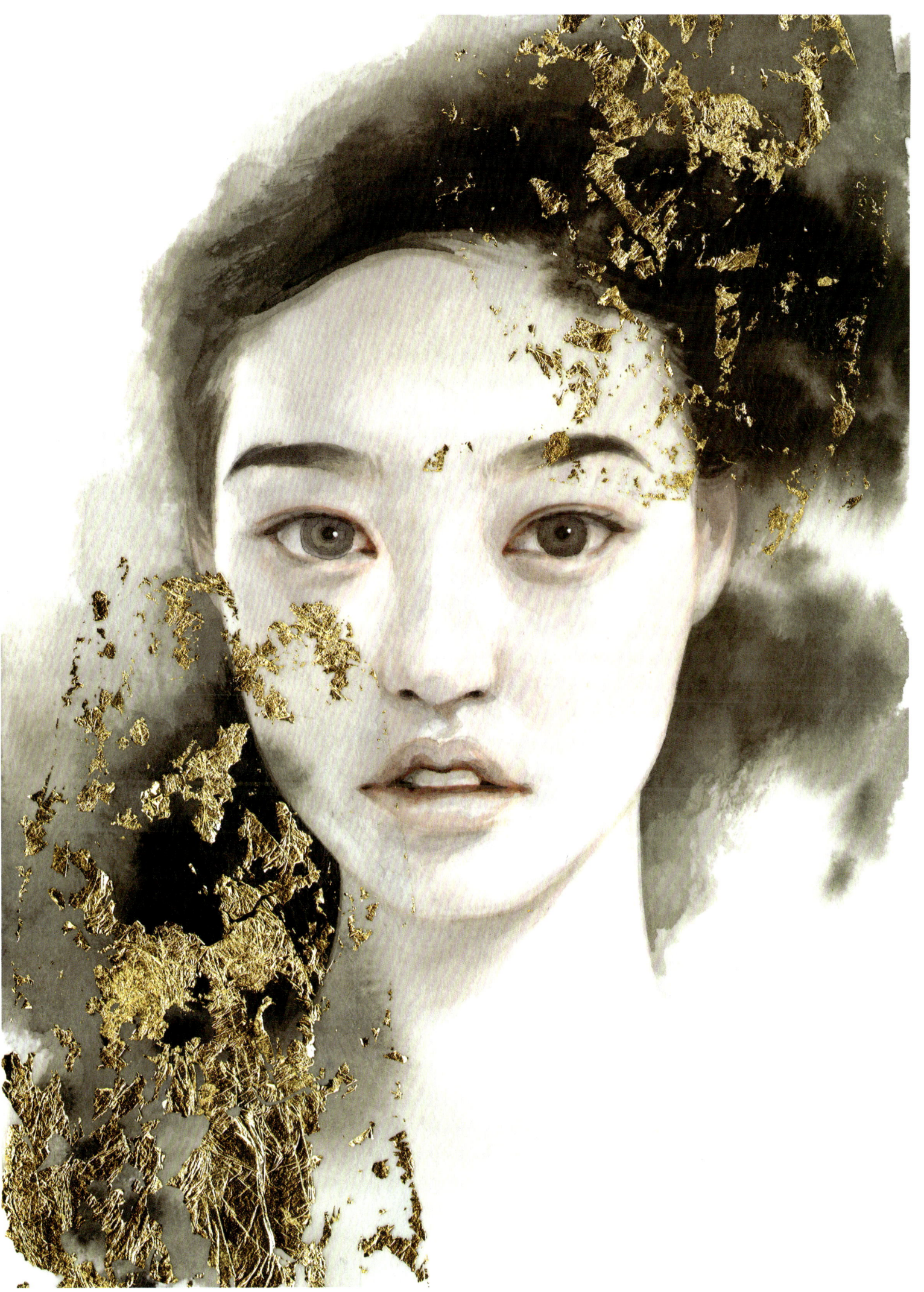

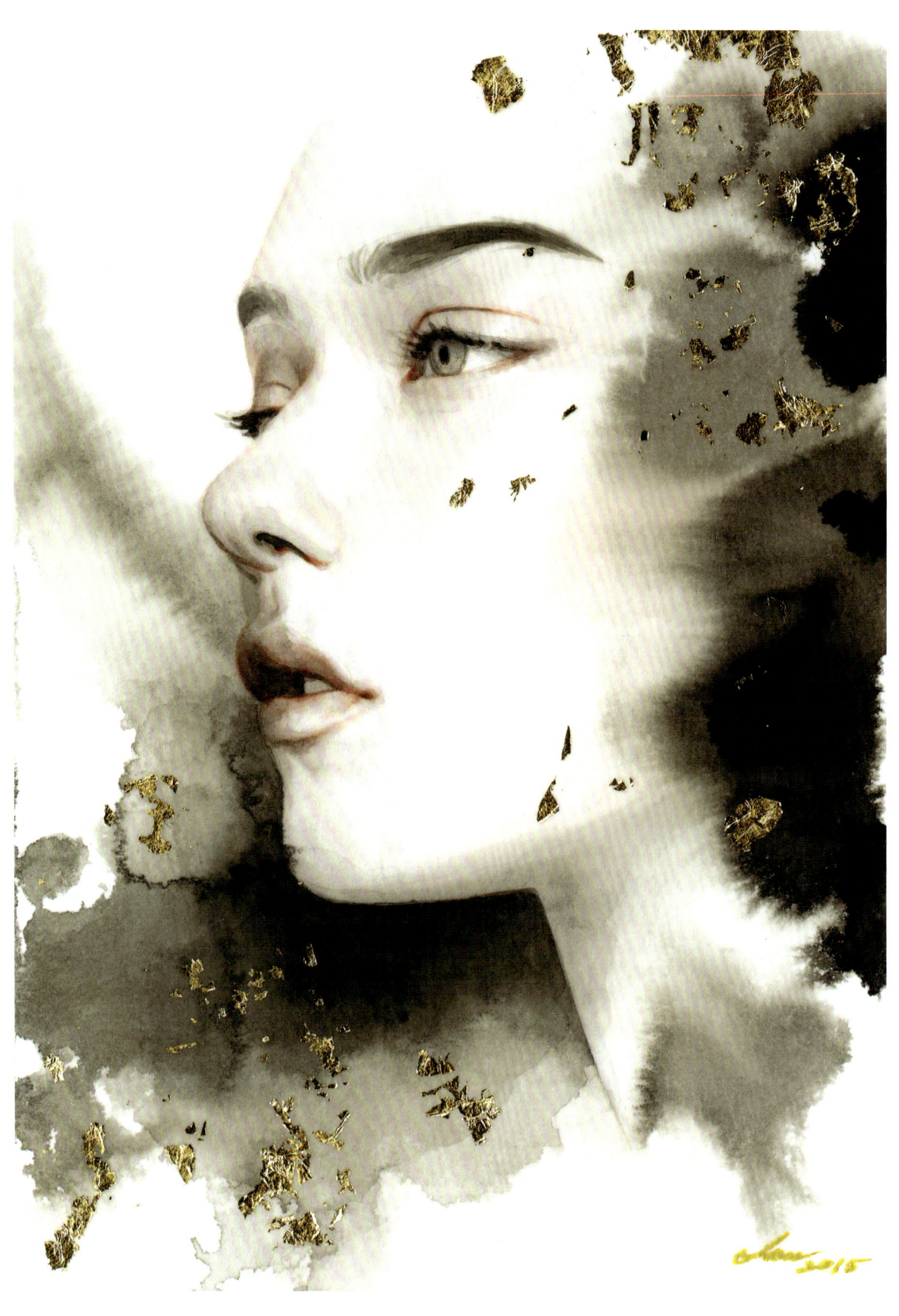

STUDY NO. 27
acrylic, colored pencil & gold leaf, 5" × 7", 2015

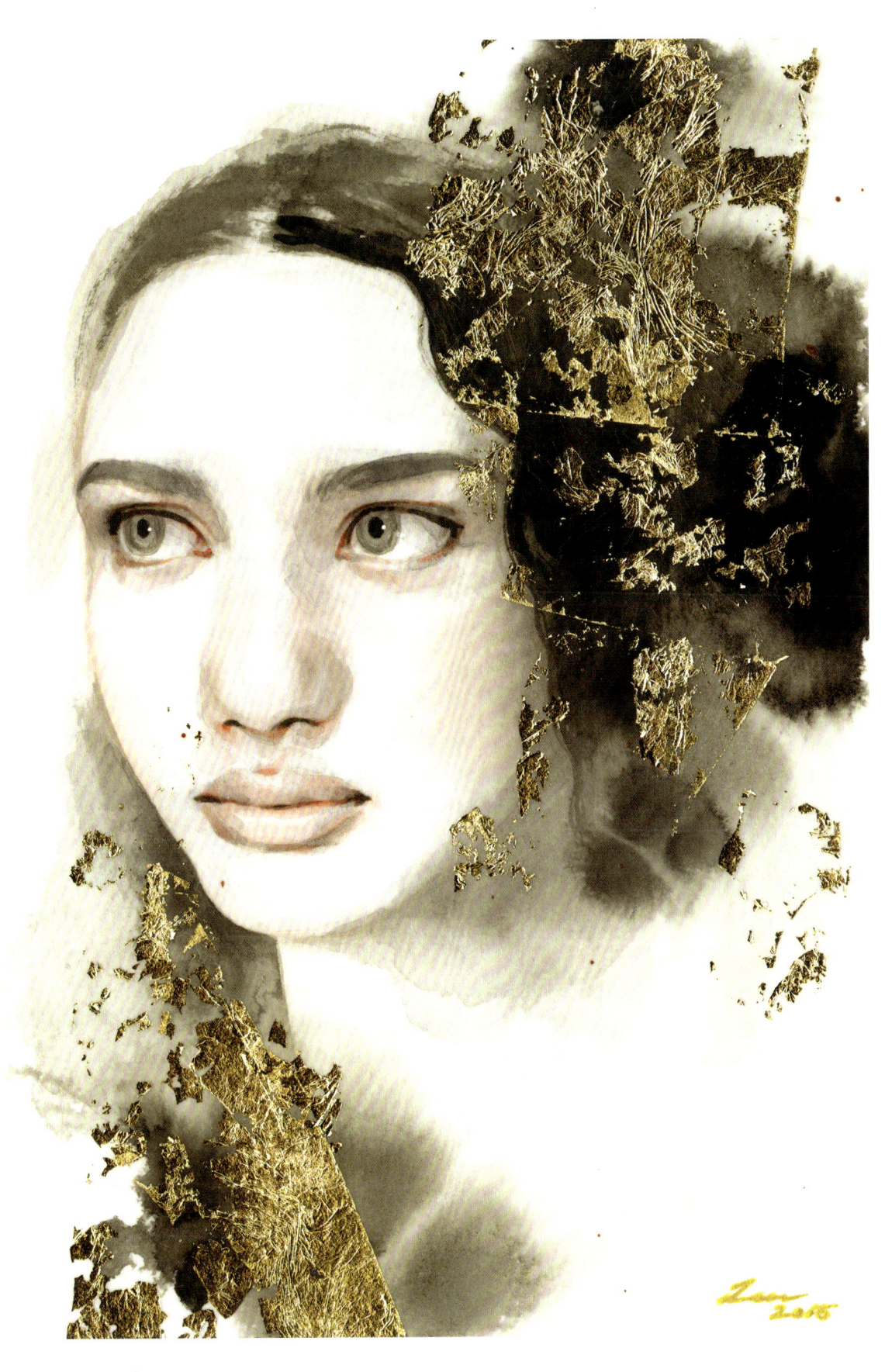

STUDY NO. 28
acrylic, colored pencil & gold leaf, 5" × 7", 2015

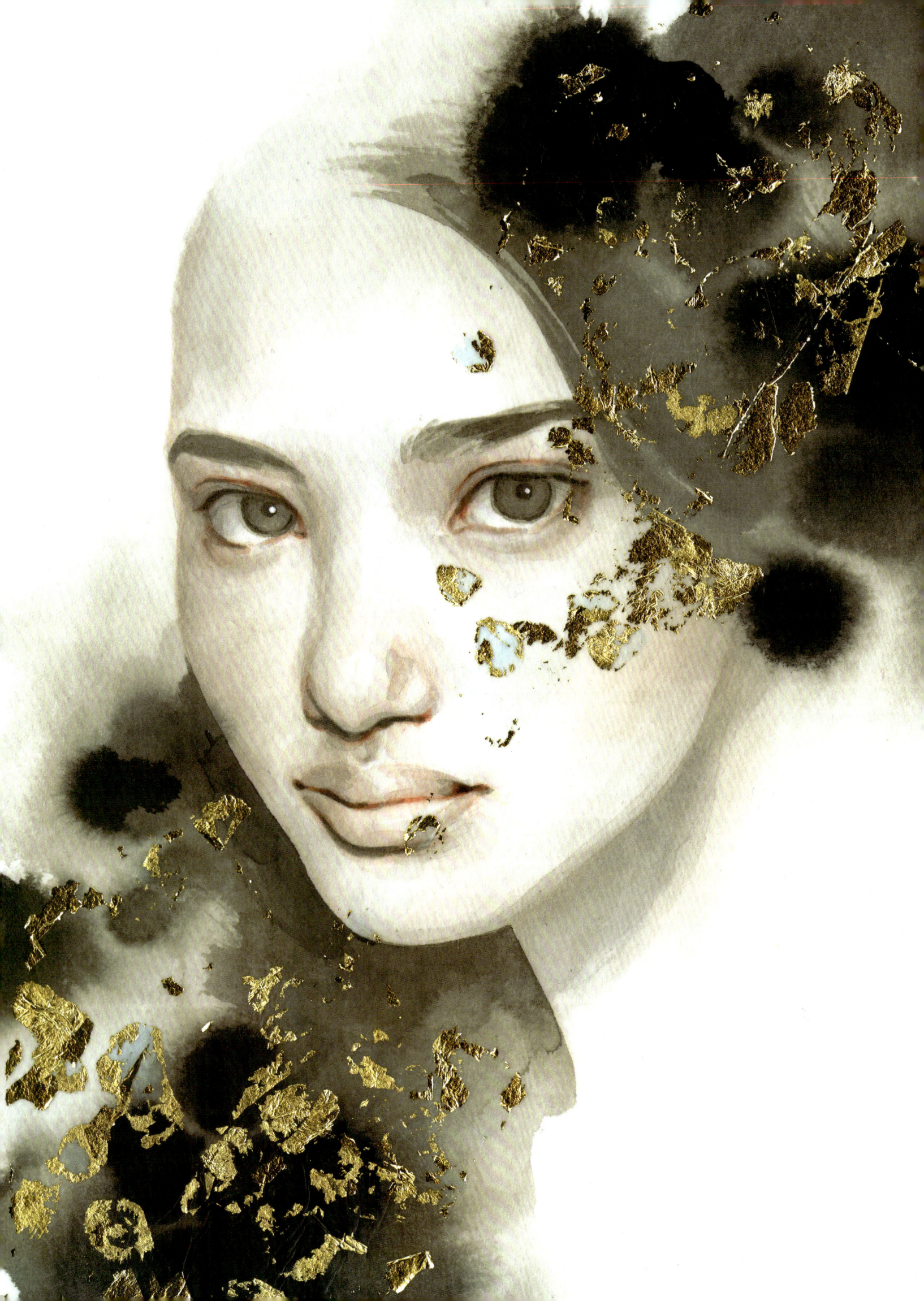

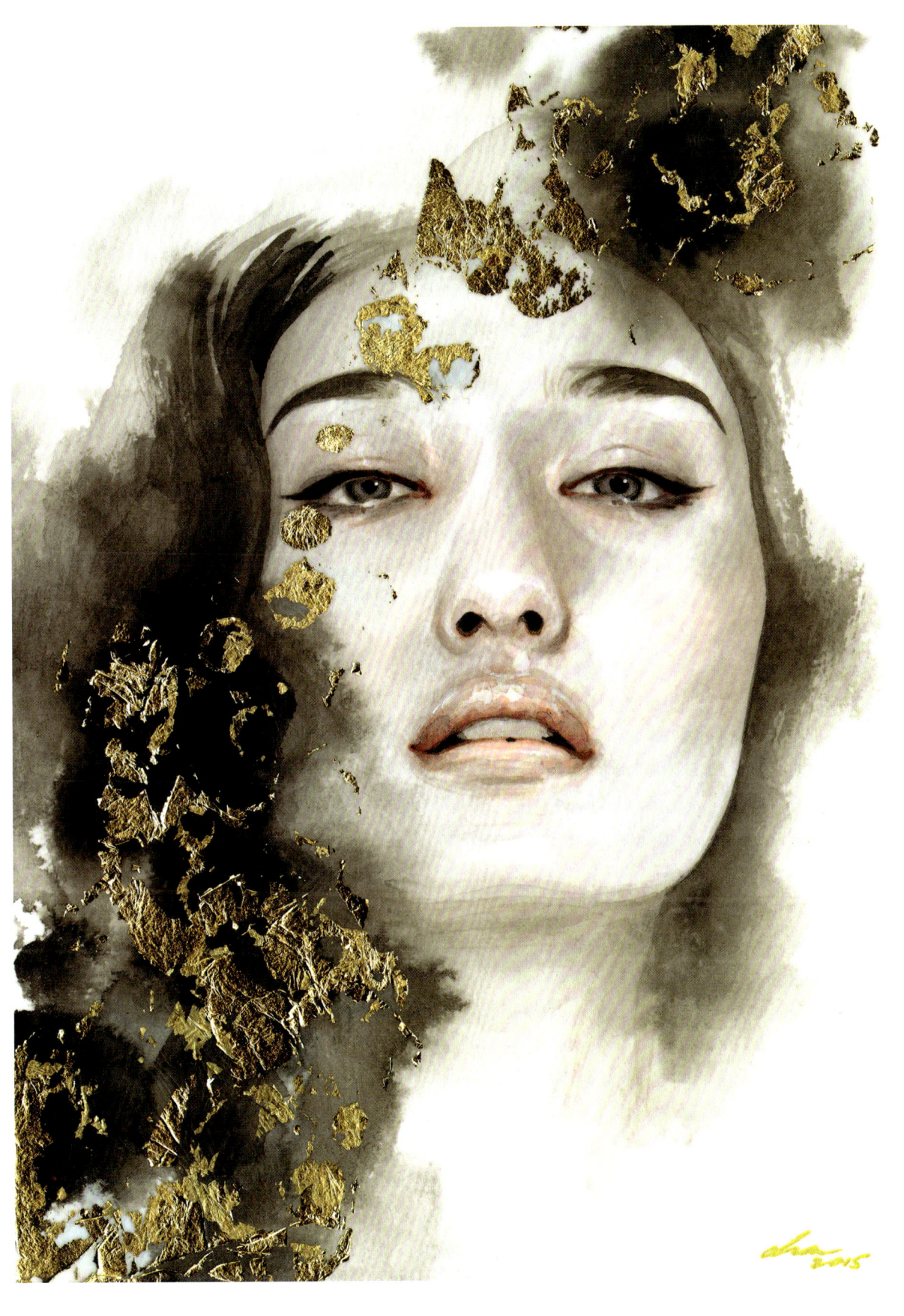

left
STUDY NO. 29
acrylic, colored pencil & gold leaf, 5" × 7", 2015

above
STUDY NO. 30
acrylic, colored pencil & gold leaf, 5" × 7", 2015

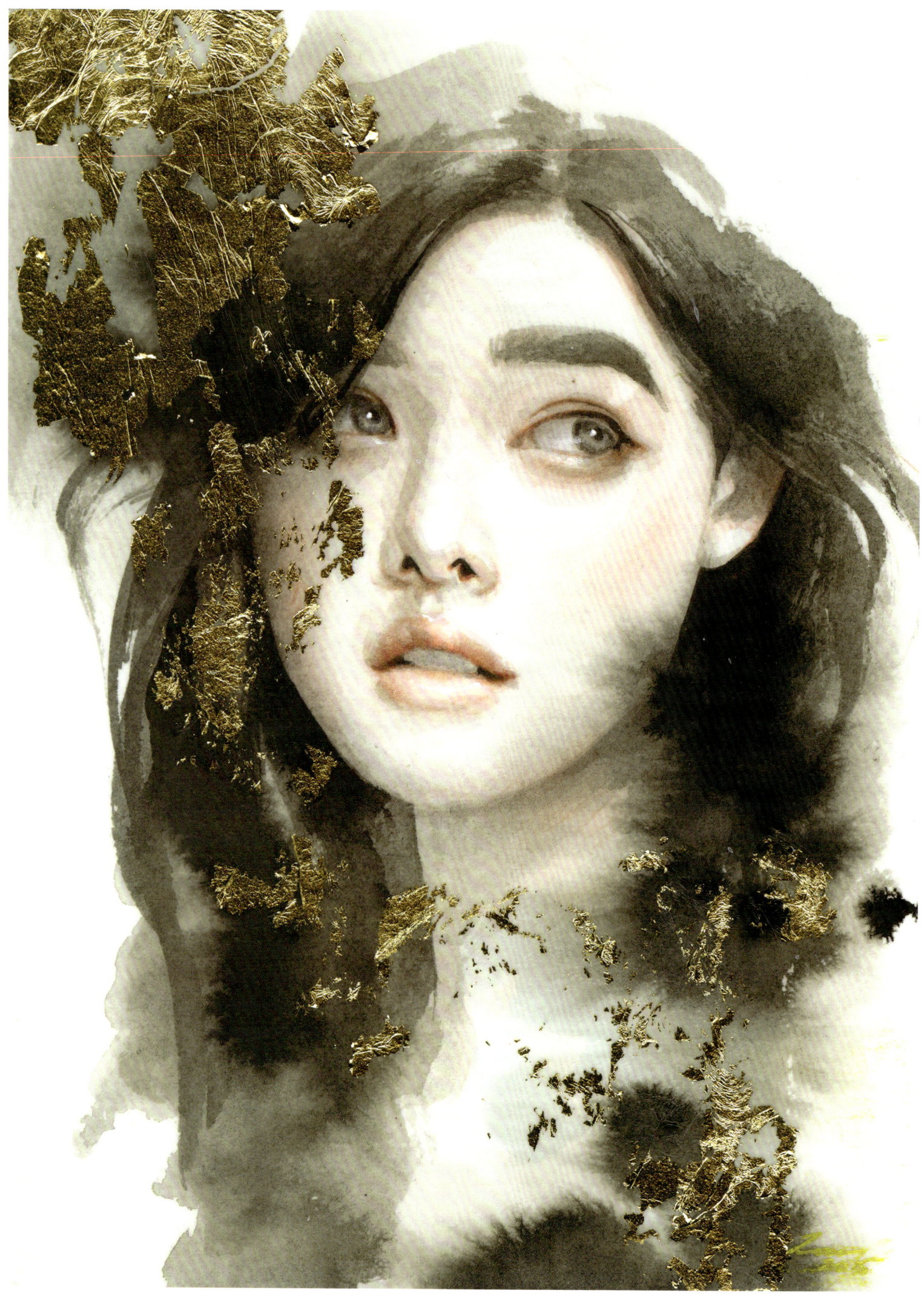

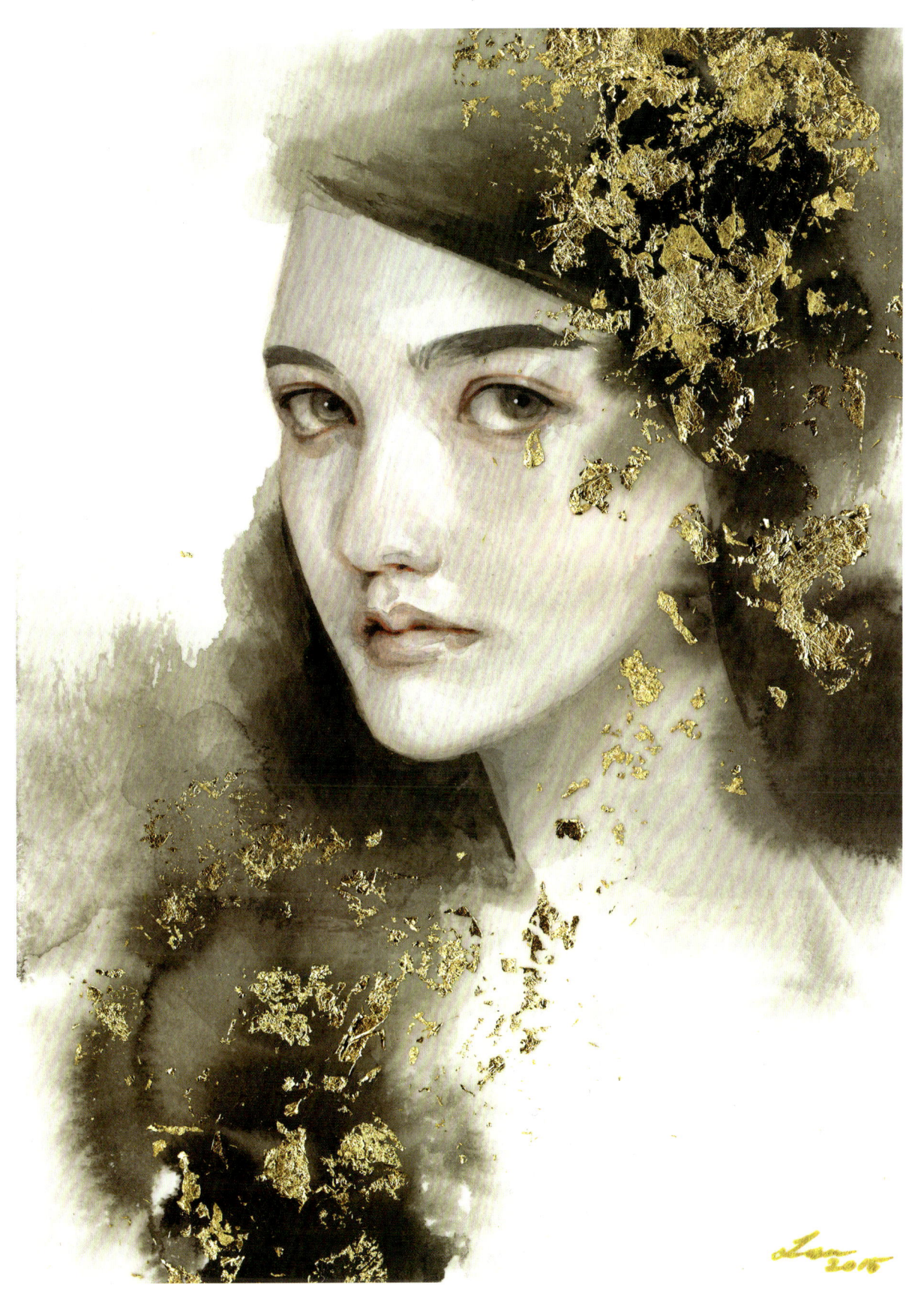

left
STUDY NO. 31
acrylic, colored pencil & gold leaf, 5" × 7", 2015

above
STUDY NO. 33
acrylic, colored pencil & gold leaf, 5" × 7", 2015

73

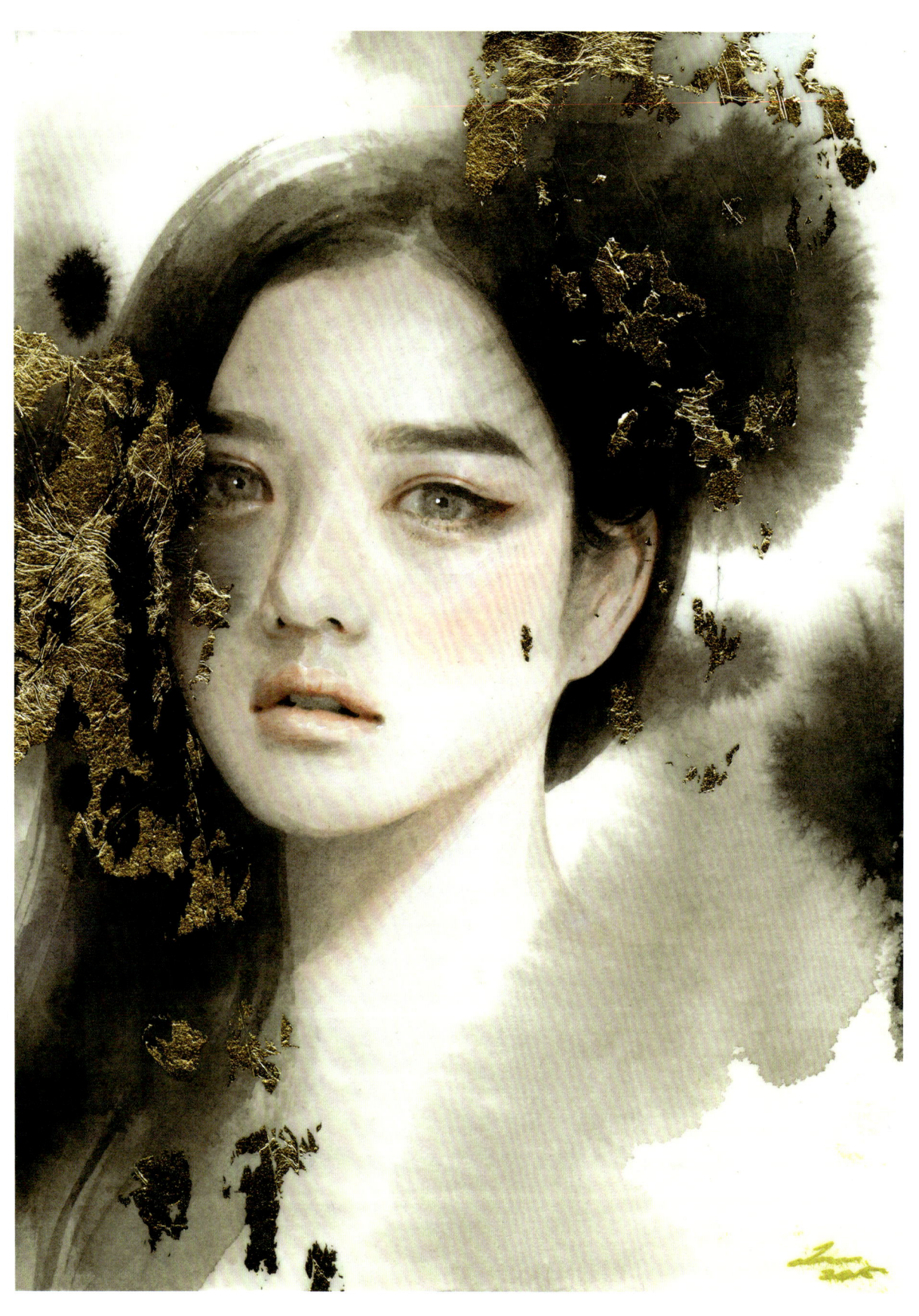

above
STUDY NO. 34
acrylic, colored pencil & gold leaf, 5" × 7", 2015

right
STUDY NO. 70
acrylic, ink & silver leaf, 5" × 7", 2018

74

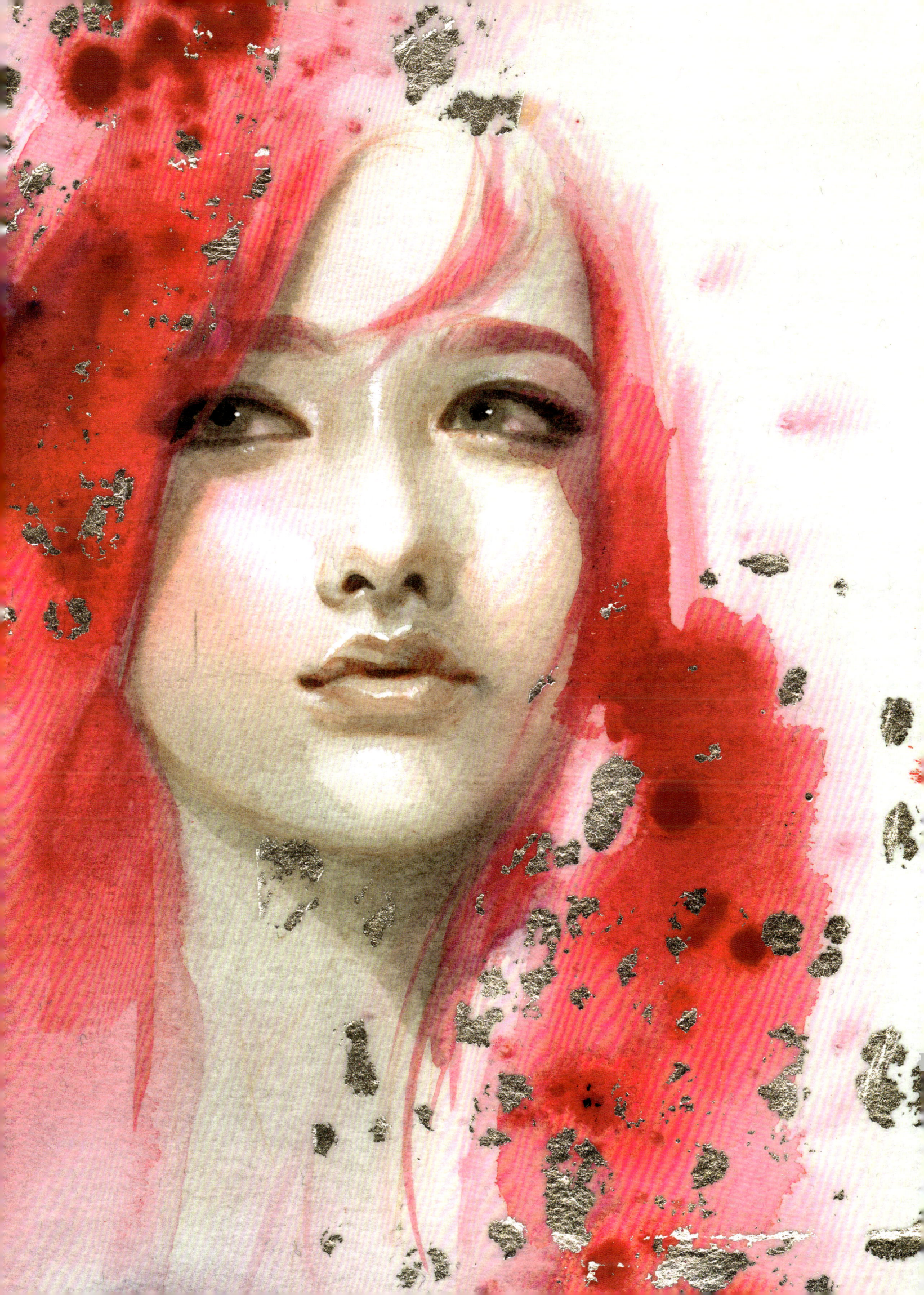

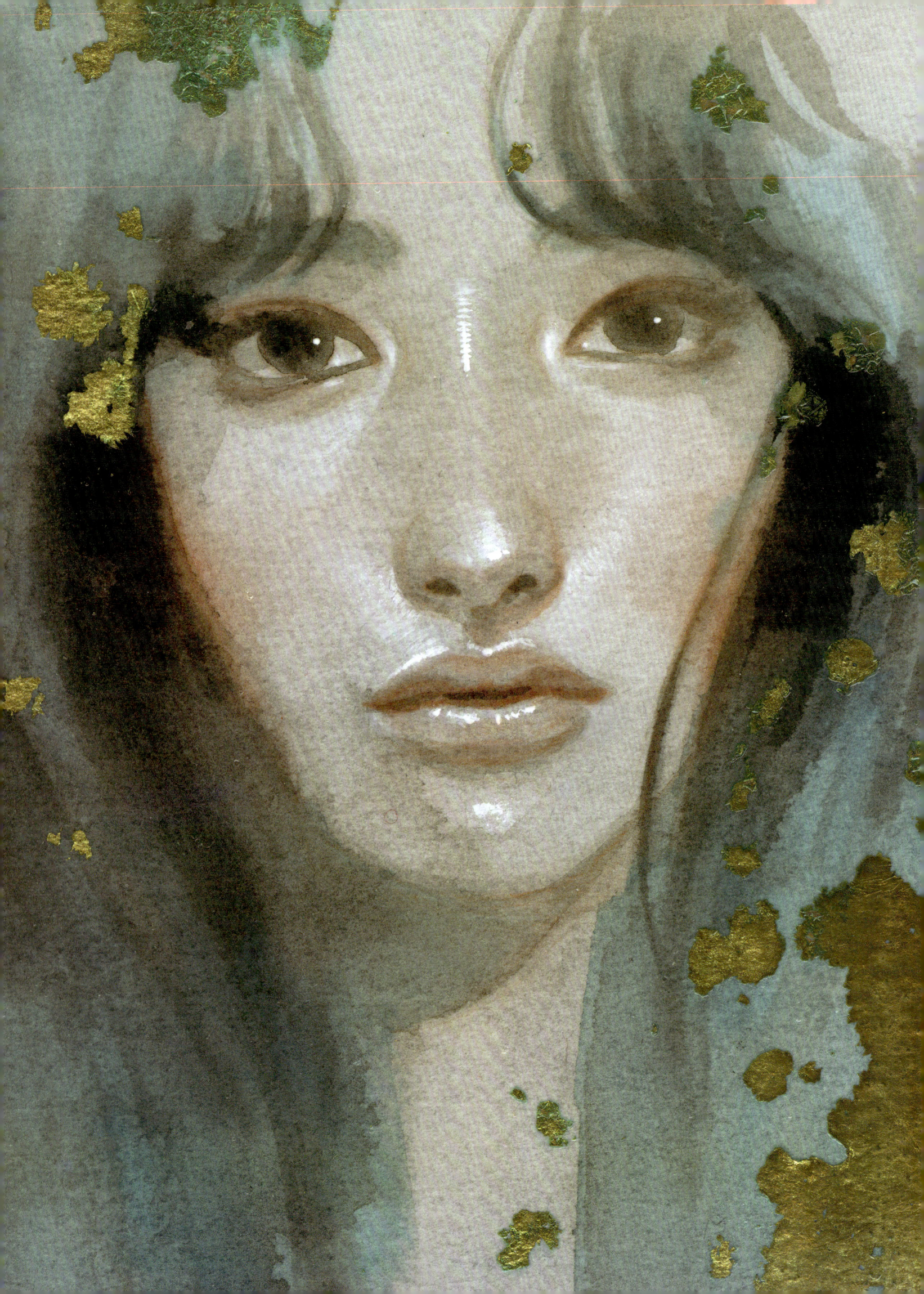

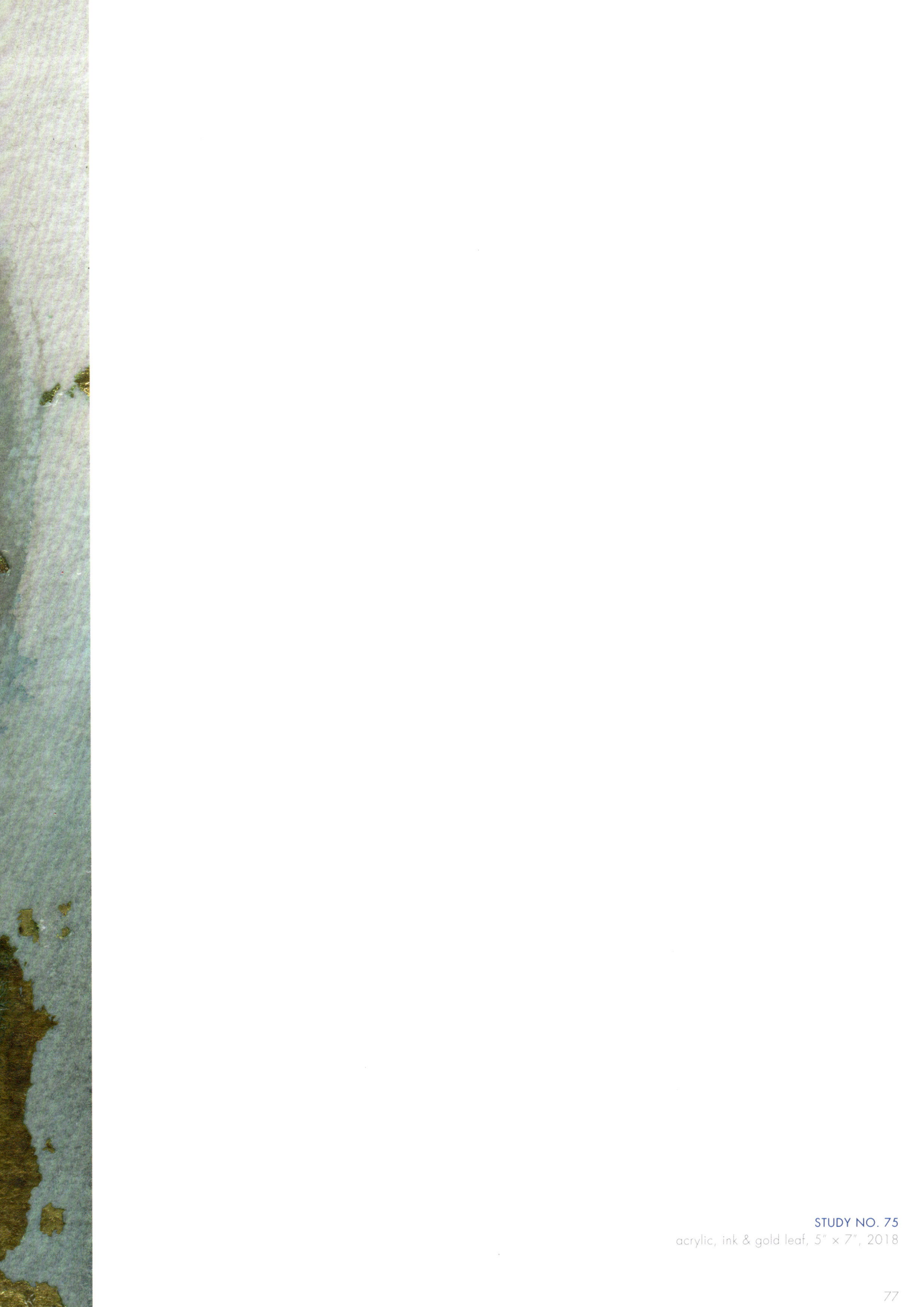

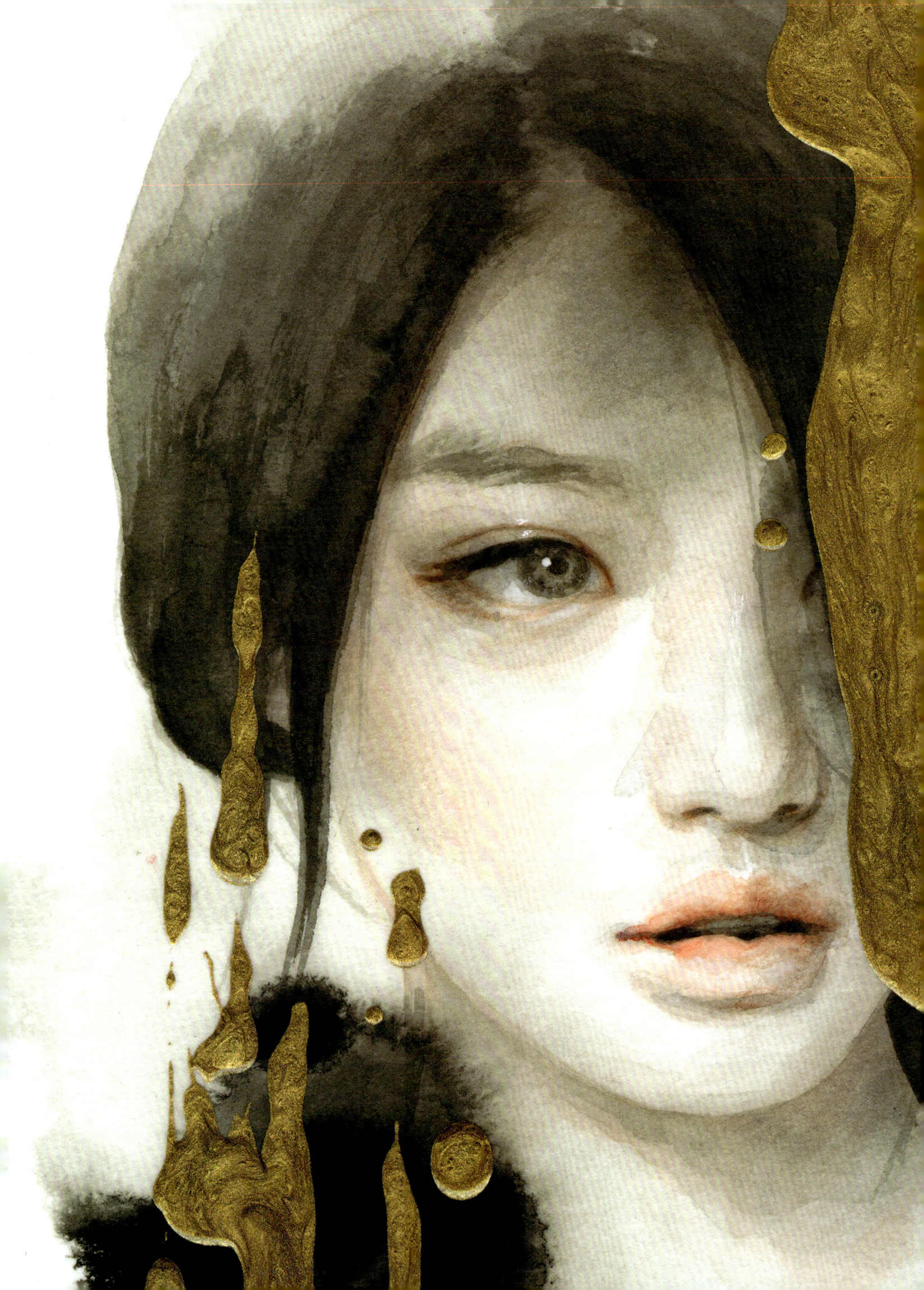

PAINT DRIP

EXPERIMENTS WITH PEBEO COLORS

I discovered Pebeo colors while perusing my local art-supply store in search of unconventional ways to embellish my studies. Using their line of Decorative Colours—which are oil-based, densely pigmented paints that come in a variety of luminous qualities—I began exploring the artistic possibilities of the medium.

One method of application that yields striking results is pouring the medium onto the substrate with a pipette and letting it slowly drip by tilting it at a slight angle. The size and shape of the drips are controlled by the amount of pressure used when handling the pipette. The flow of the iridescent colors against drips of paint adds movement to the static image.

Similar to impasto, they appear to be coming out of the paper, giving it a new level of dimension. Because the pigment can be unpredictable, mistakes are permanent, and I've learned to embrace the imperfections. The studies in this section consist of lustrous, multi-toned textures achieved with Pebeo paint.

STUDY NO. 11
acrylic, colored pencil & pebeo paint, 5" × 7", 2014

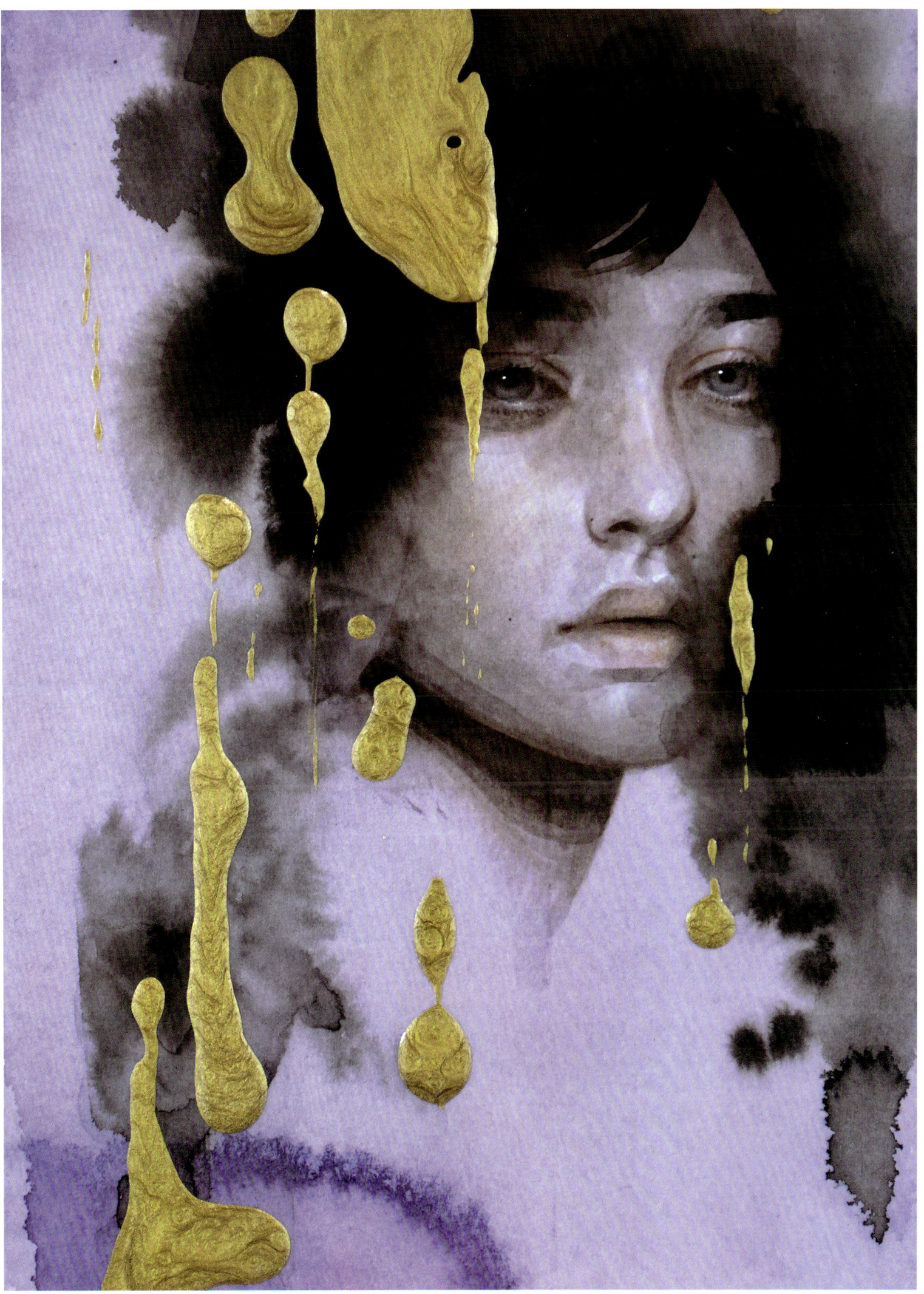

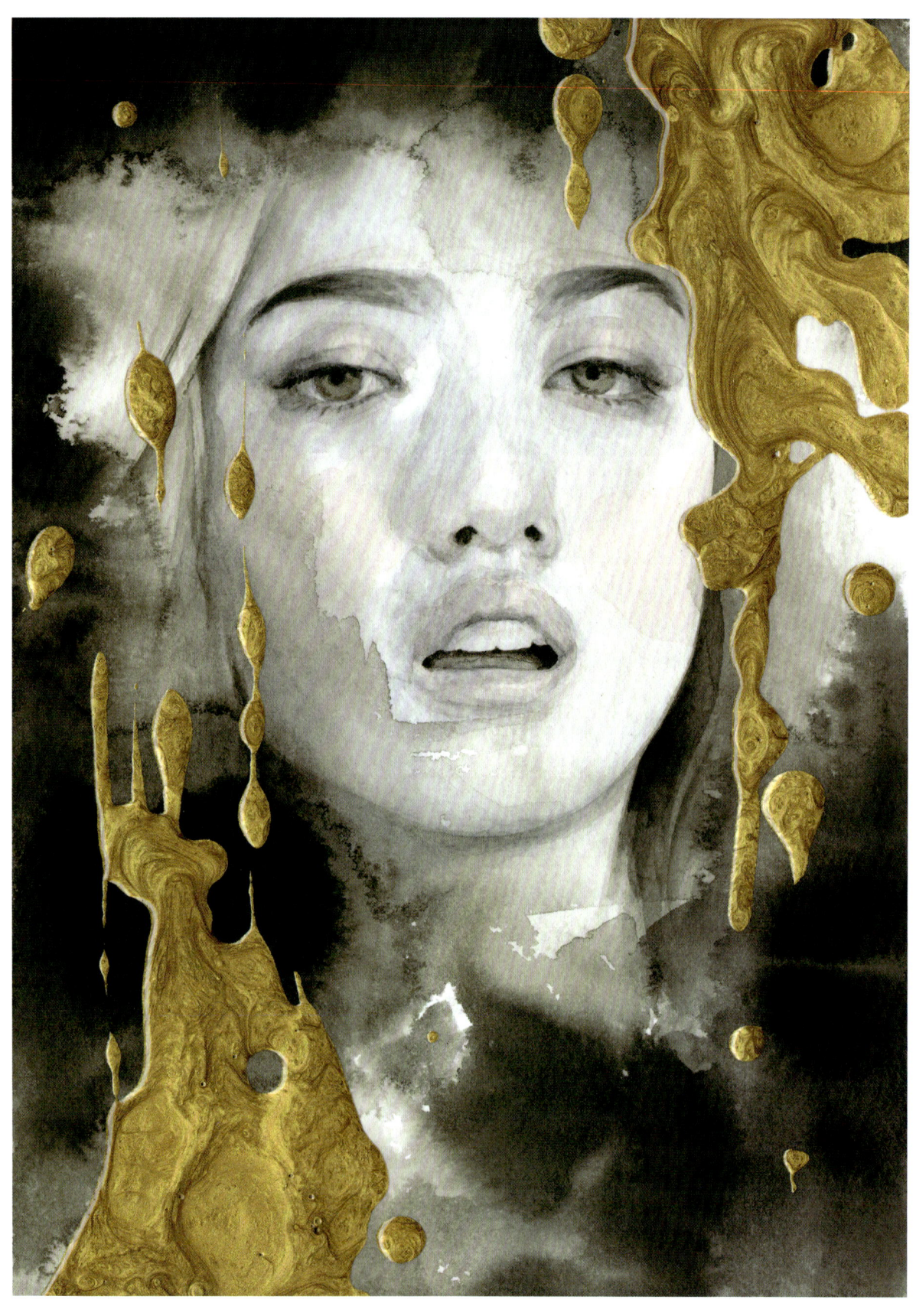

above
STUDY NO. 23
acrylic, colored pencil & pebeo paint, 5" x 7", 2015

right
STUDY NO. 24
acrylic, colored pencil & pebeo paint, 5" x 7", 2015

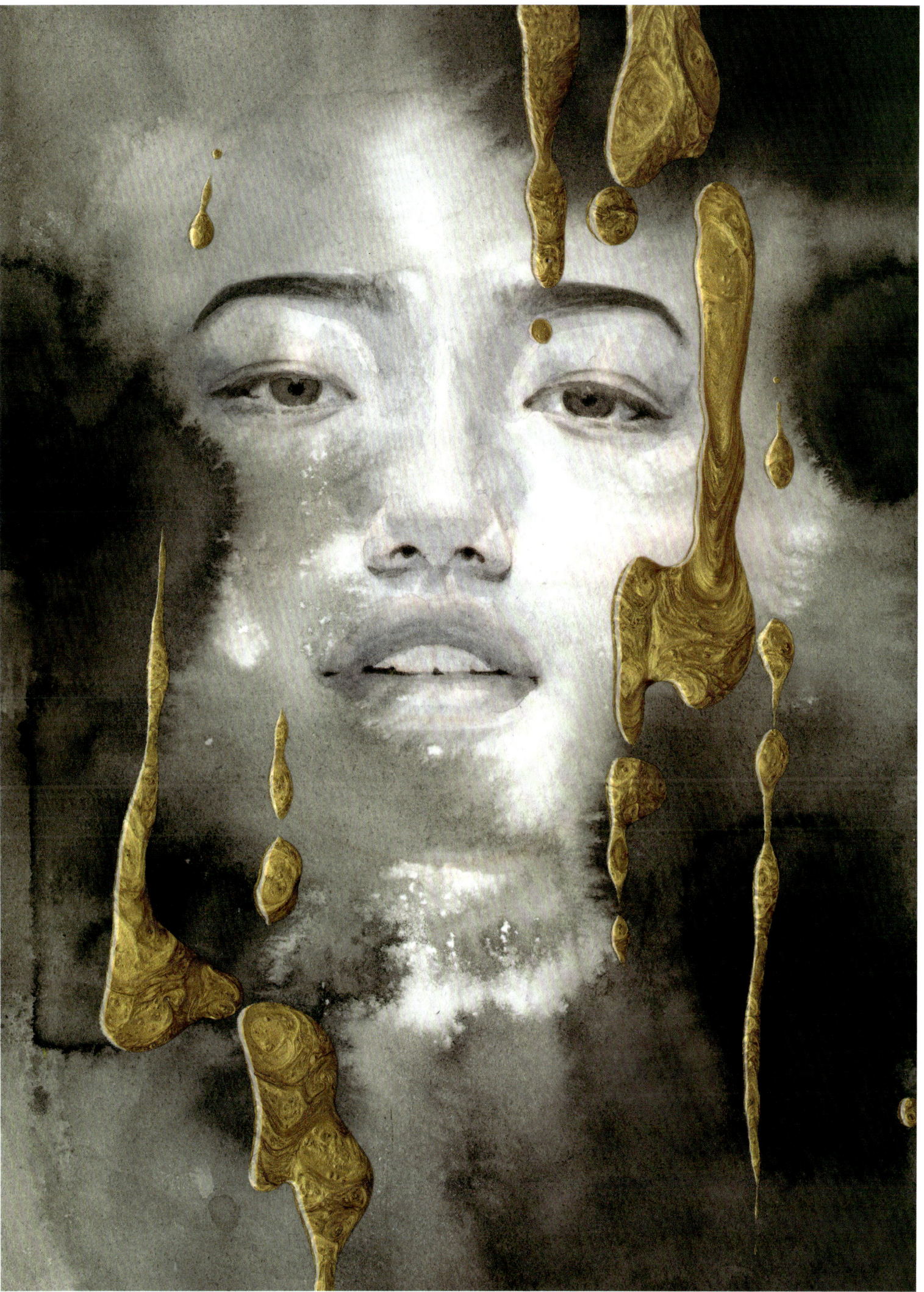

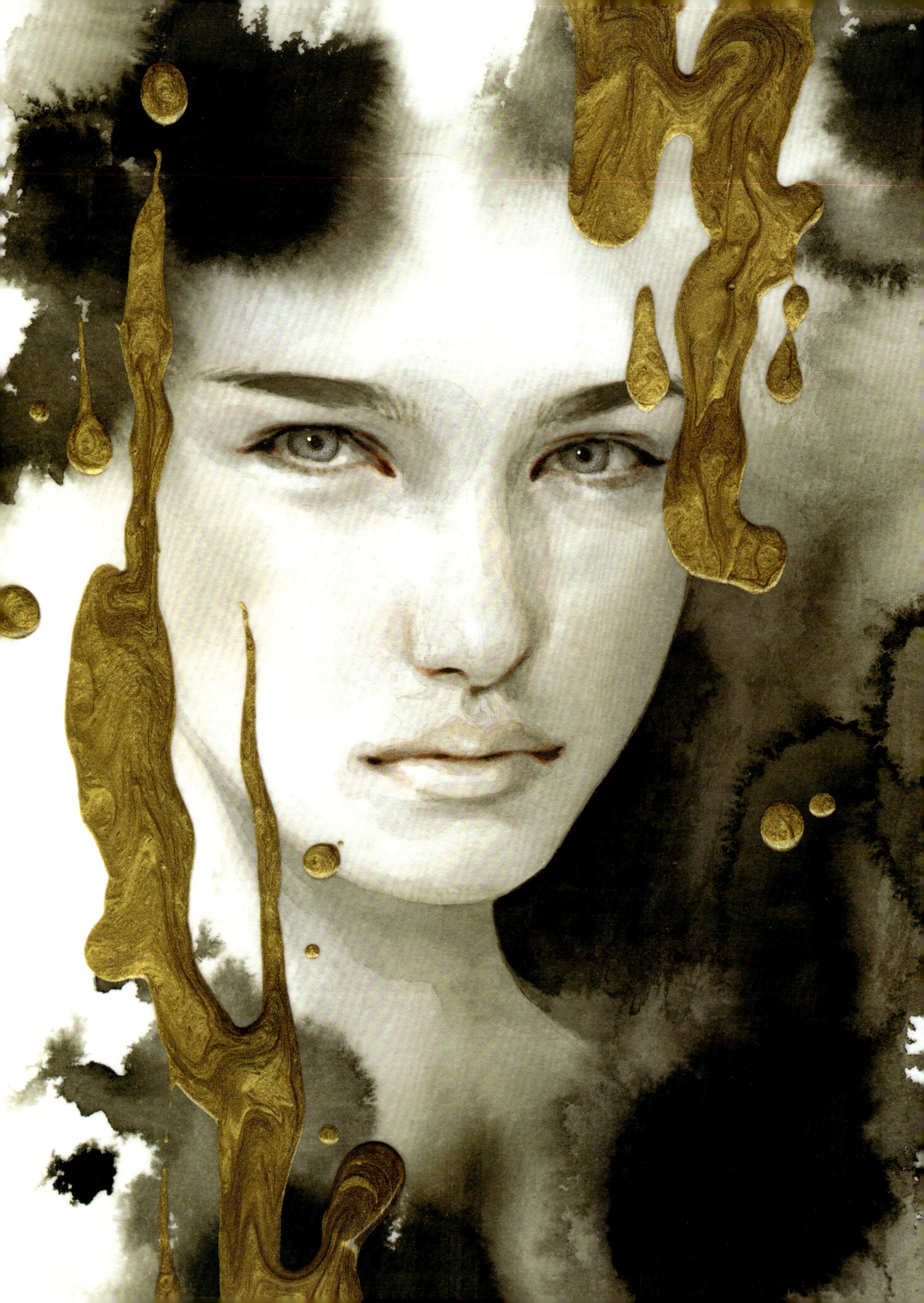

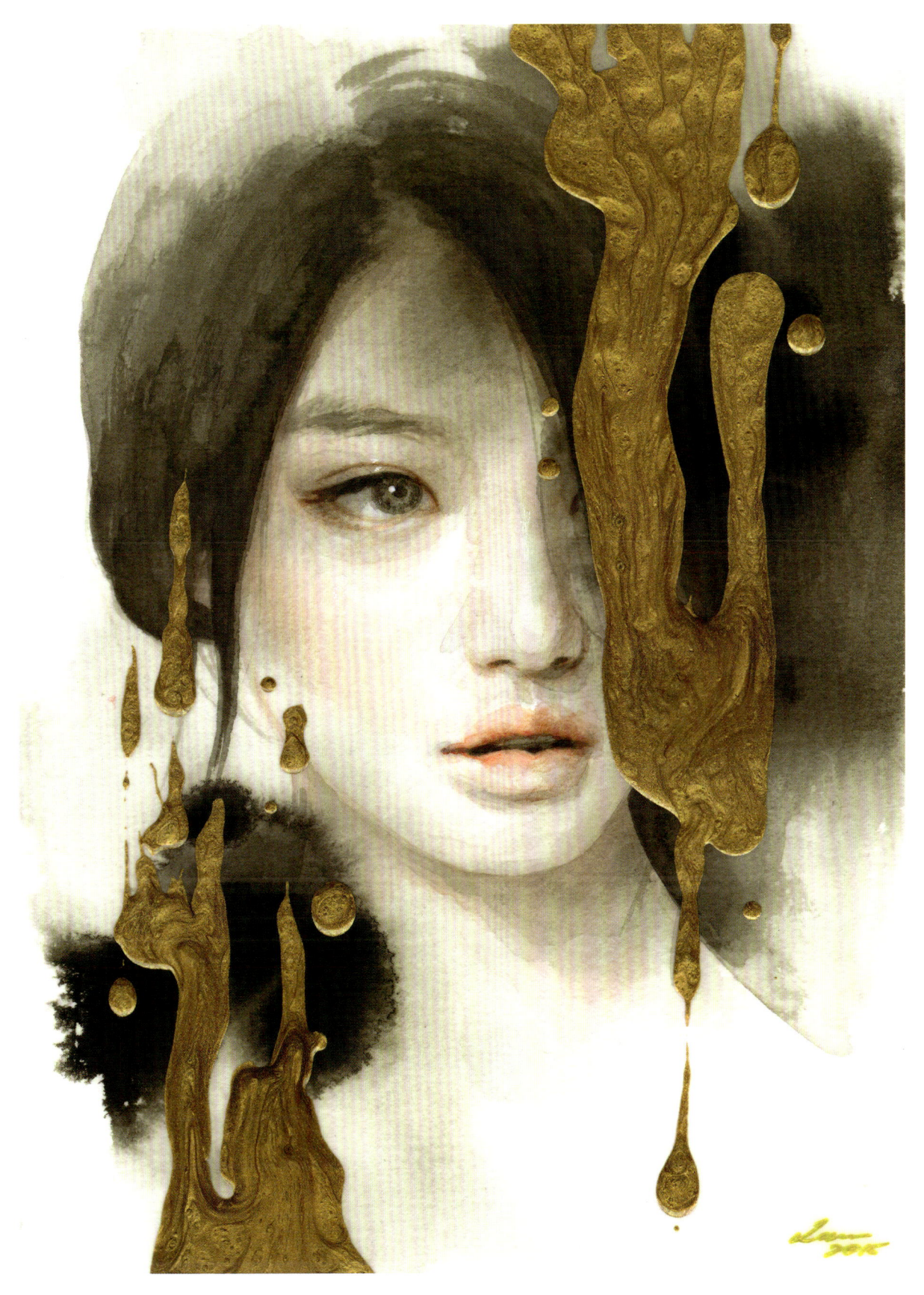

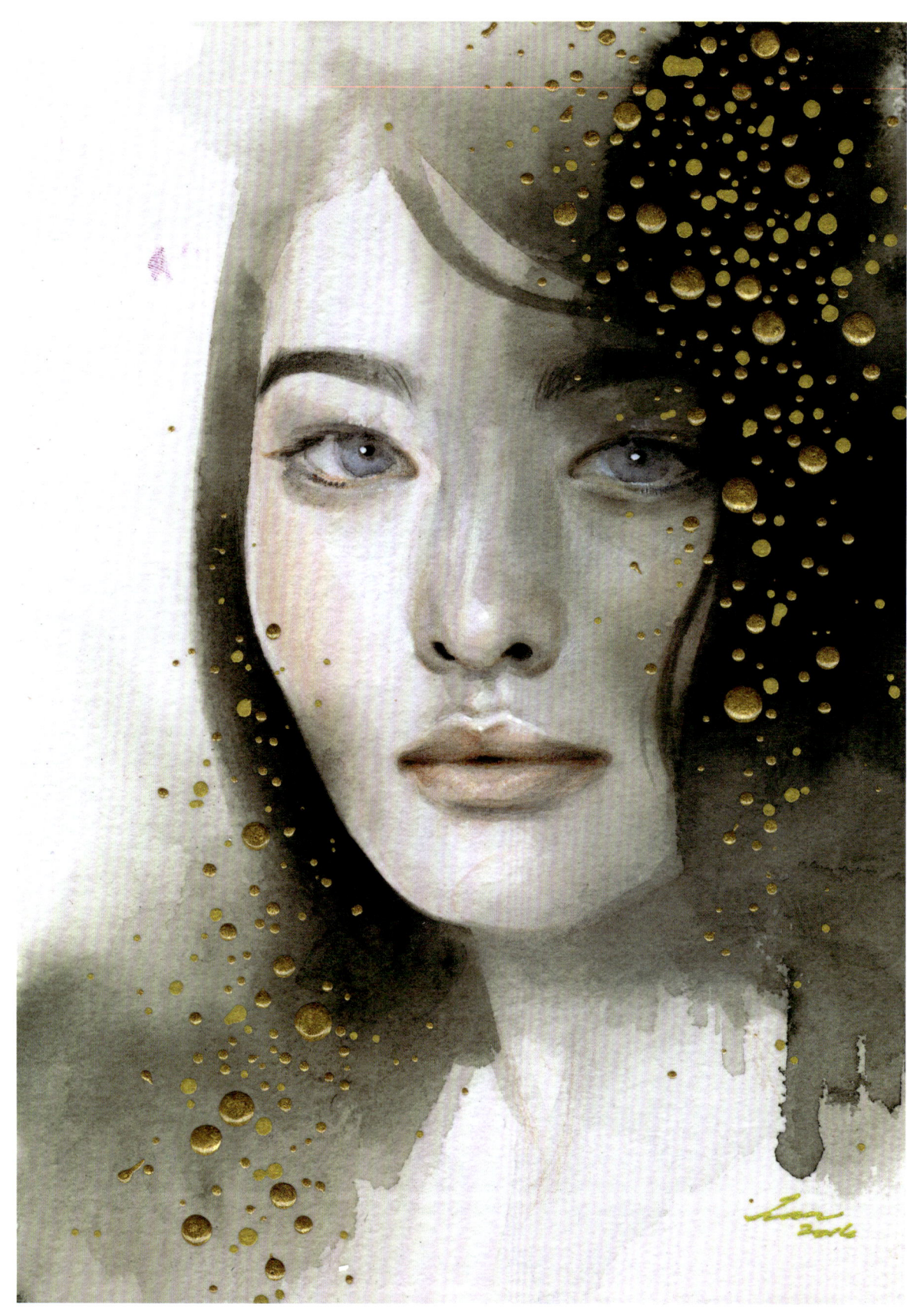

above
STUDY NO. 38
acrylic, colored pencil & pebeo paint, 5" × 7", 2016

right
STUDY NO. 41
acrylic, colored pencil & pebeo paint, 5" × 7", 2016

86

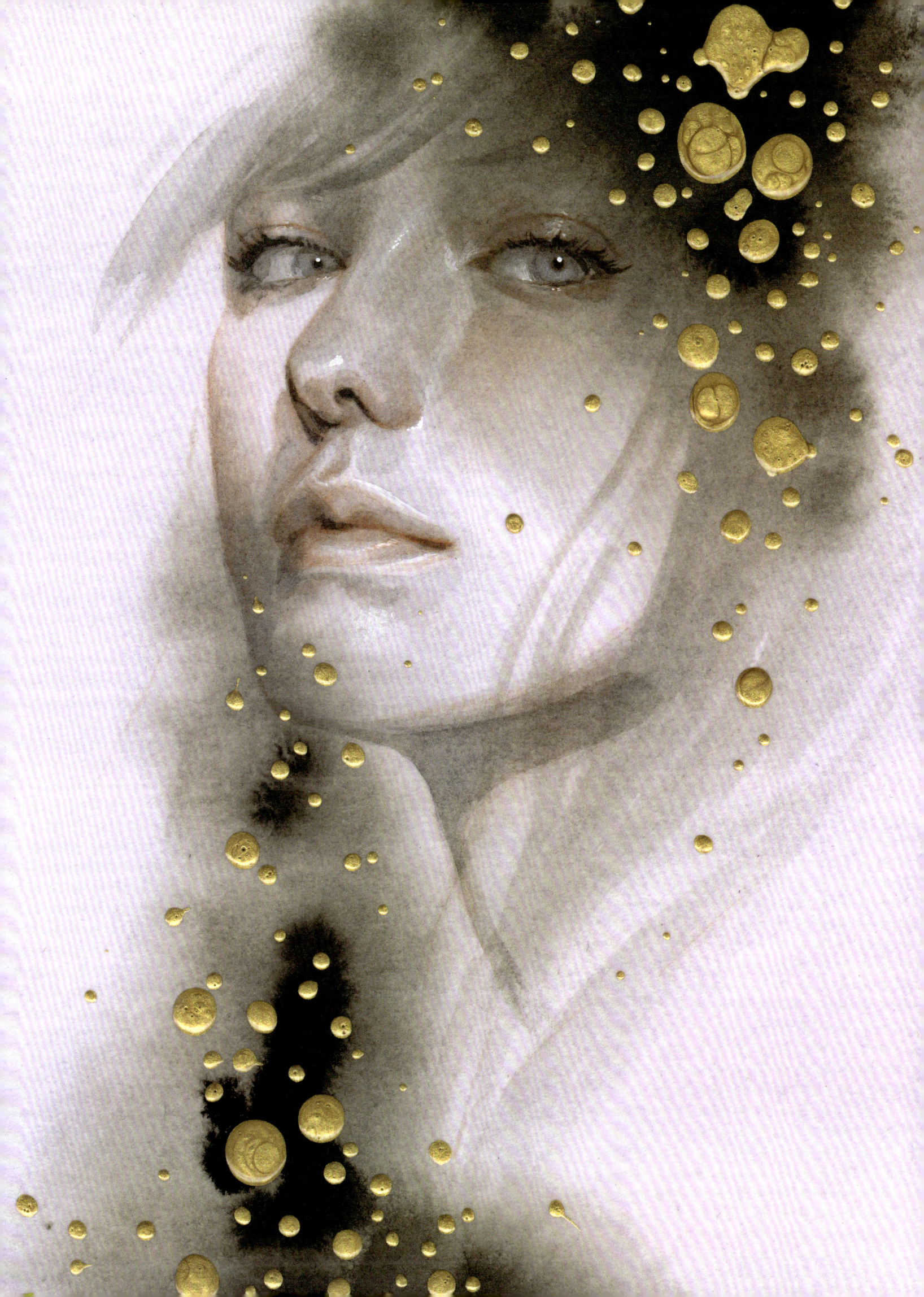

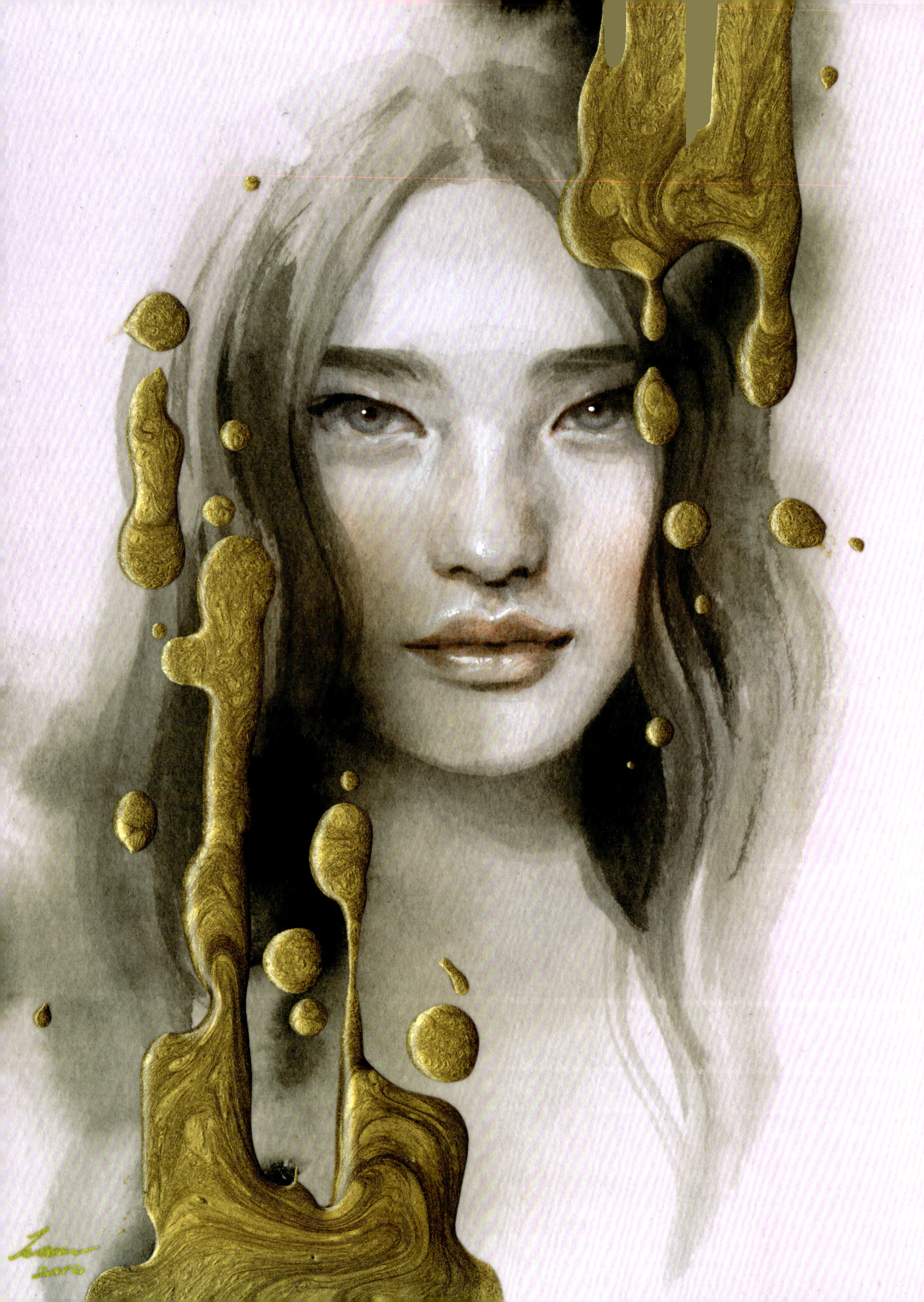

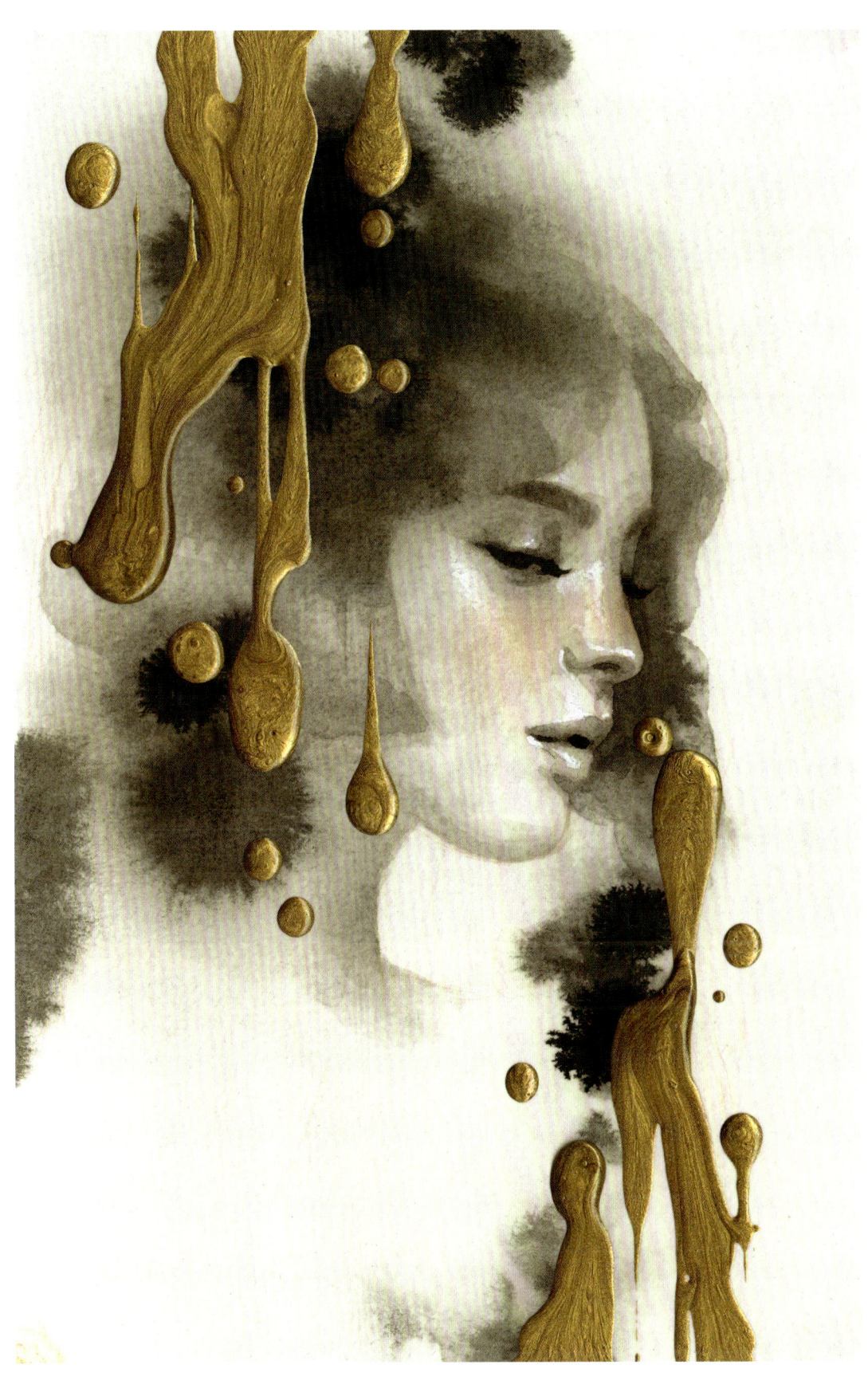

left
STUDY NO. 42
acrylic, colored pencil & pebeo paint, 5" × 7", 2016

above
STUDY NO. 52
ink, colored pencil & pebeo paint, 5.5" x 8.5", 2017

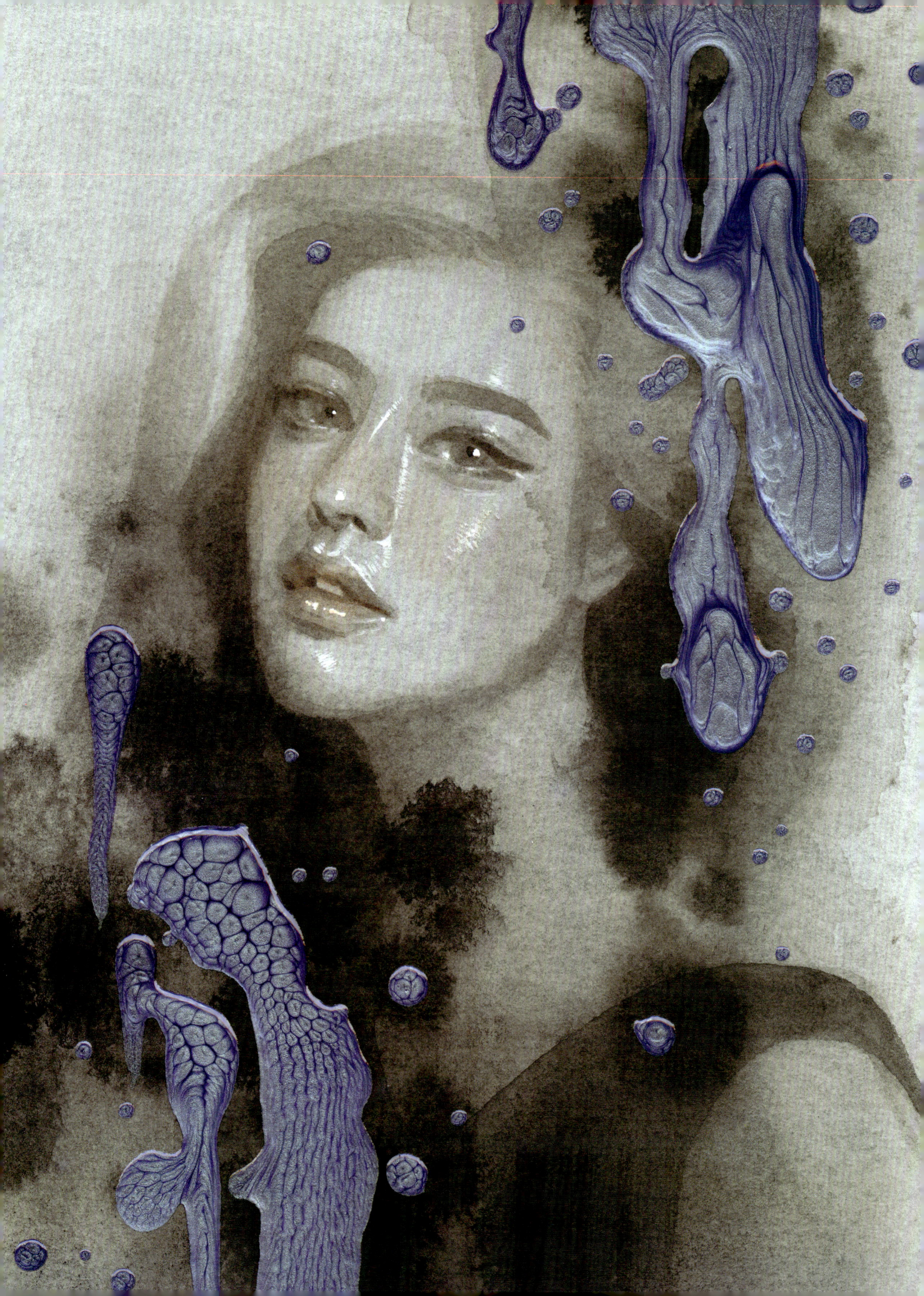

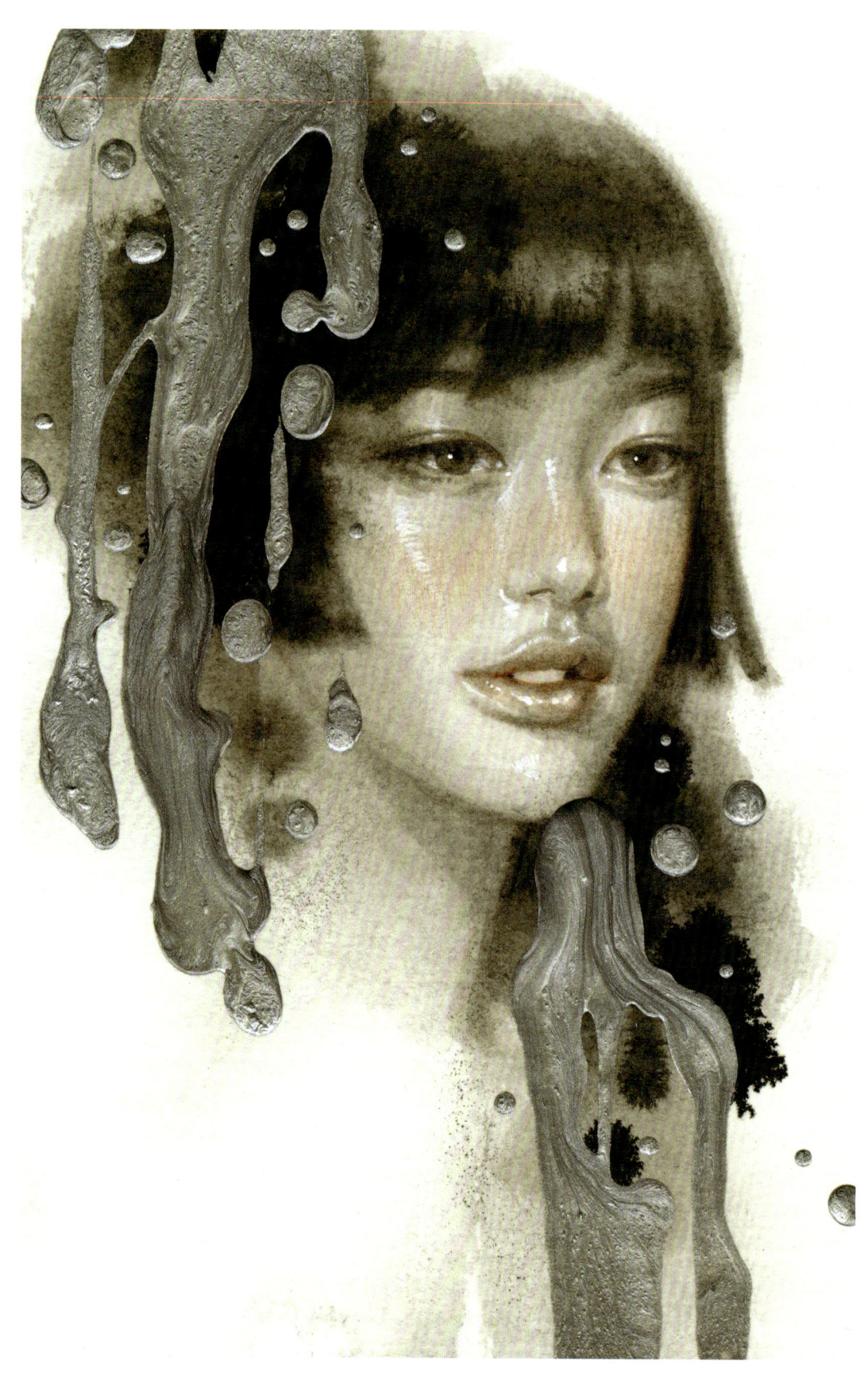

STUDY NO. 63
ink, colored pencil & pebeo paint, 5.5" x 8.5", 2017

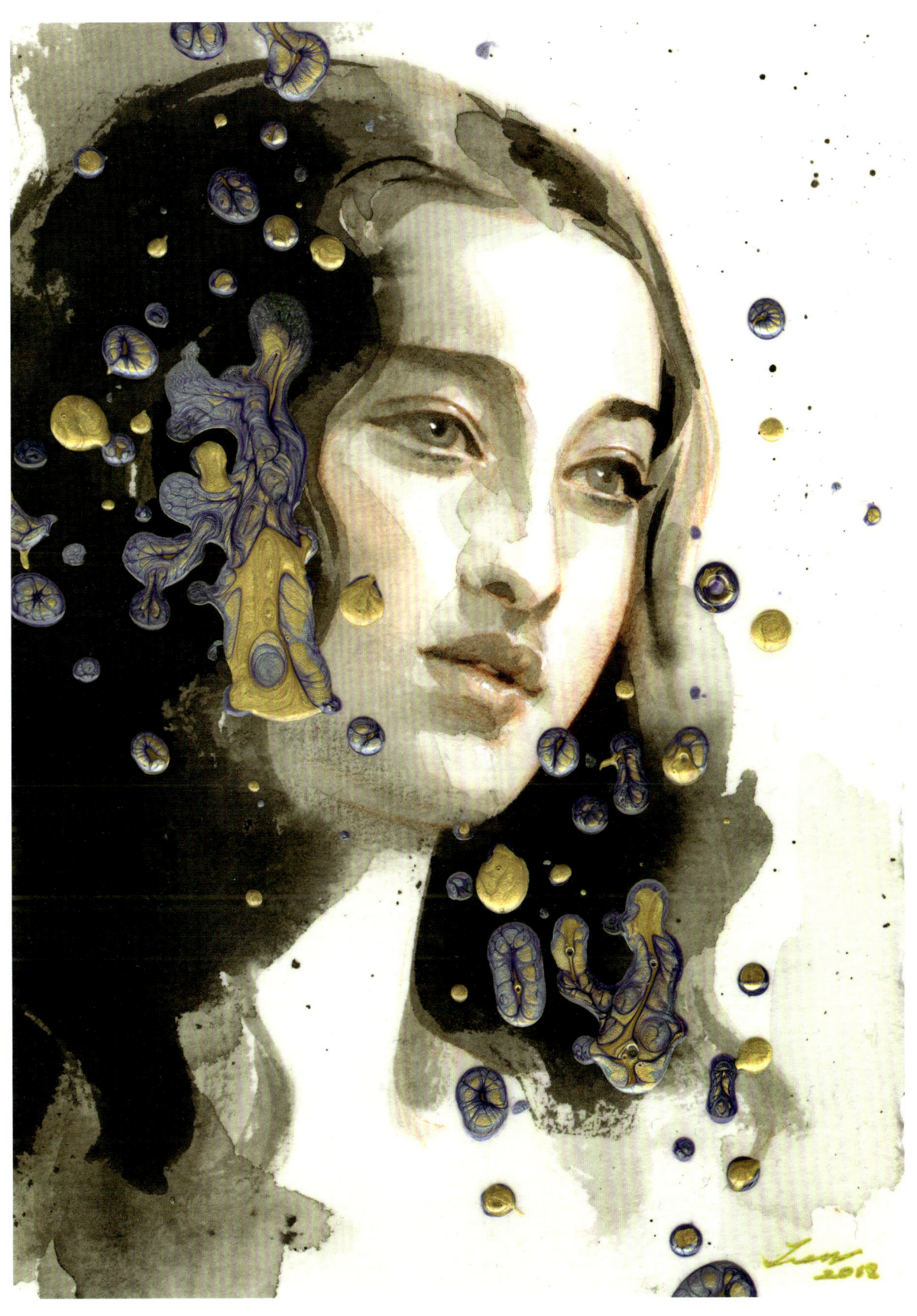

STUDY NO. 68
ink, acrylic & pebeo paint, 5" × 7", 2018

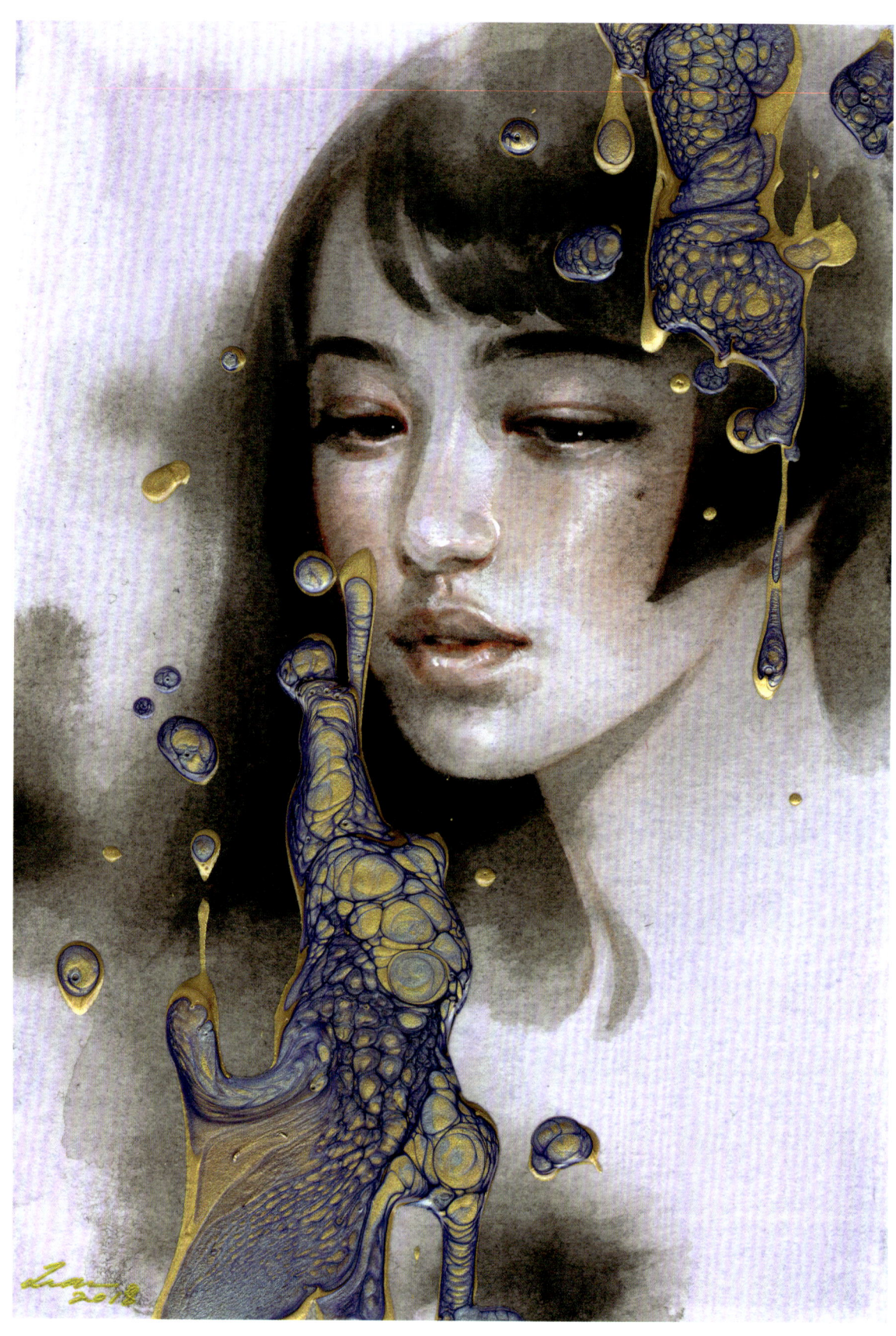

above
STUDY NO. 71
ink, acrylic & pebeo paint, 5" × 7", 2018

right
STUDY NO. 72
ink, acrylic & pebeo paint, 5" × 7", 2018

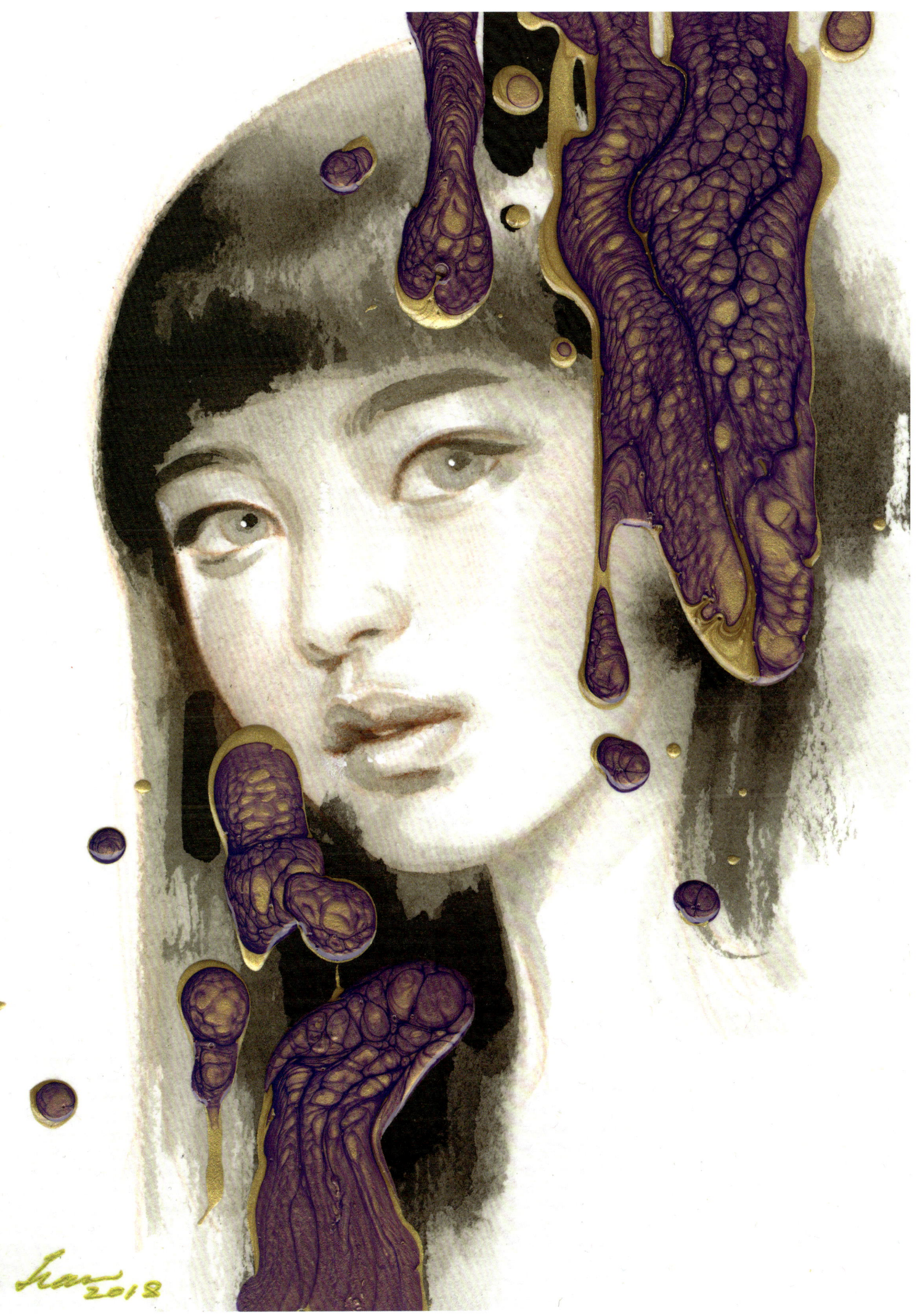

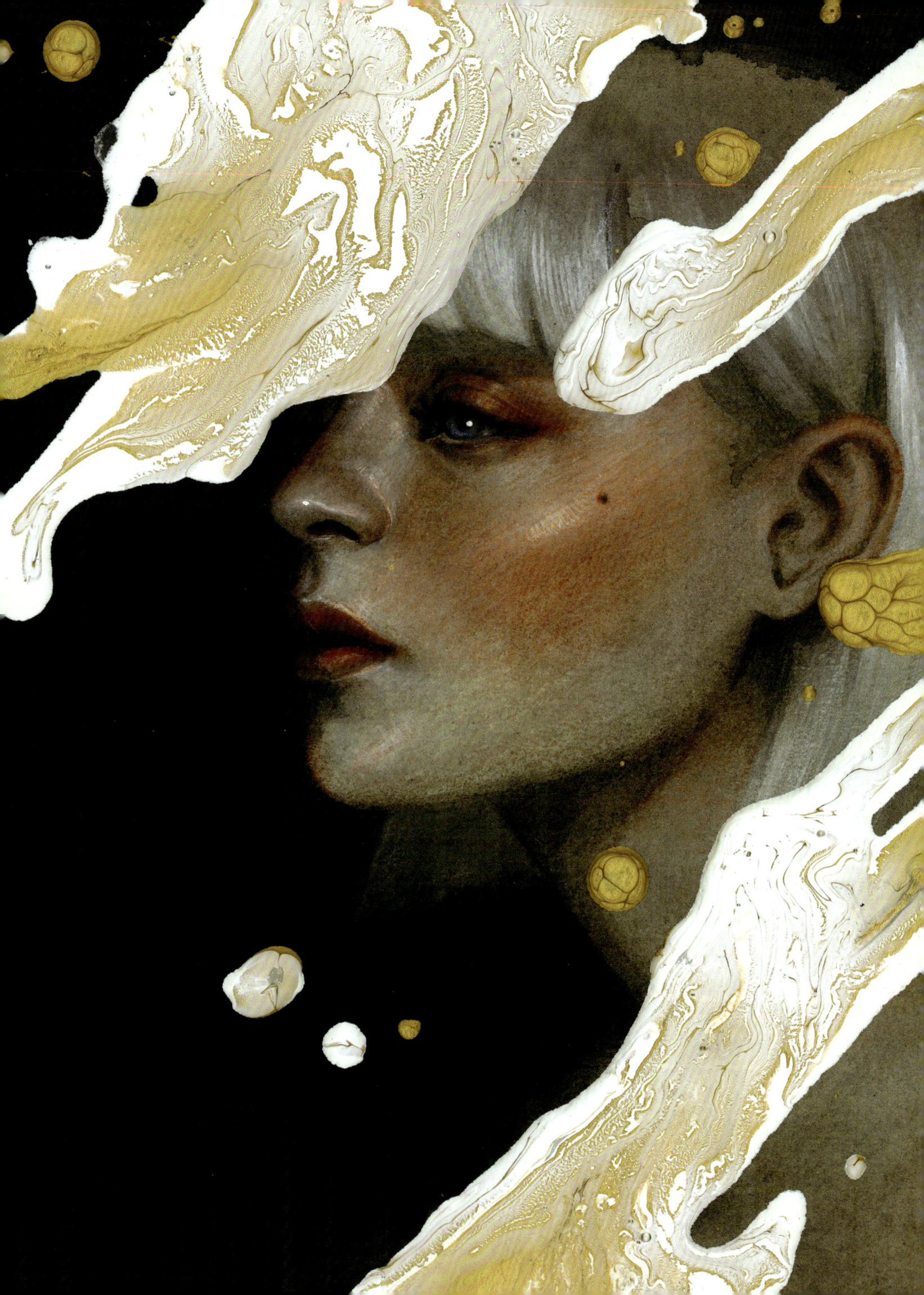

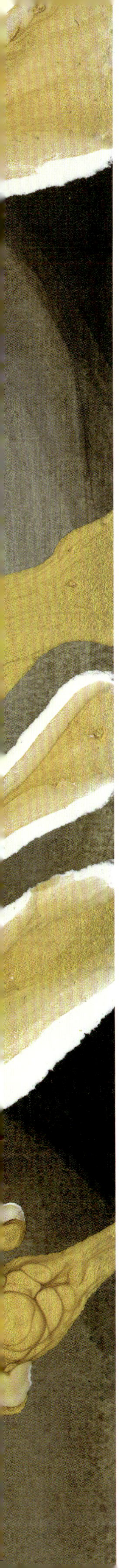

STUDY NO. 82
acrylic, colored pencil & pebeo paint, 6″ × 9″, 2019

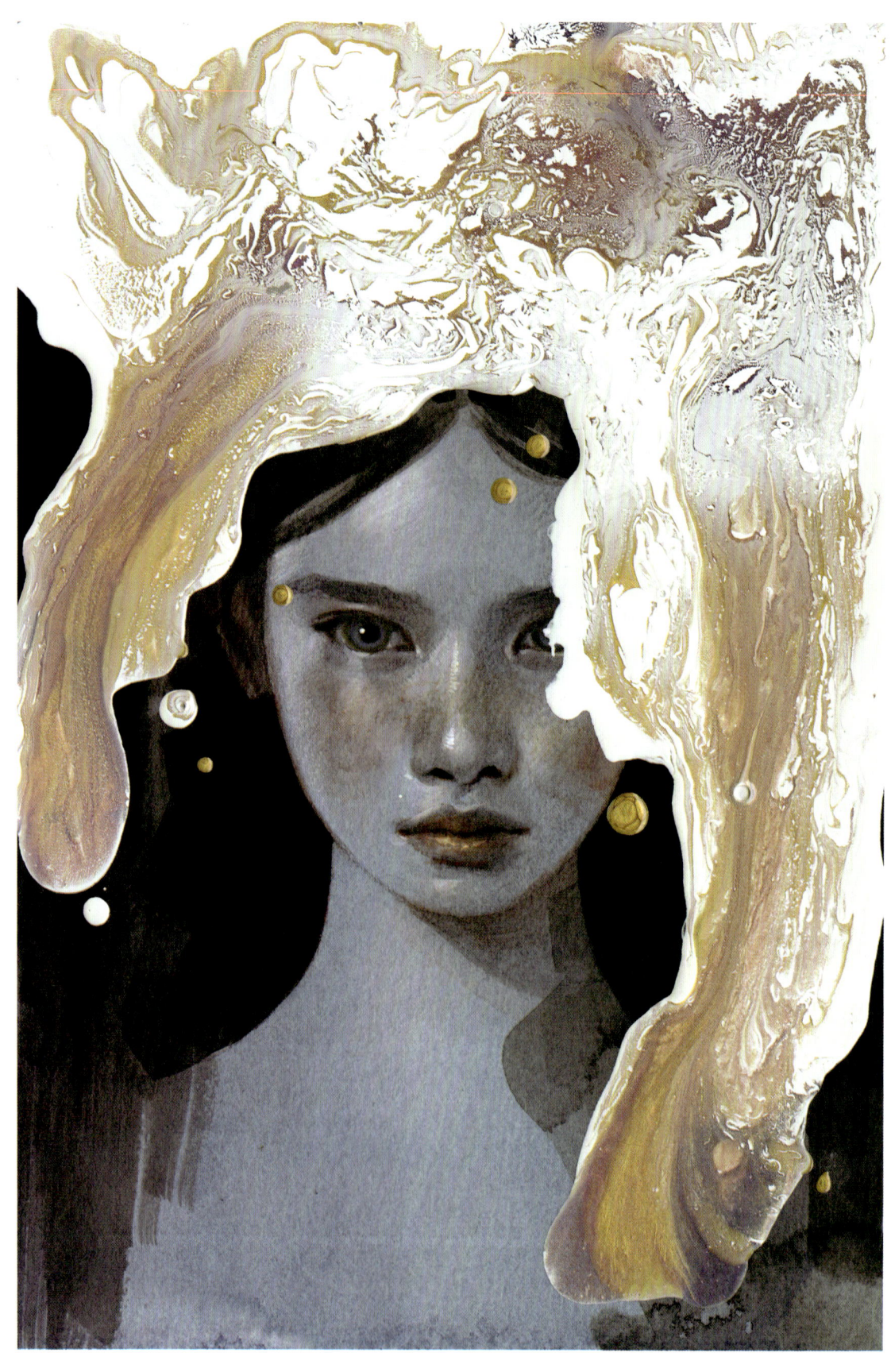

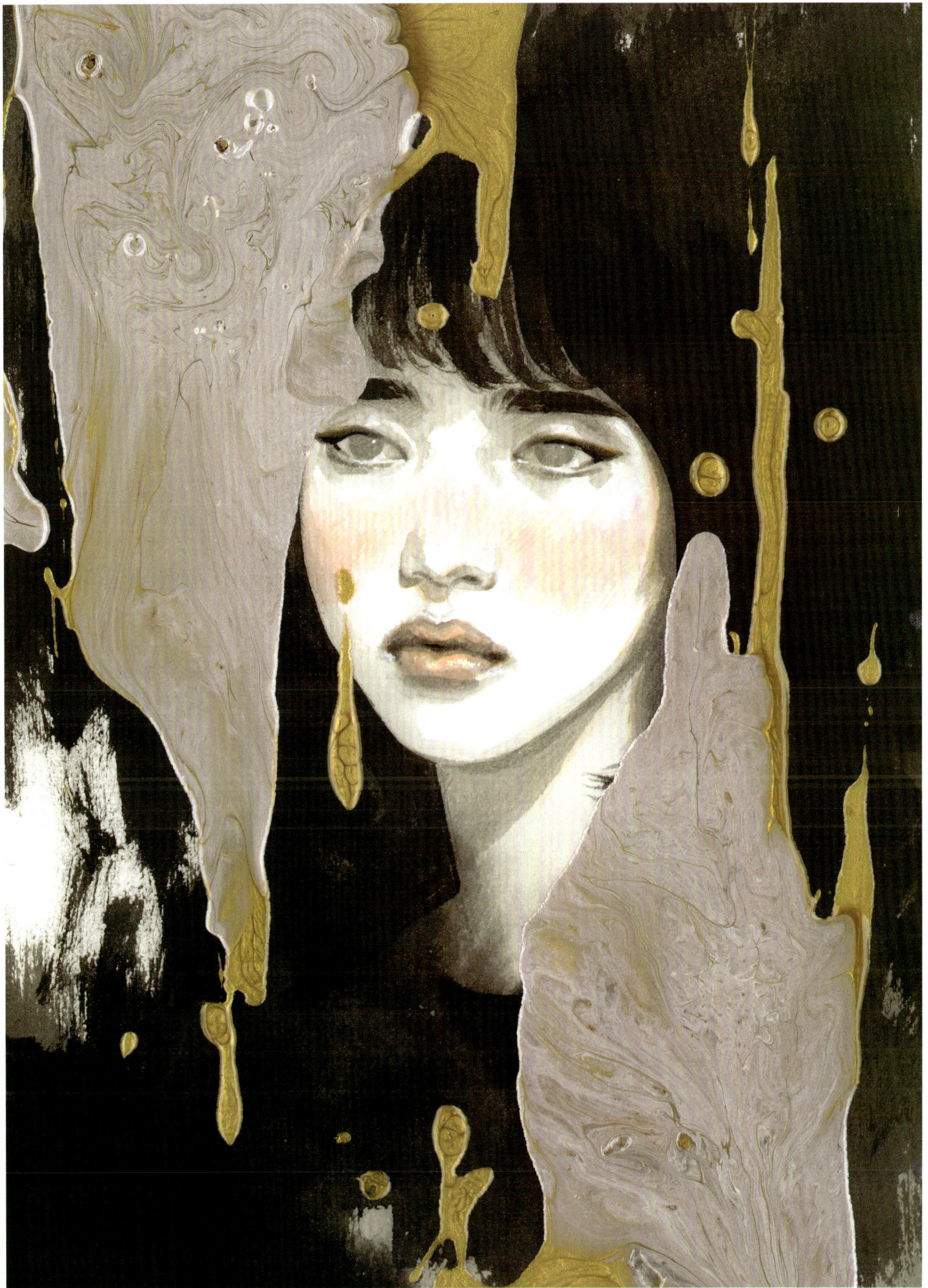

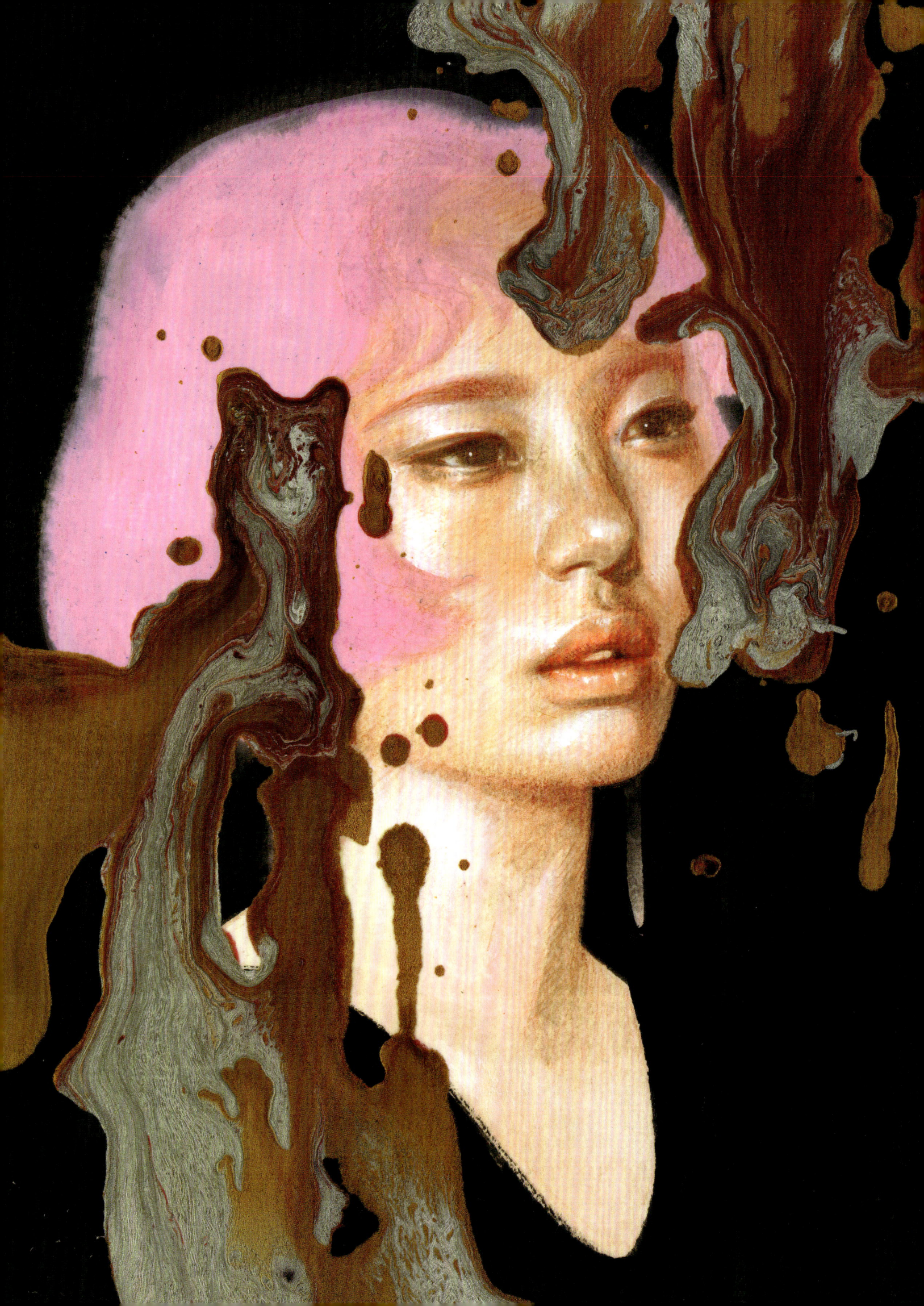

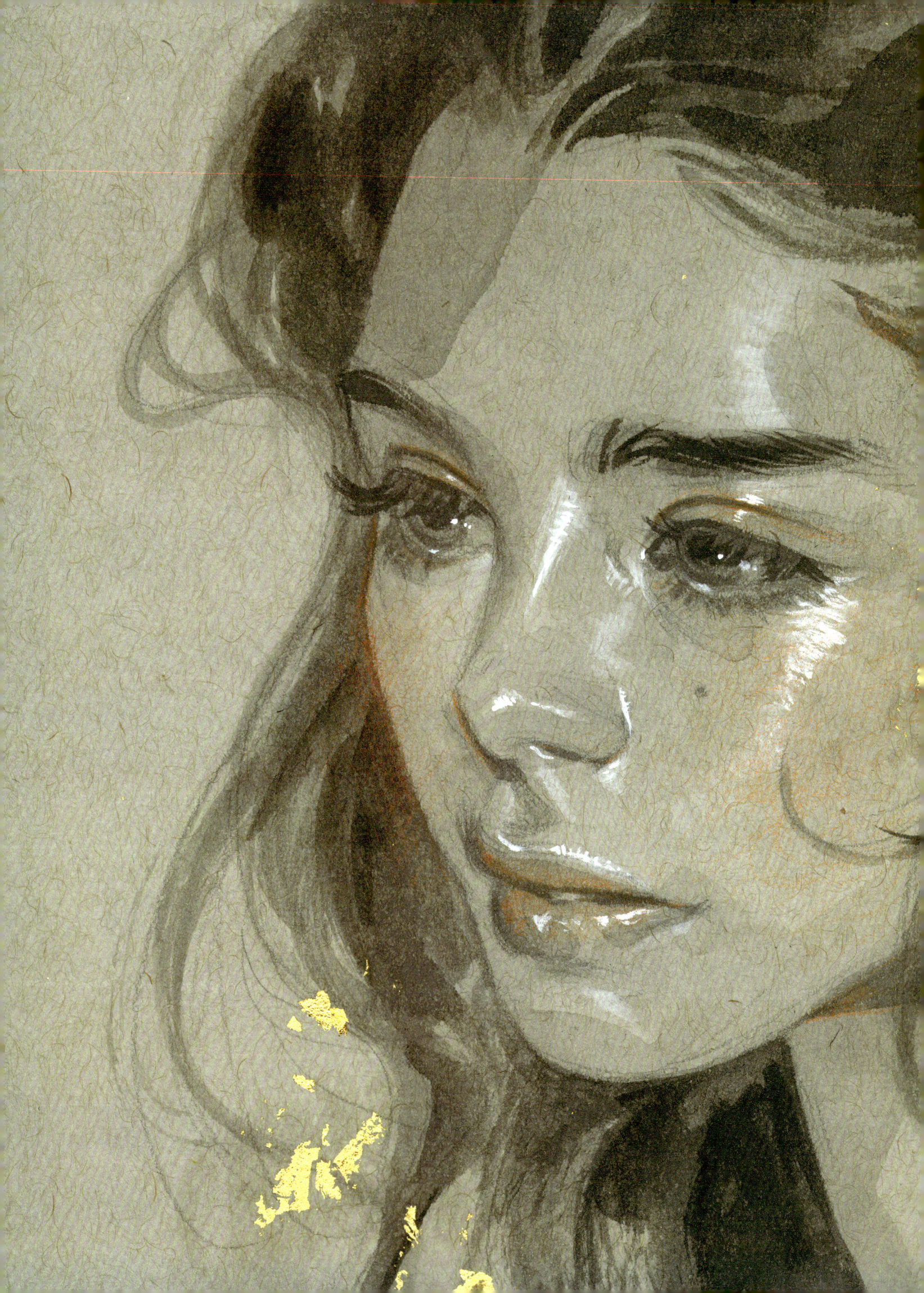

TONED PAPER

EXPERIMENTS ON MID-VALUE COLORED PAPER

In college, I worked with toned paper and found it incredibly efficient for rendering form. With the middle value established by the color of the paper, form is achieved by applying highlights and shadows. I revisit the substrate in the following studies as a way to recalibrate how I see tonal values. I have a tendency to over-render, particularly in faces, which dulls the natural movement of gestural brushstrokes. When working on colored paper, I'm more mindful of how lights and darks are handled, restricting my compulsion to polish details.

Painting on a toned background also facilitates the illusion of depth, allowing me to contrast flat shapes with three-dimensional forms. It also unifies the picture plane and accentuates special pigments, such as metallic inks. It's highly effective in creating an impression of space on paper and realigning an artist's approach to value.

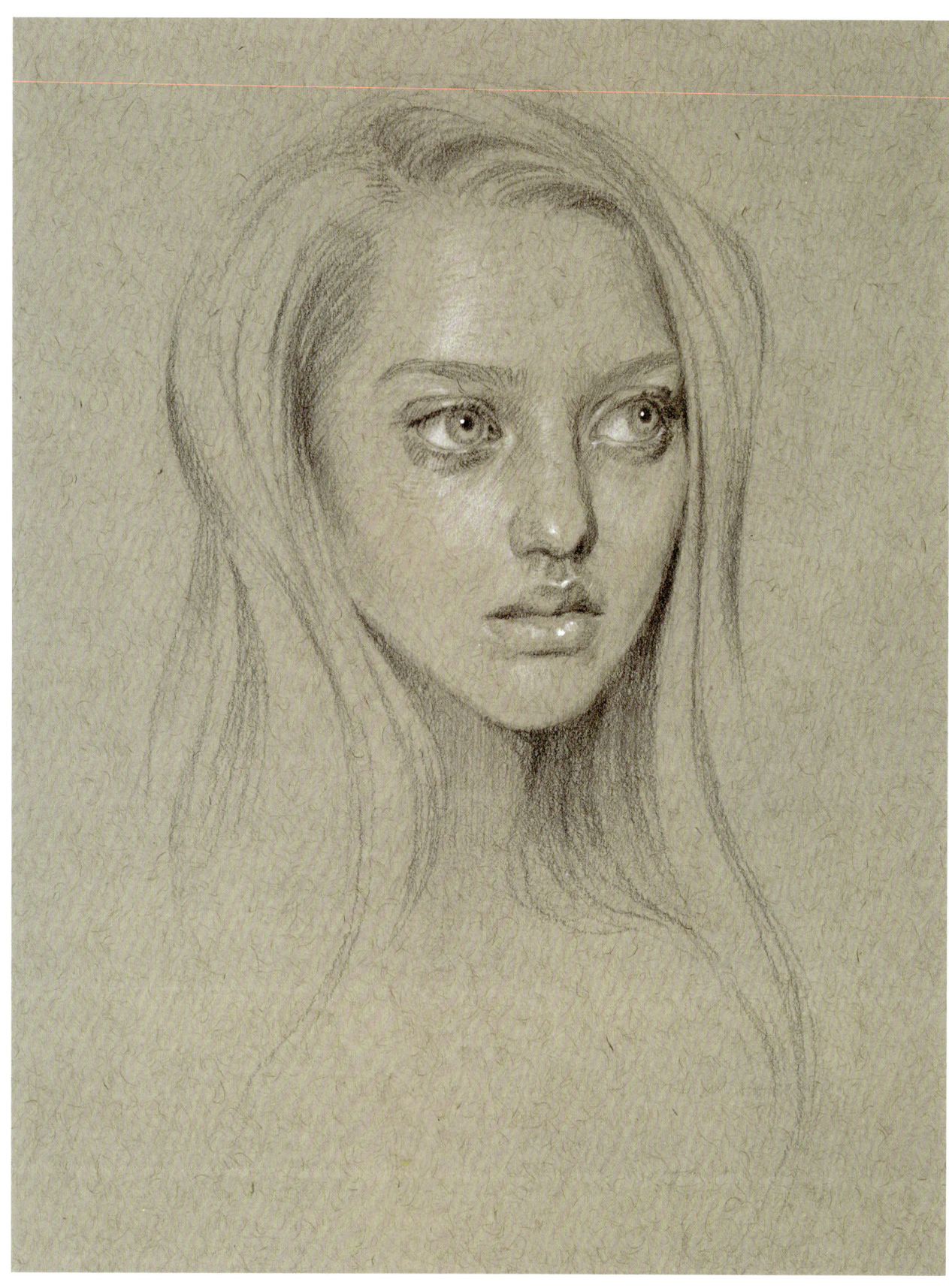

above
STUDY NO. P5
graphite on toned paper, 9" x 12", 2017

right
STUDY NO. 95
ink & colored pencil on toned paper, 9" x 12", 2020

104

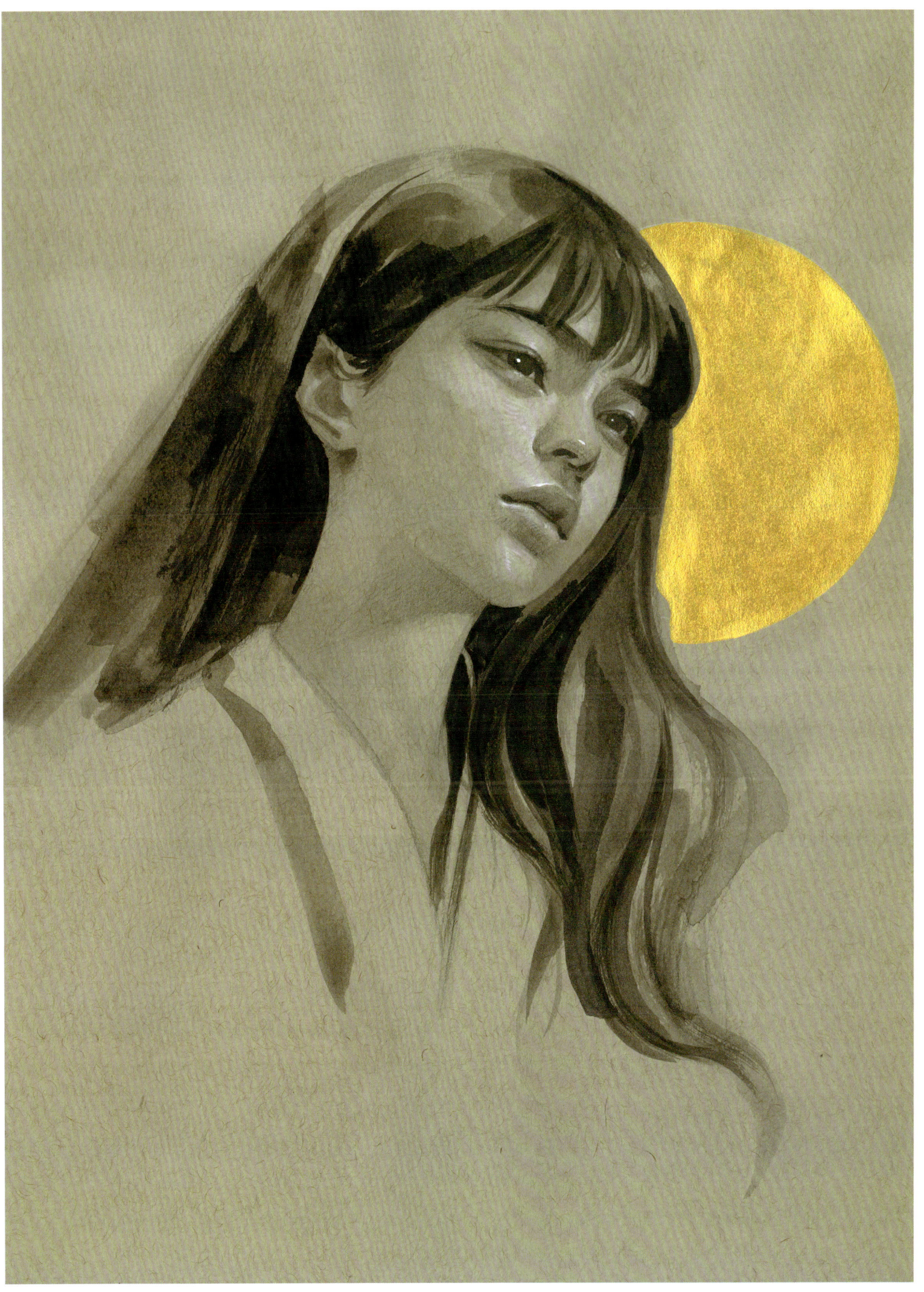

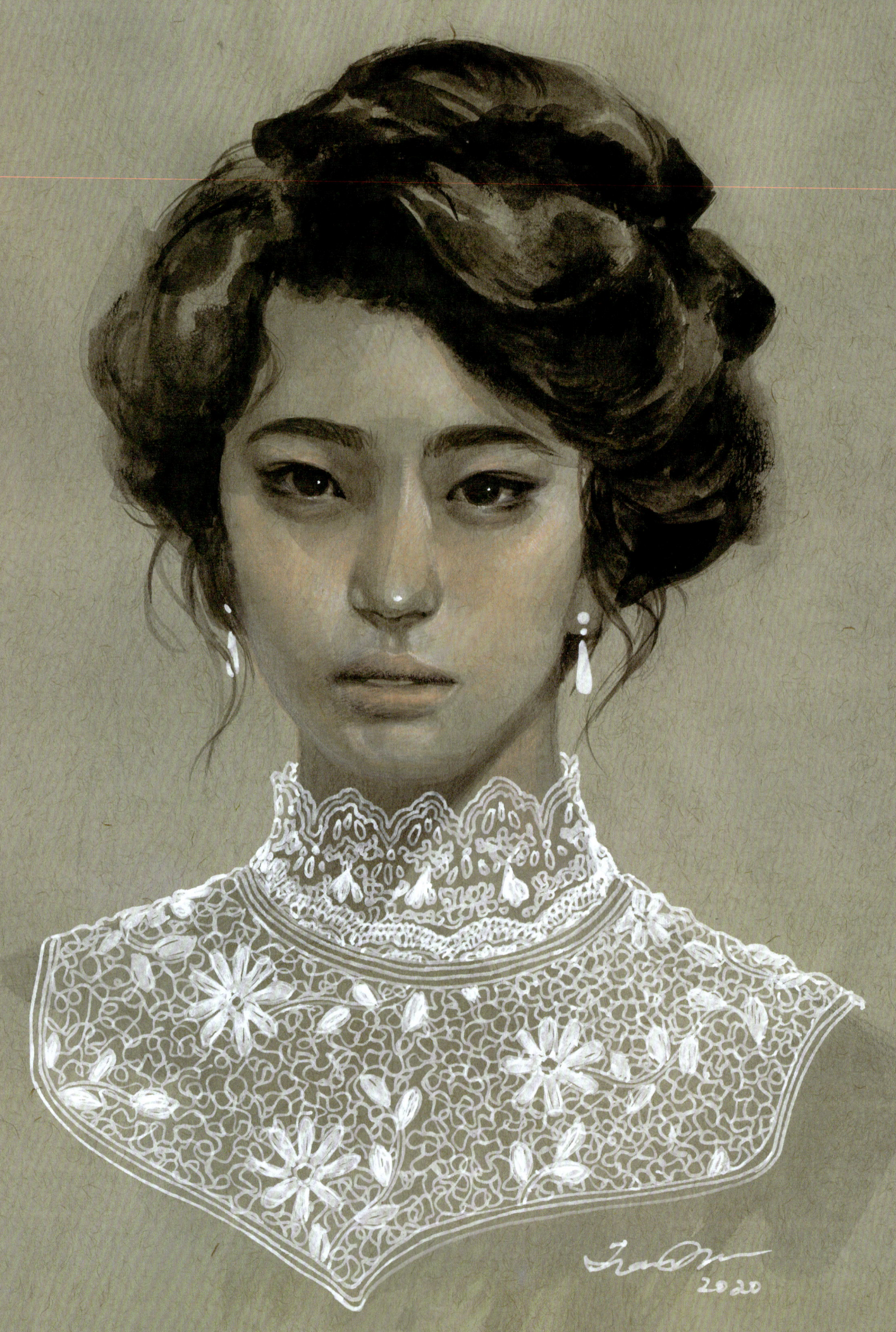

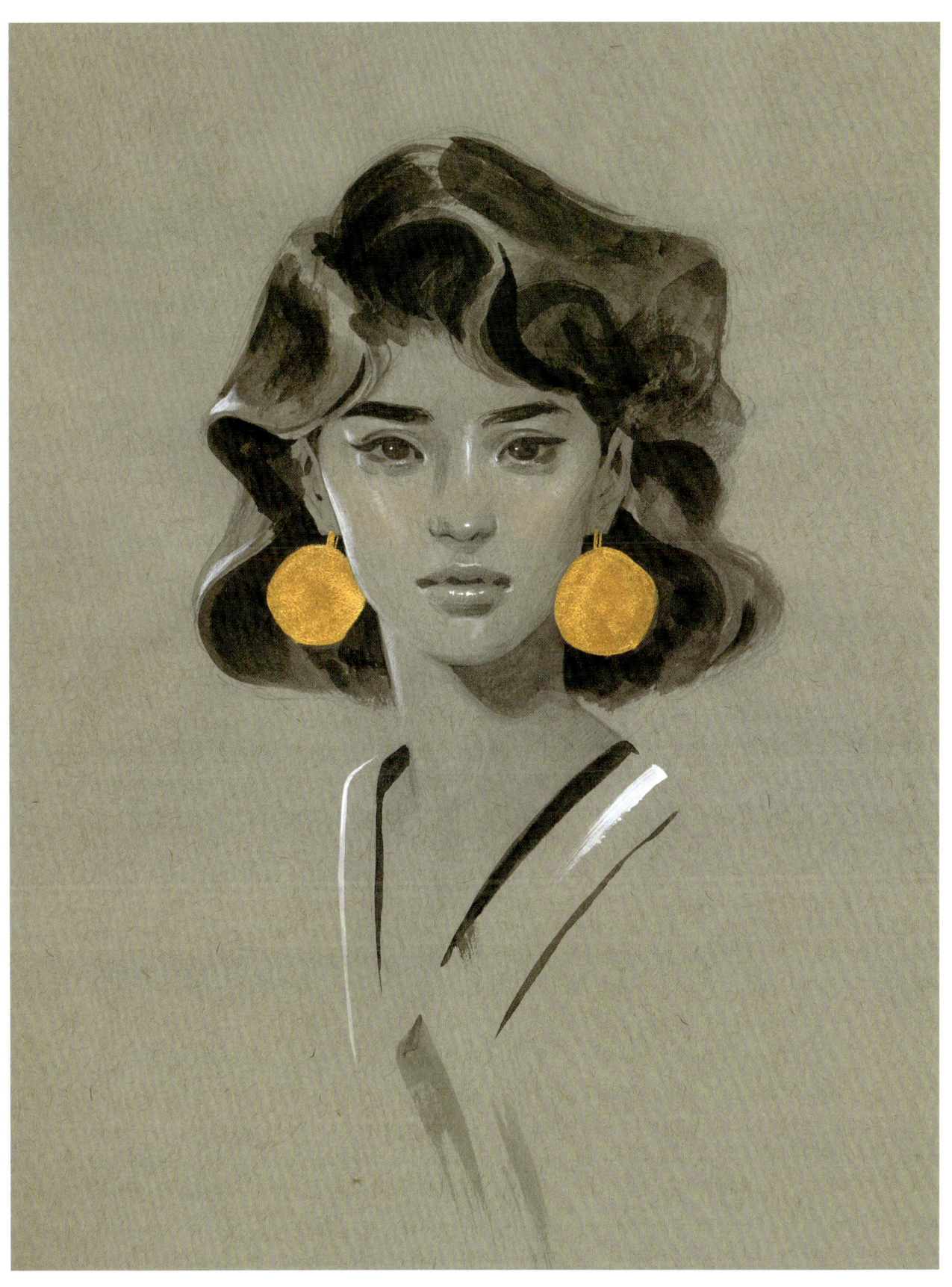

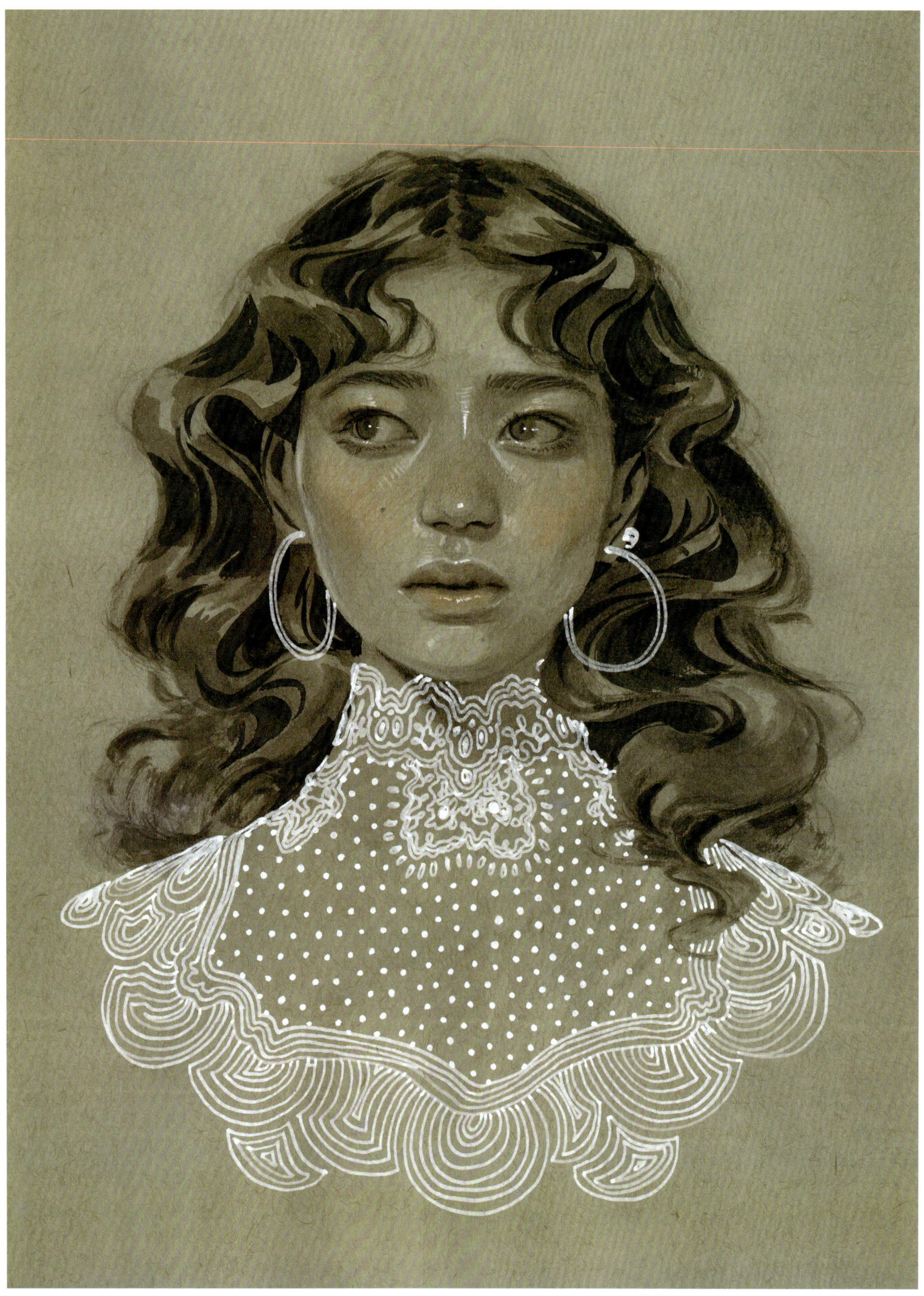

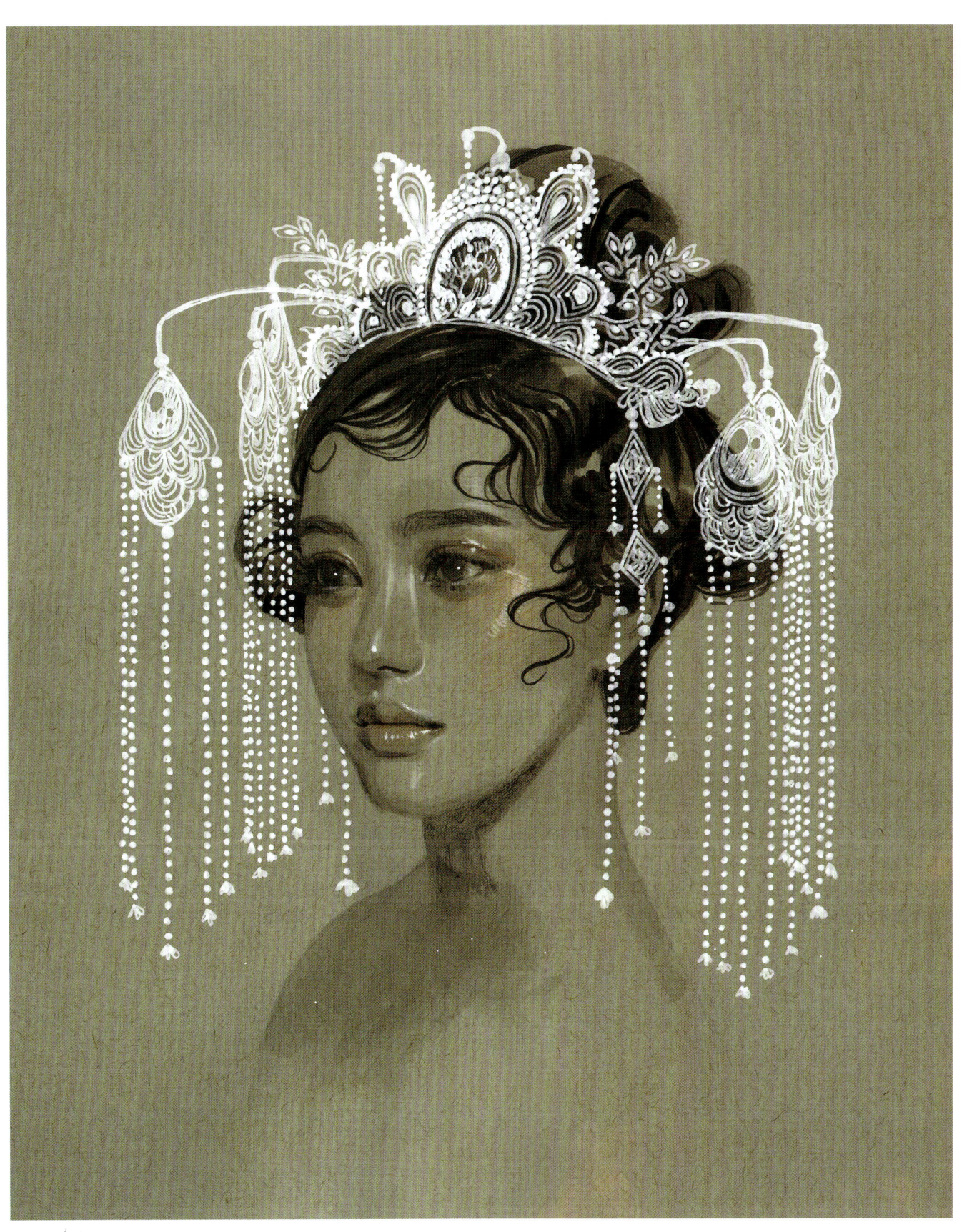

left
STUDY NO. 98
ink & colored pencil on toned paper, 9″ x 12″, 2020

above
STUDY NO. 99
ink & colored pencil on toned paper, 9″ x 12″, 2020

109

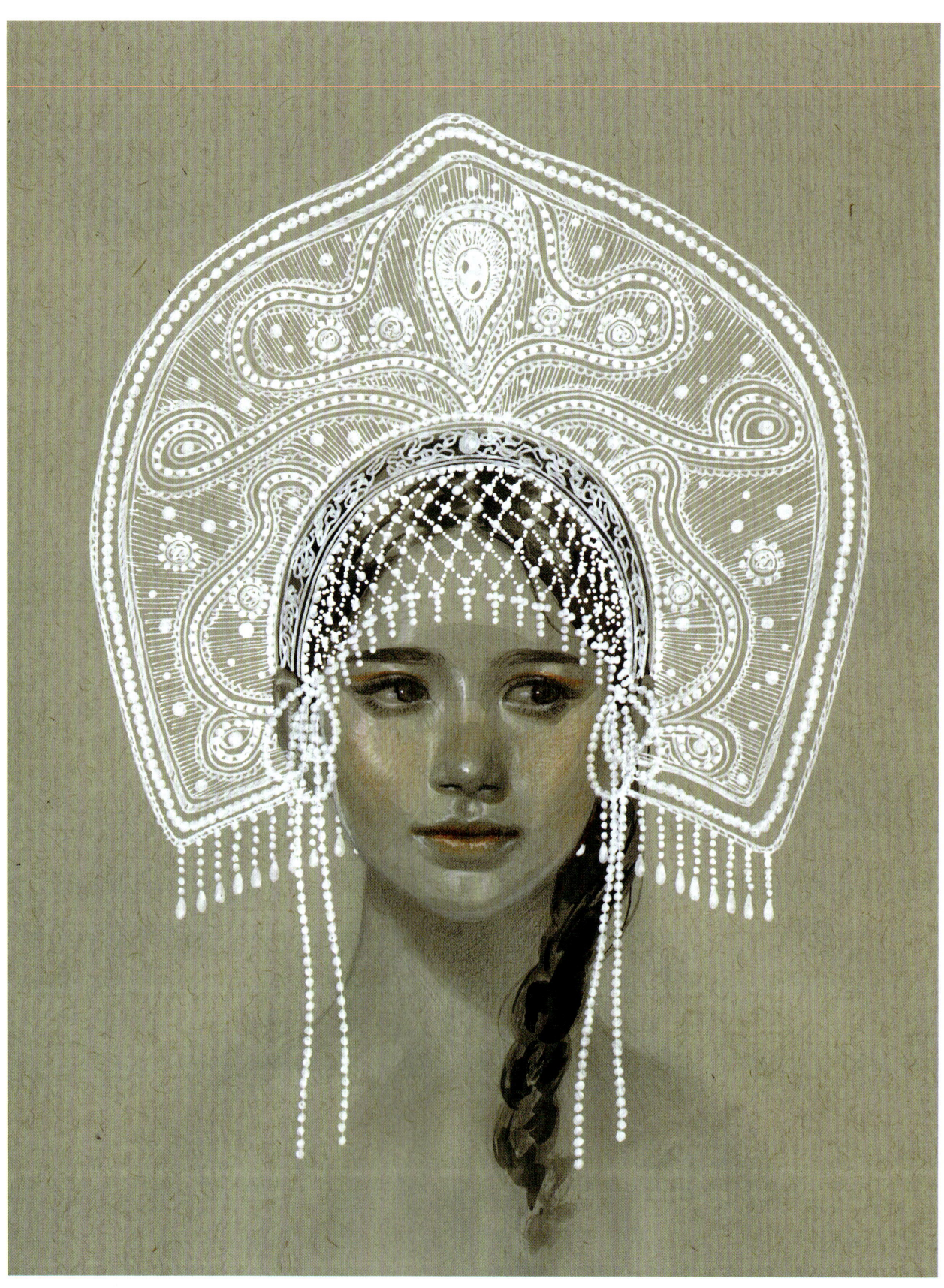

above

STUDY NO. 100

ink & colored pencil on toned paper, 9" x 12", 2020

right

STUDY NO. 101

ink & colored pencil on toned paper, 9" x 12", 2020

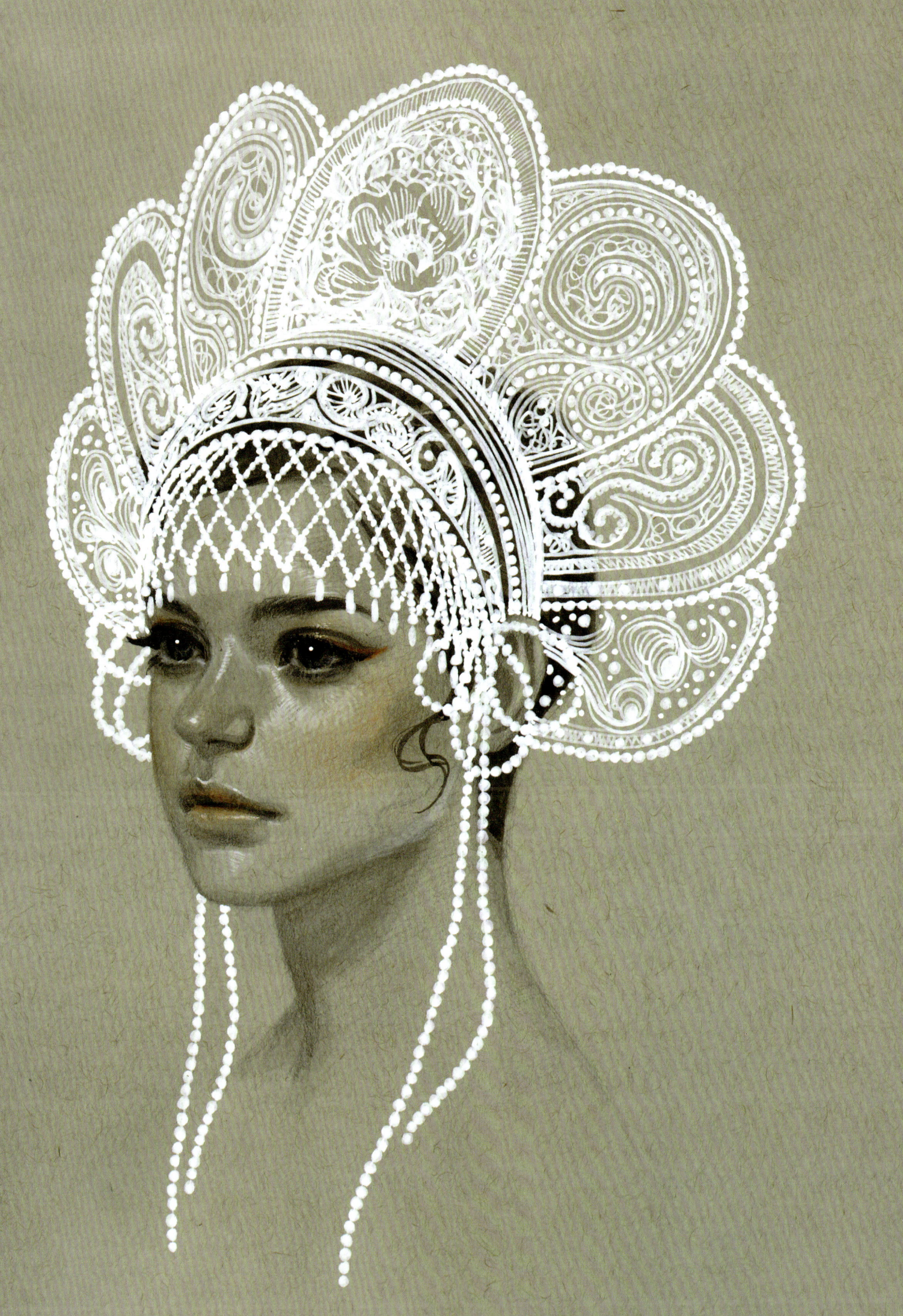

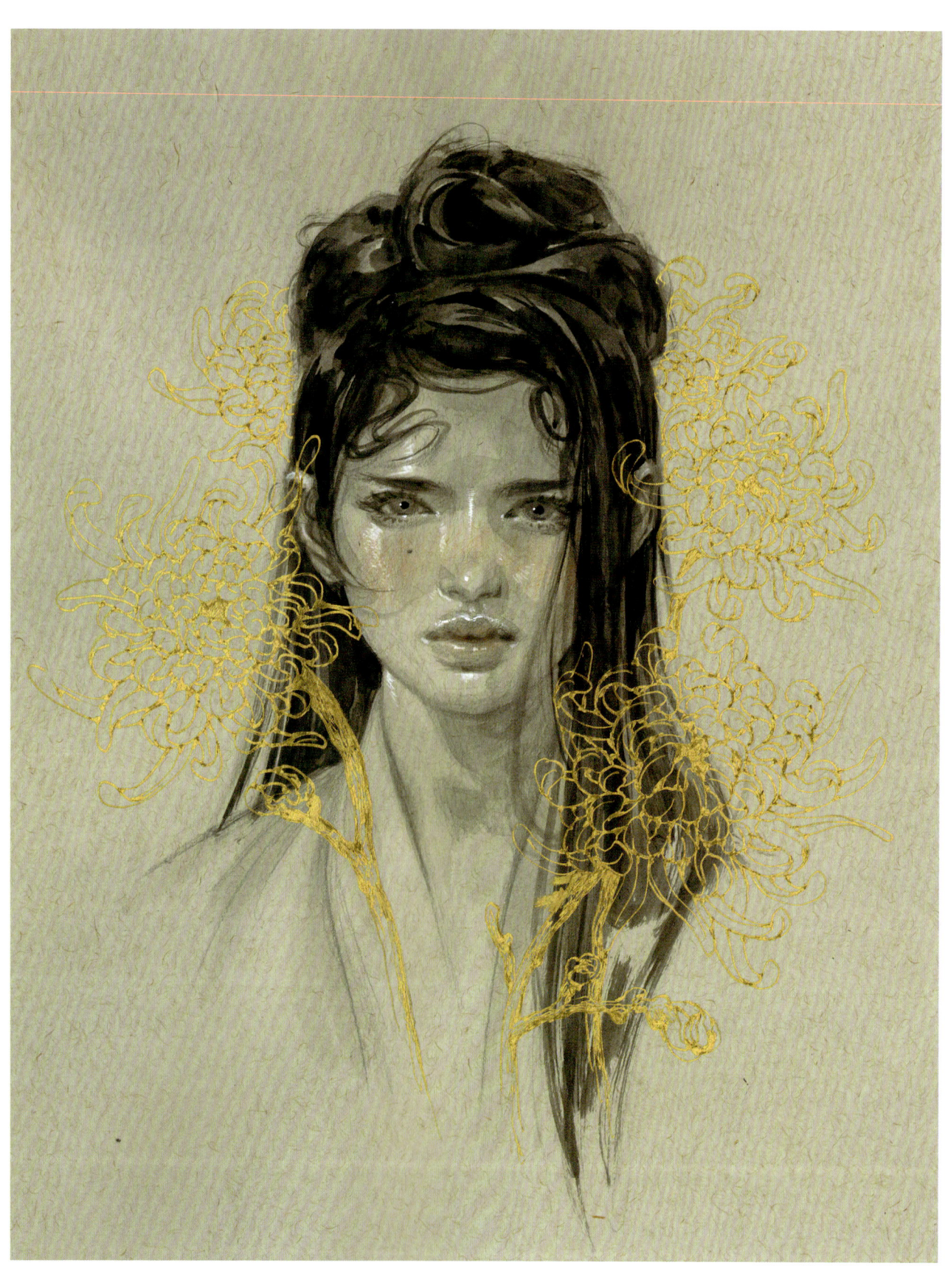

STUDY NO. 102
ink & colored pencil on toned paper, 9" × 12", 2021

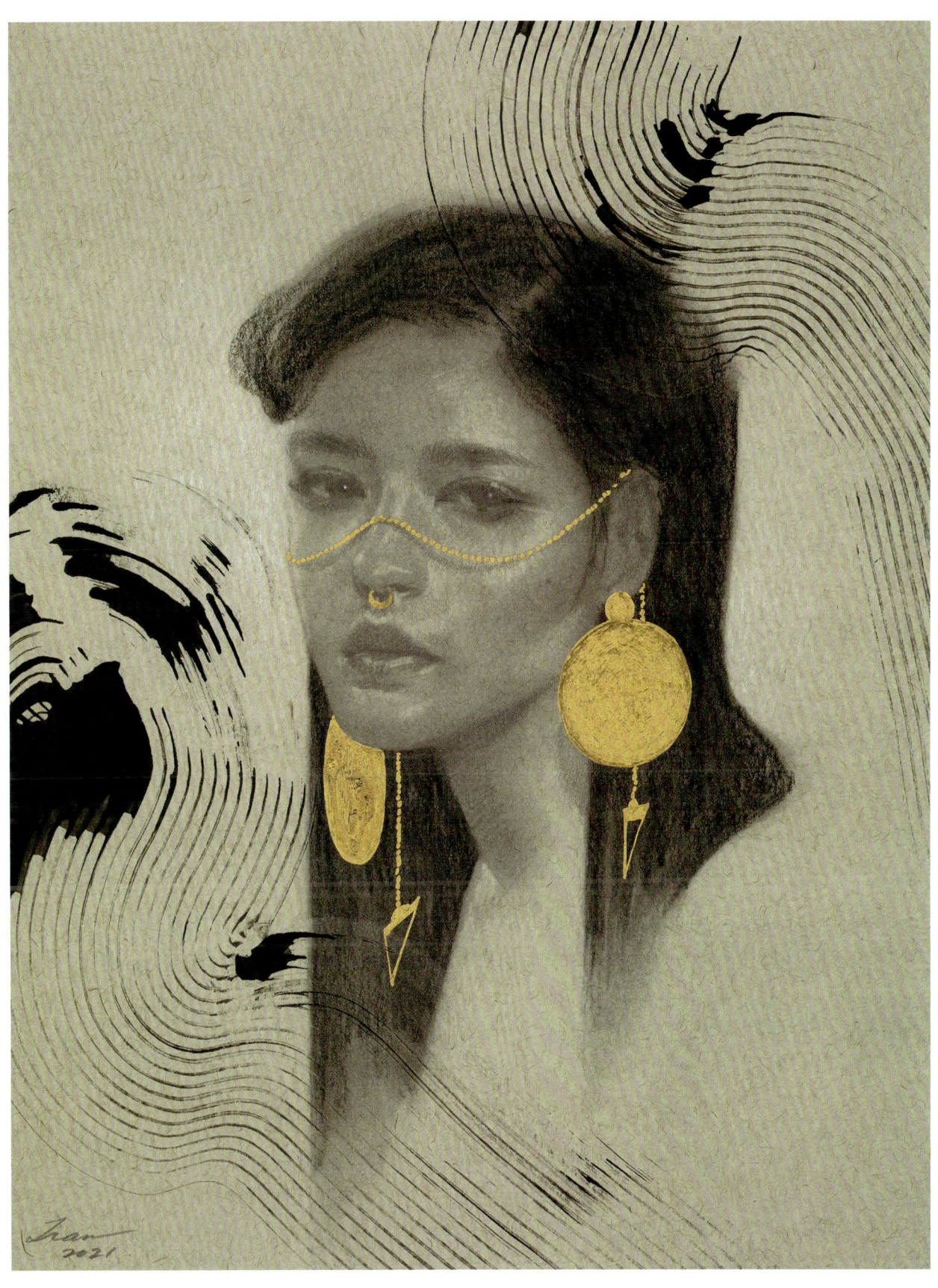

STUDY NO. 103
graphite, charcoal & acrylic on toned paper, 9" × 12", 2021

113

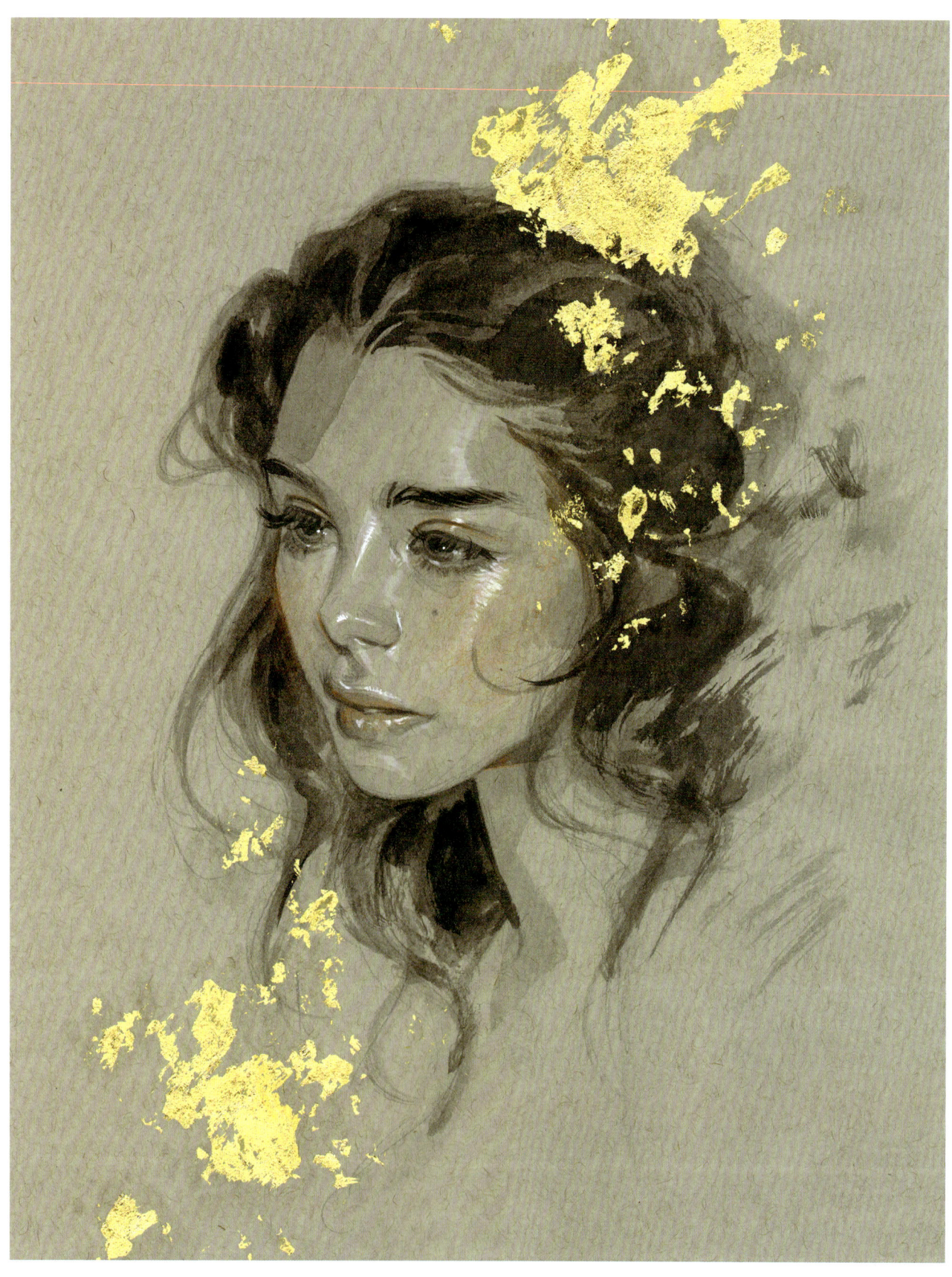

above
STUDY NO. 104
ink, colored pencil & gold leaf on toned paper, 9" x 12", 2021

right
STUDY NO. 105
ink, gold leaf & ginkgo leaf on toned paper, 9" x 12", 2021

114

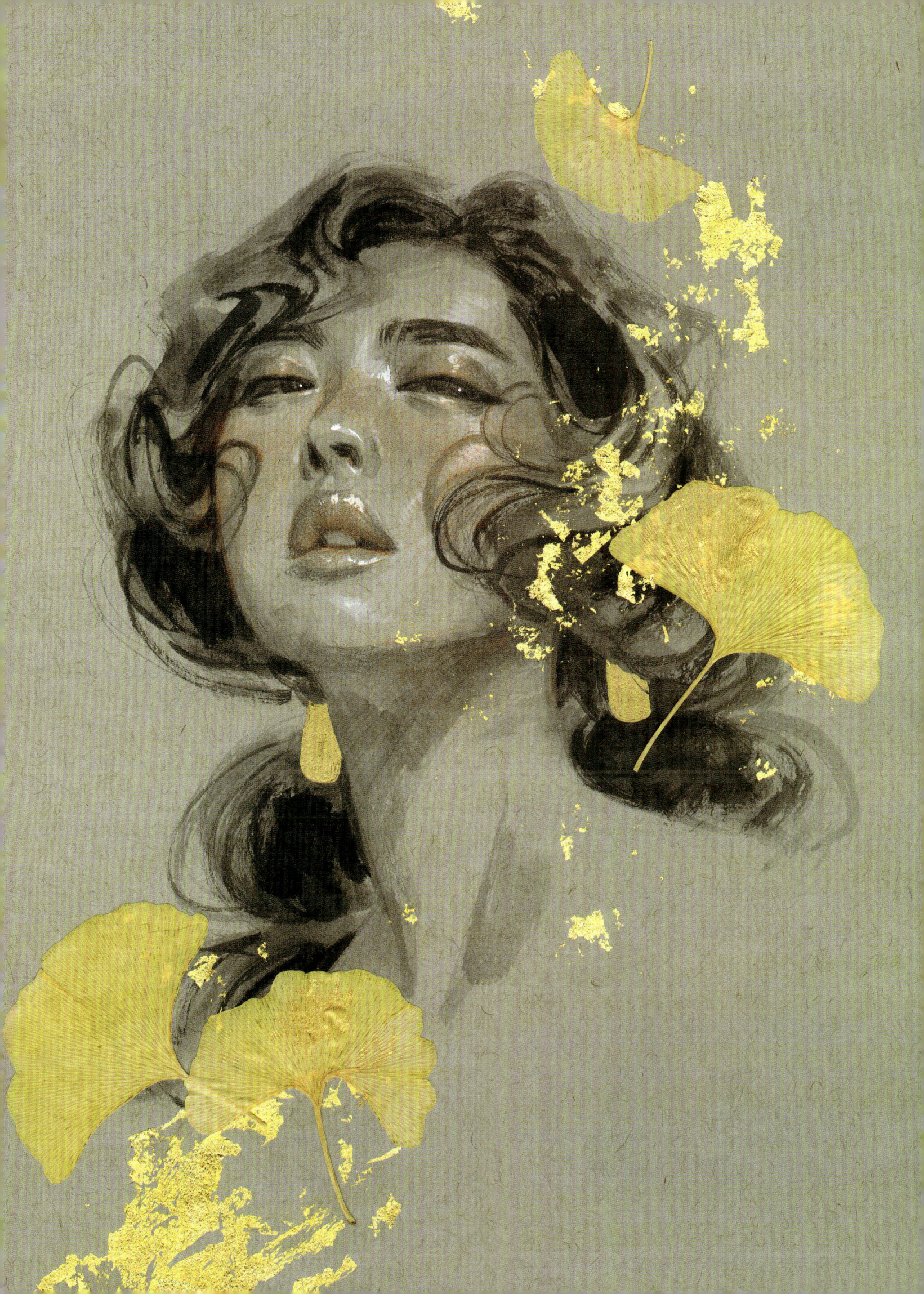

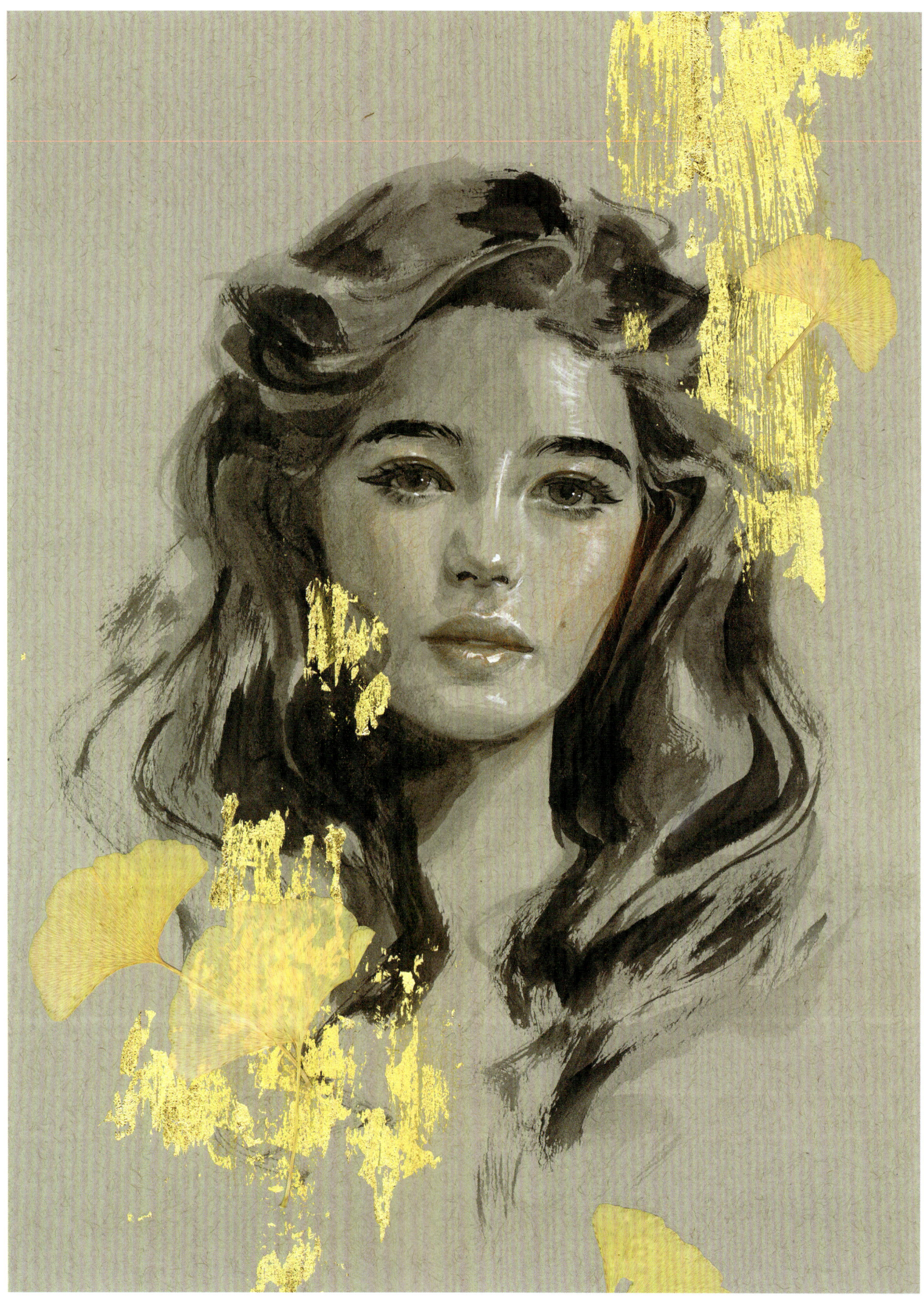

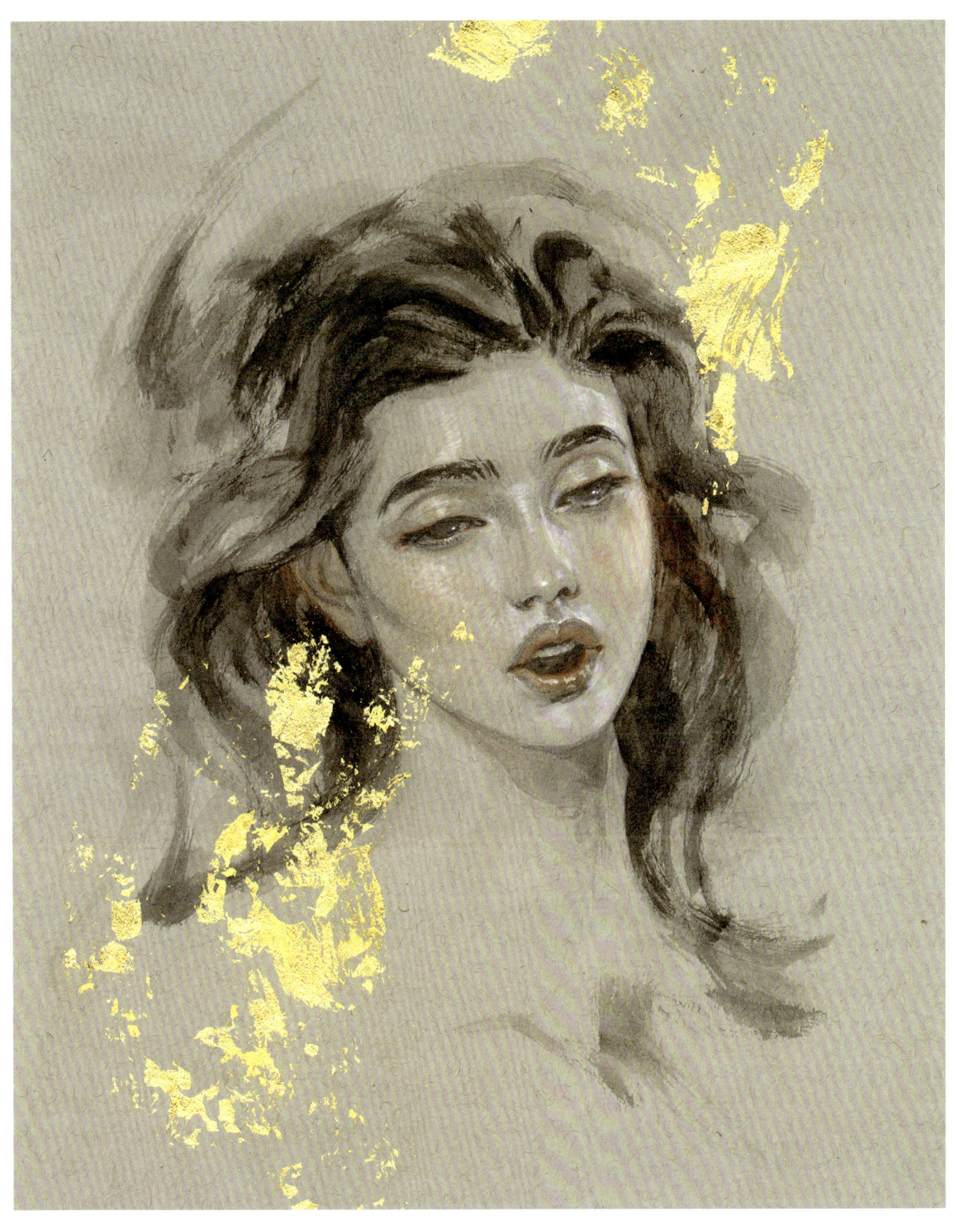

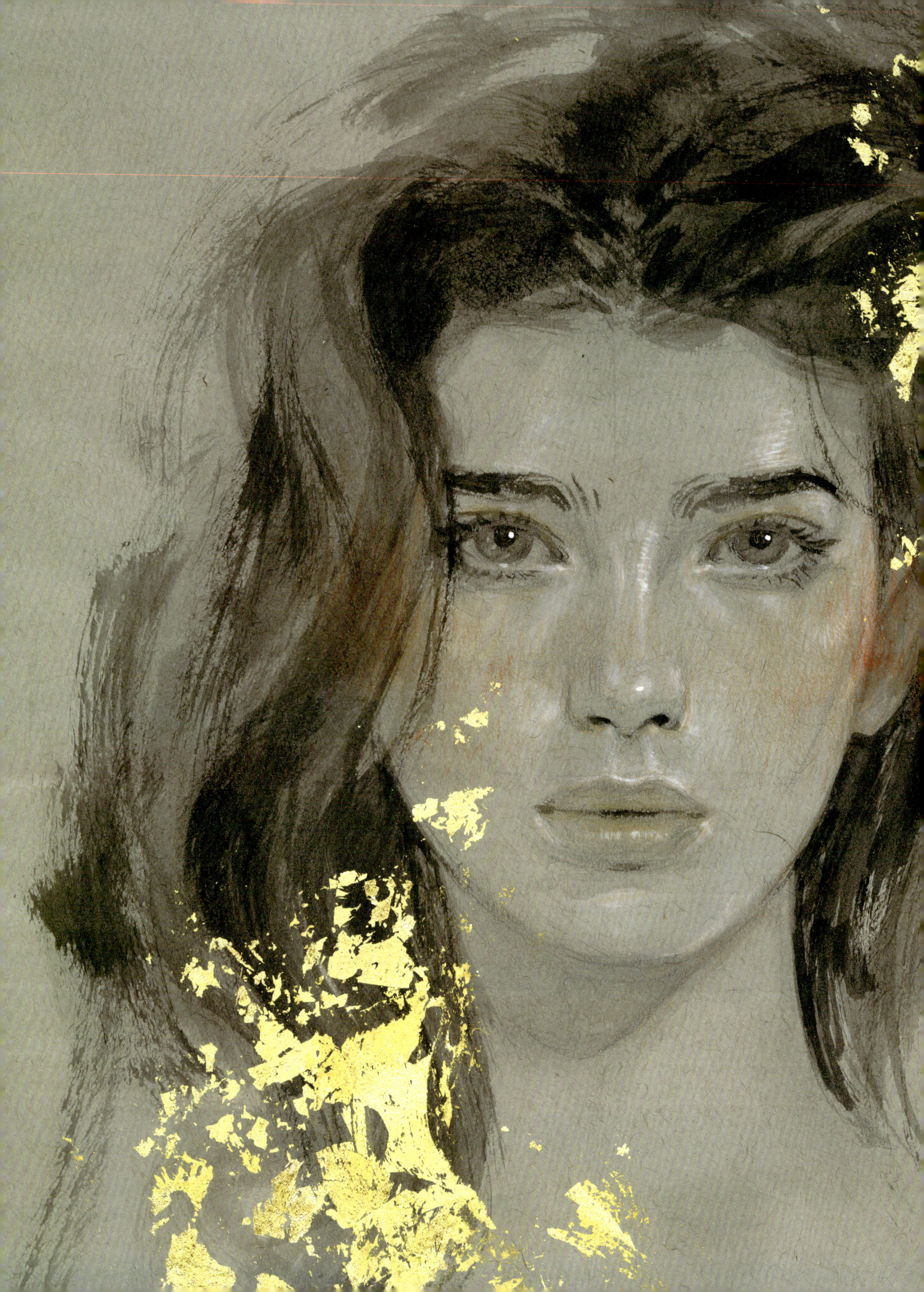

STUDY NO. 119
ink, colored pencil & pebeo paint on toned paper, 9" × 12", 2023

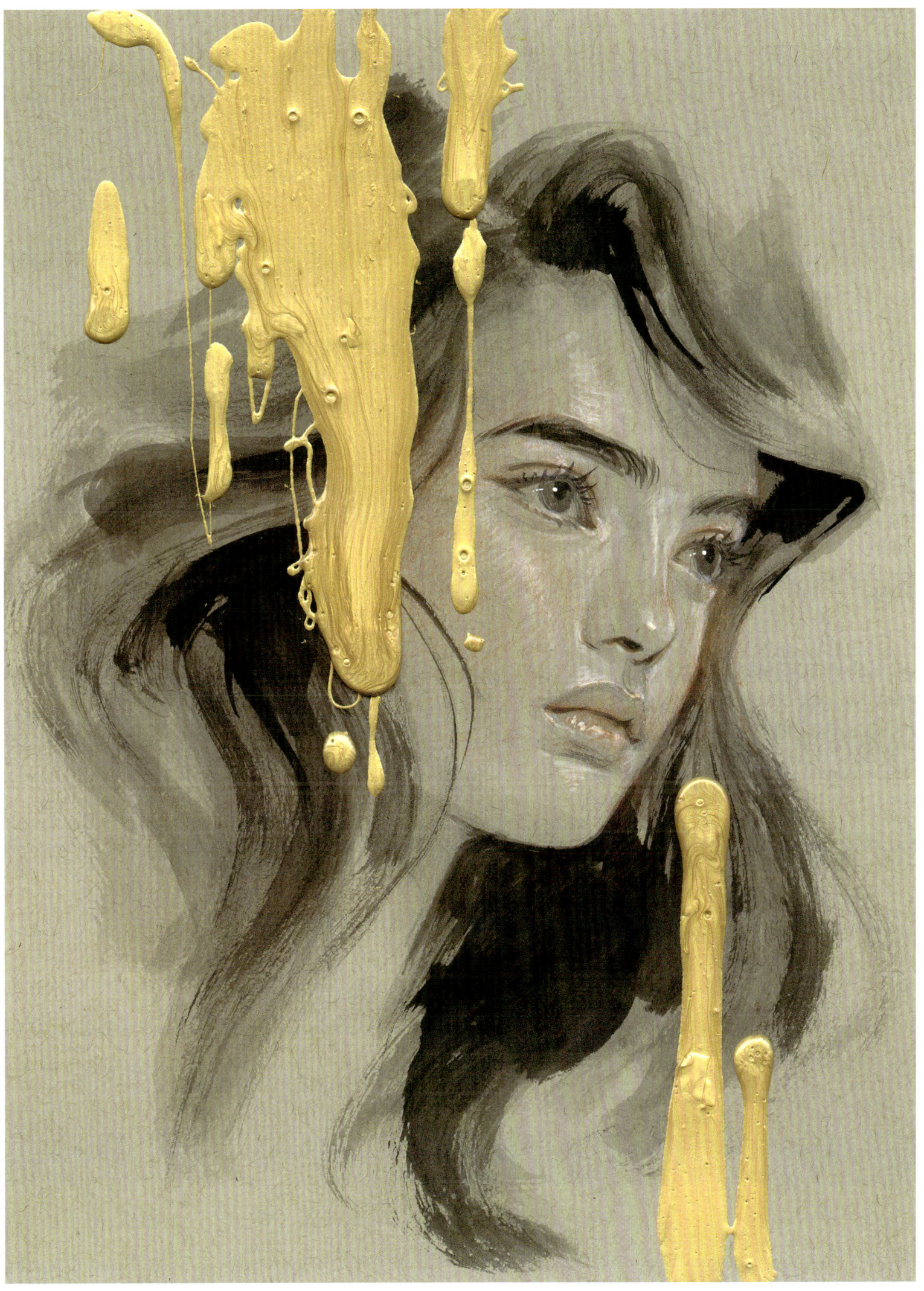

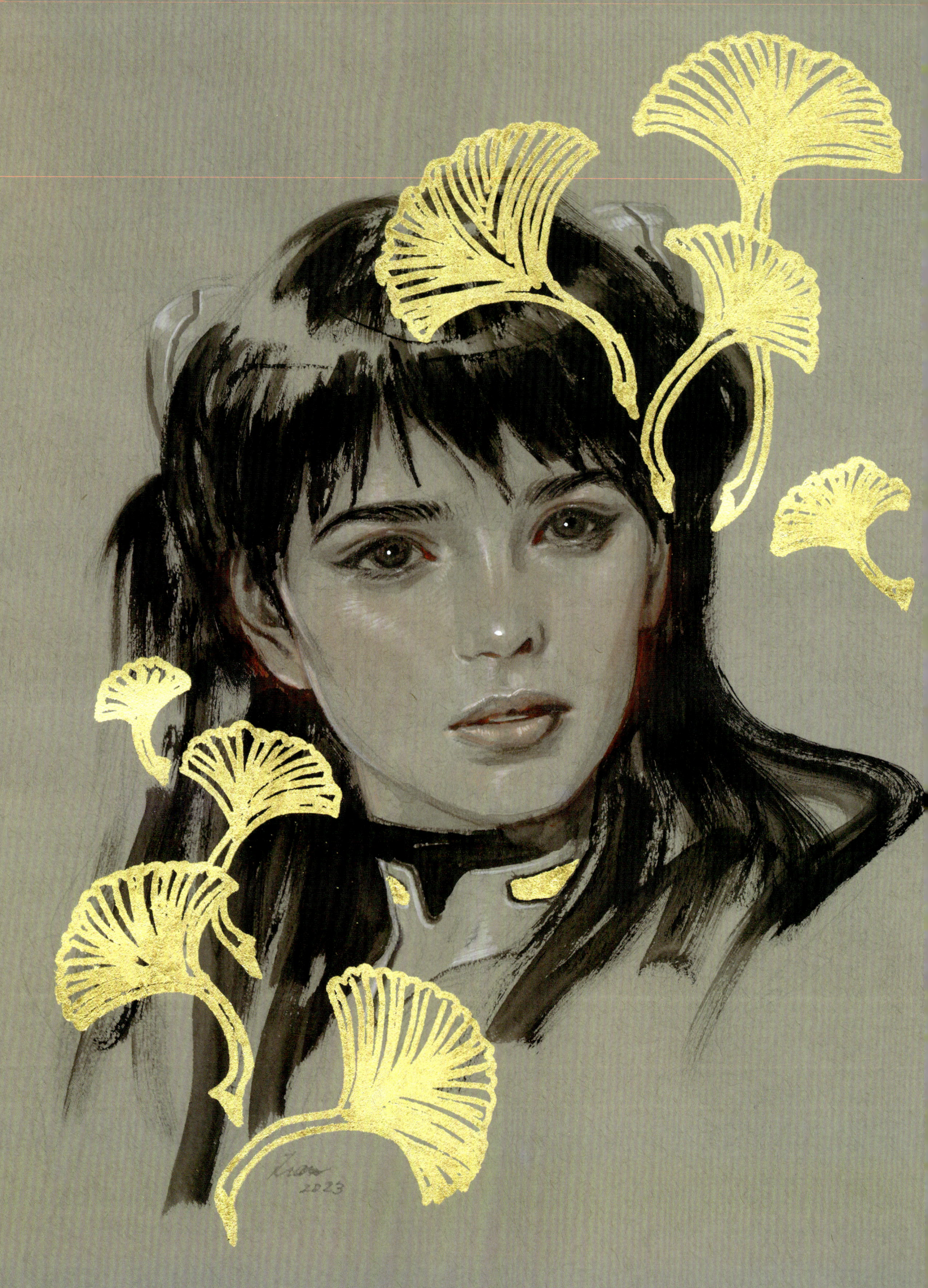

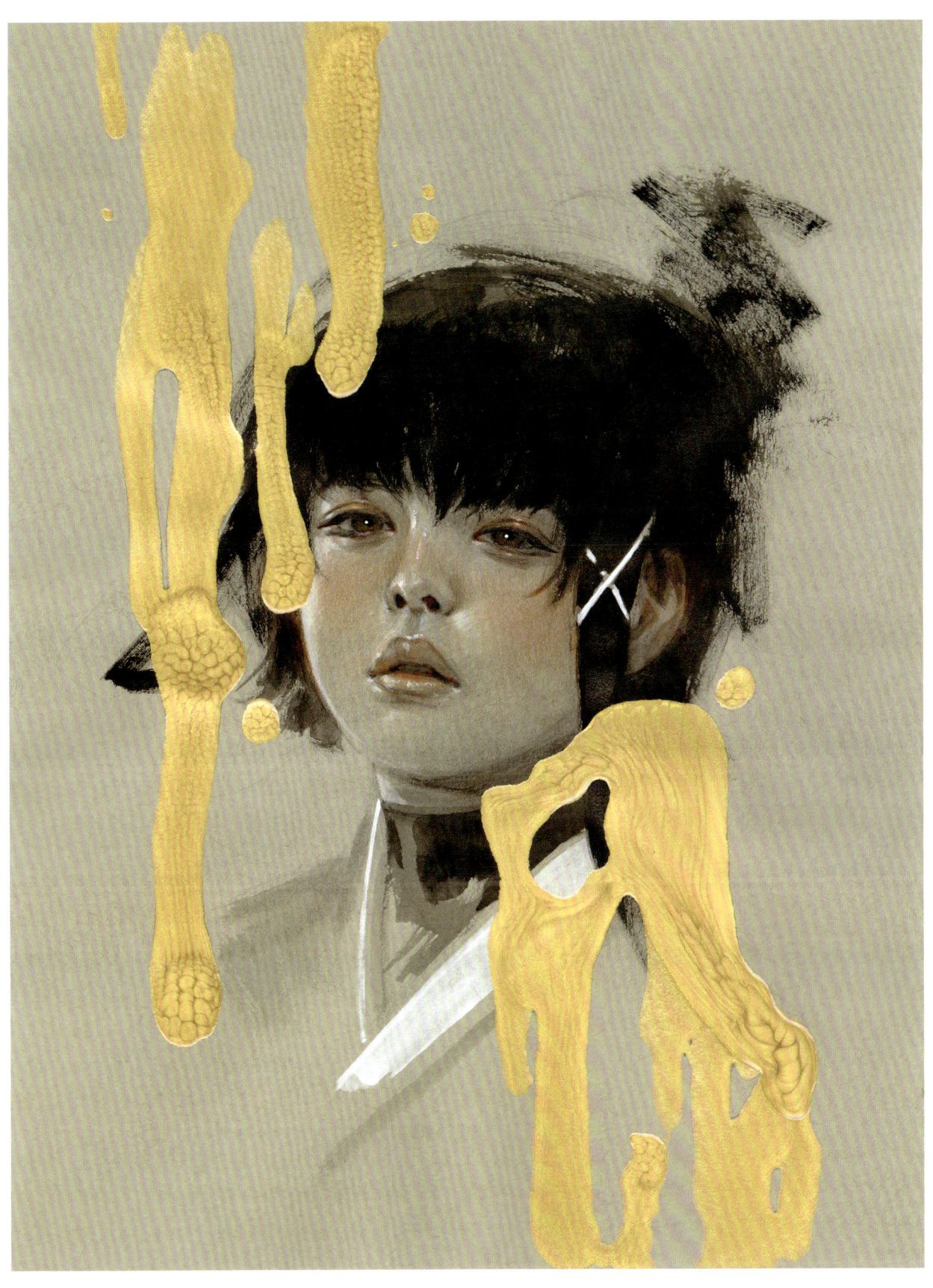

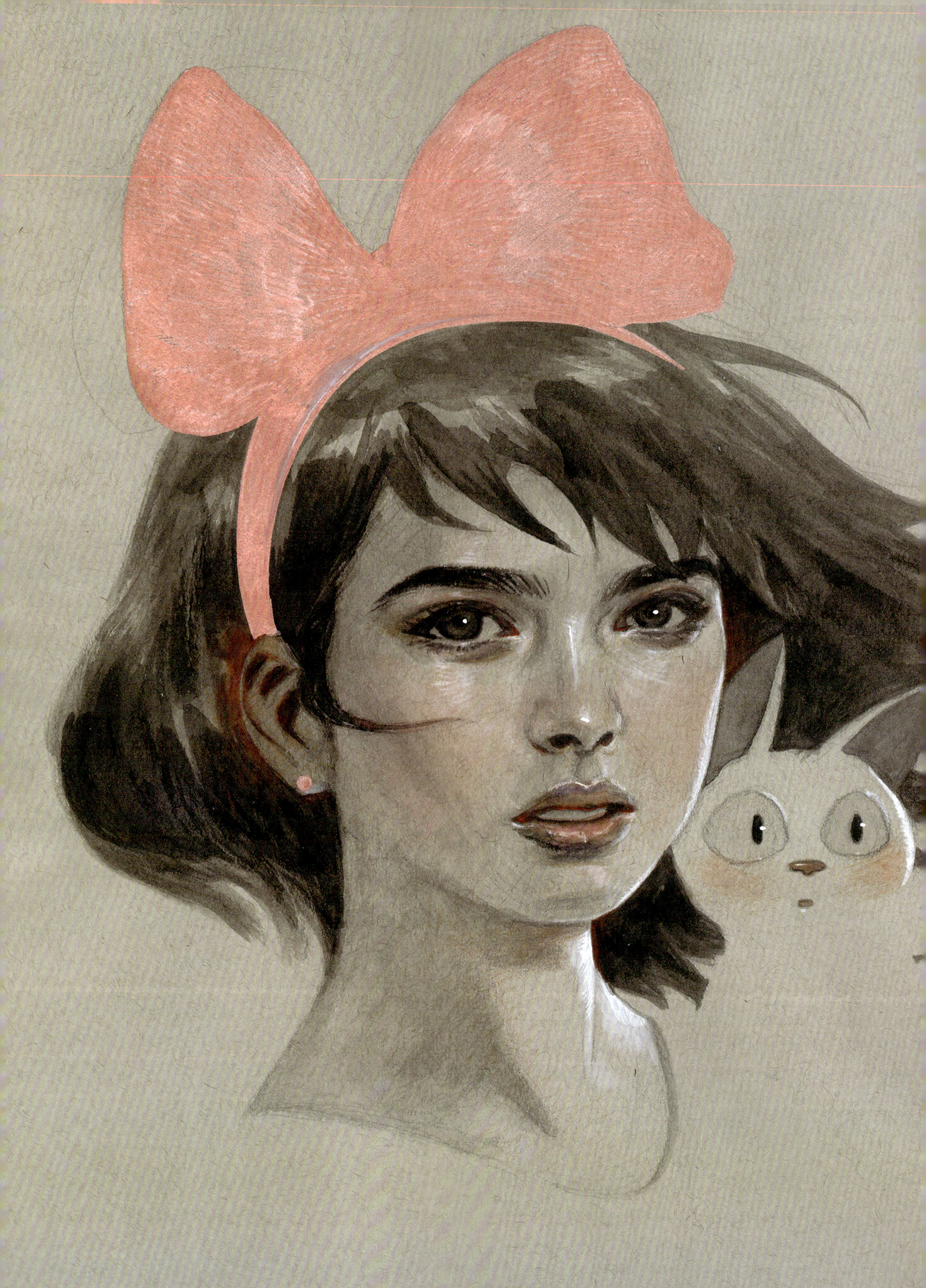

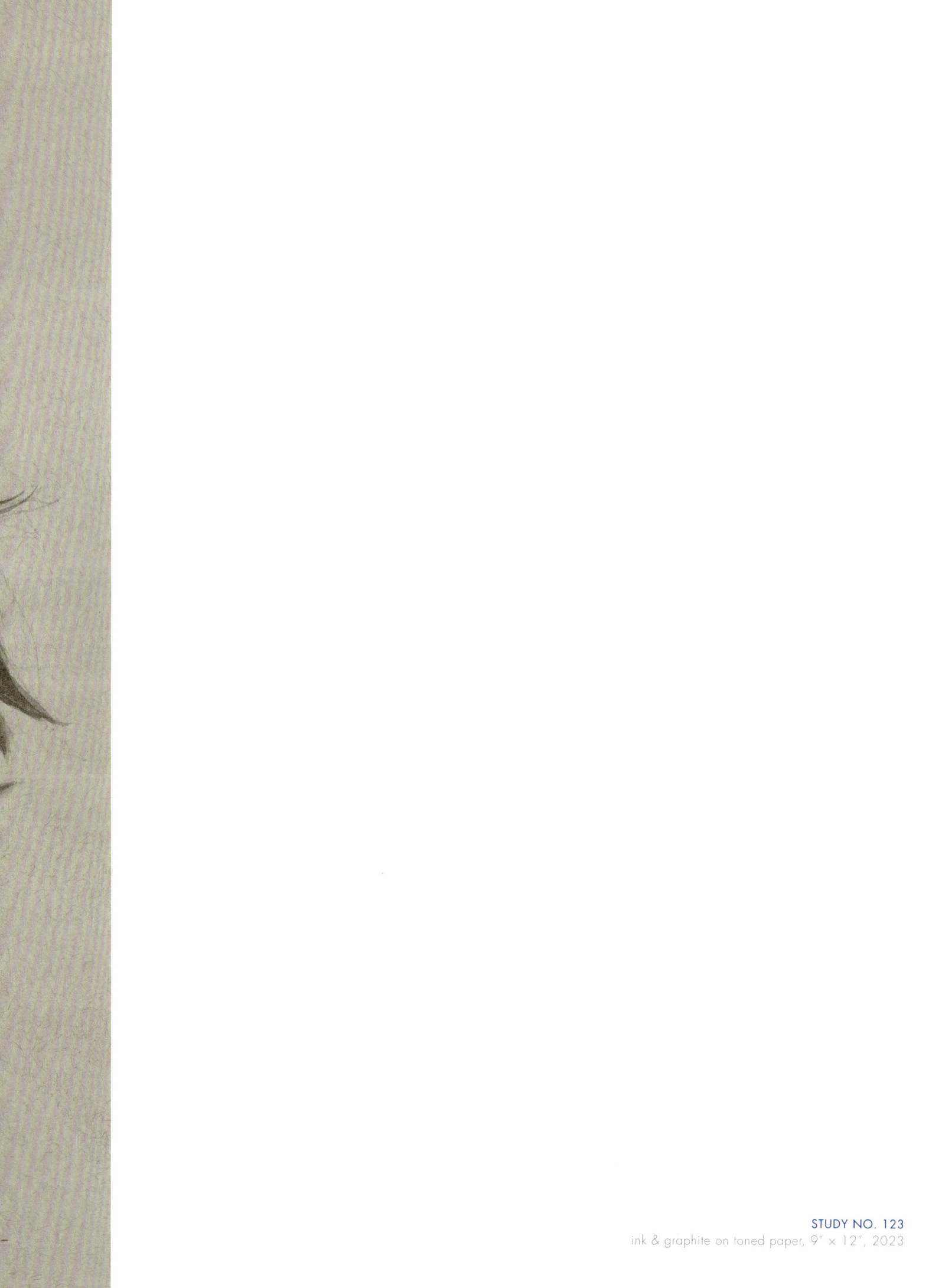

STUDY NO. 123
ink & graphite on toned paper, 9″ × 12″, 2023

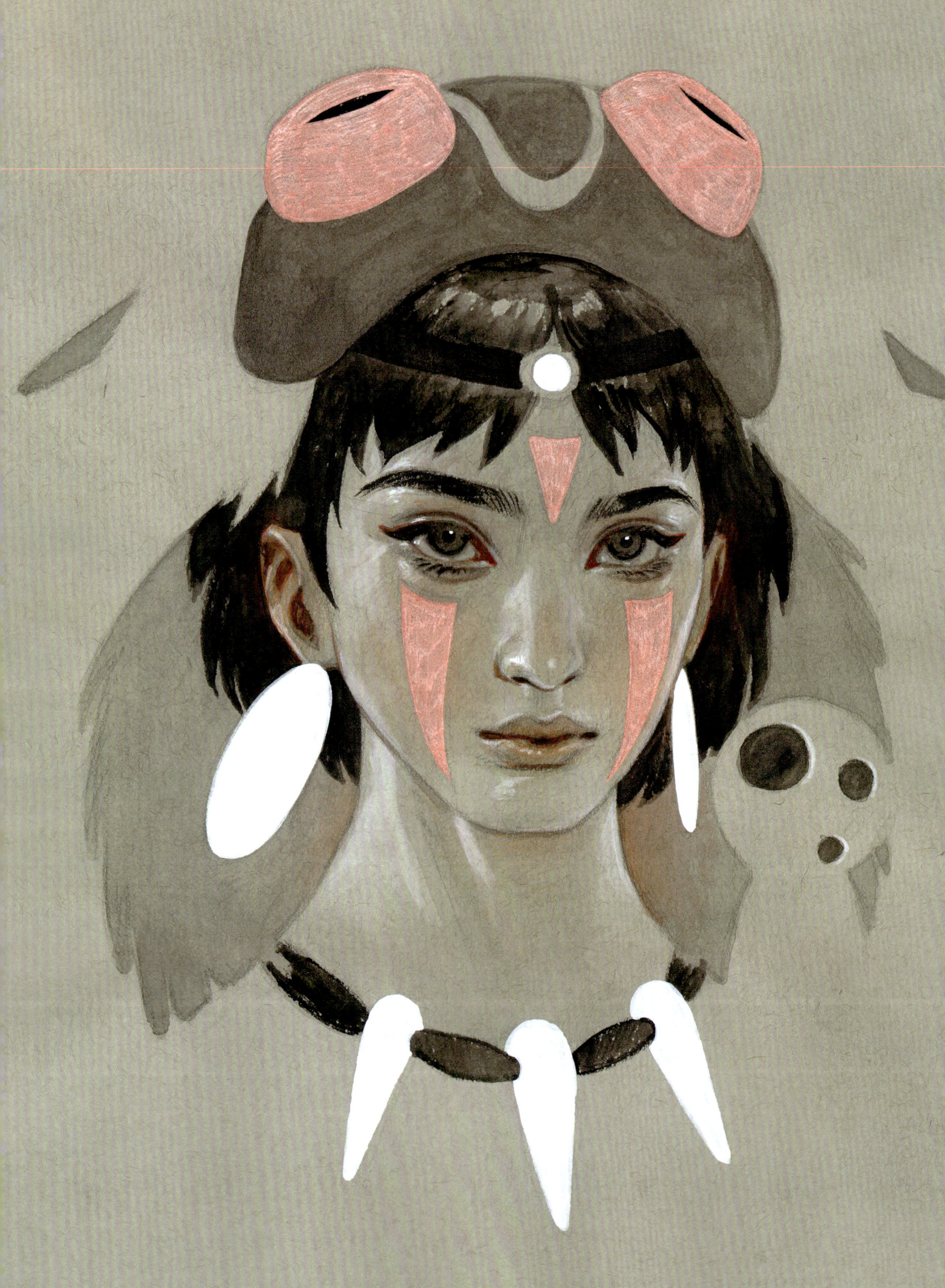

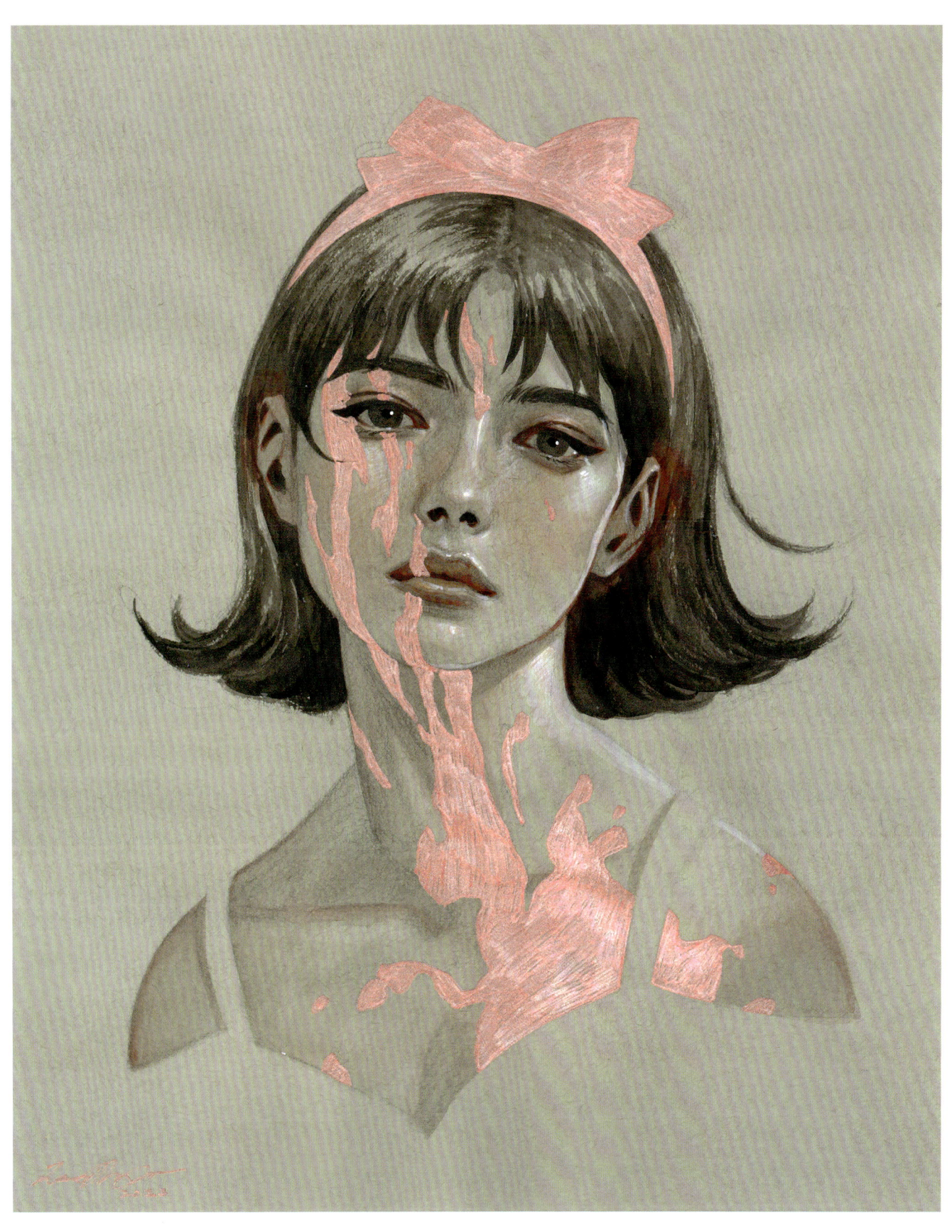

left
STUDY NO. 124
ink & graphite on toned paper, 9" × 12", 2023

above
STUDY NO. 125
ink & graphite on toned paper, 9" × 12", 2023

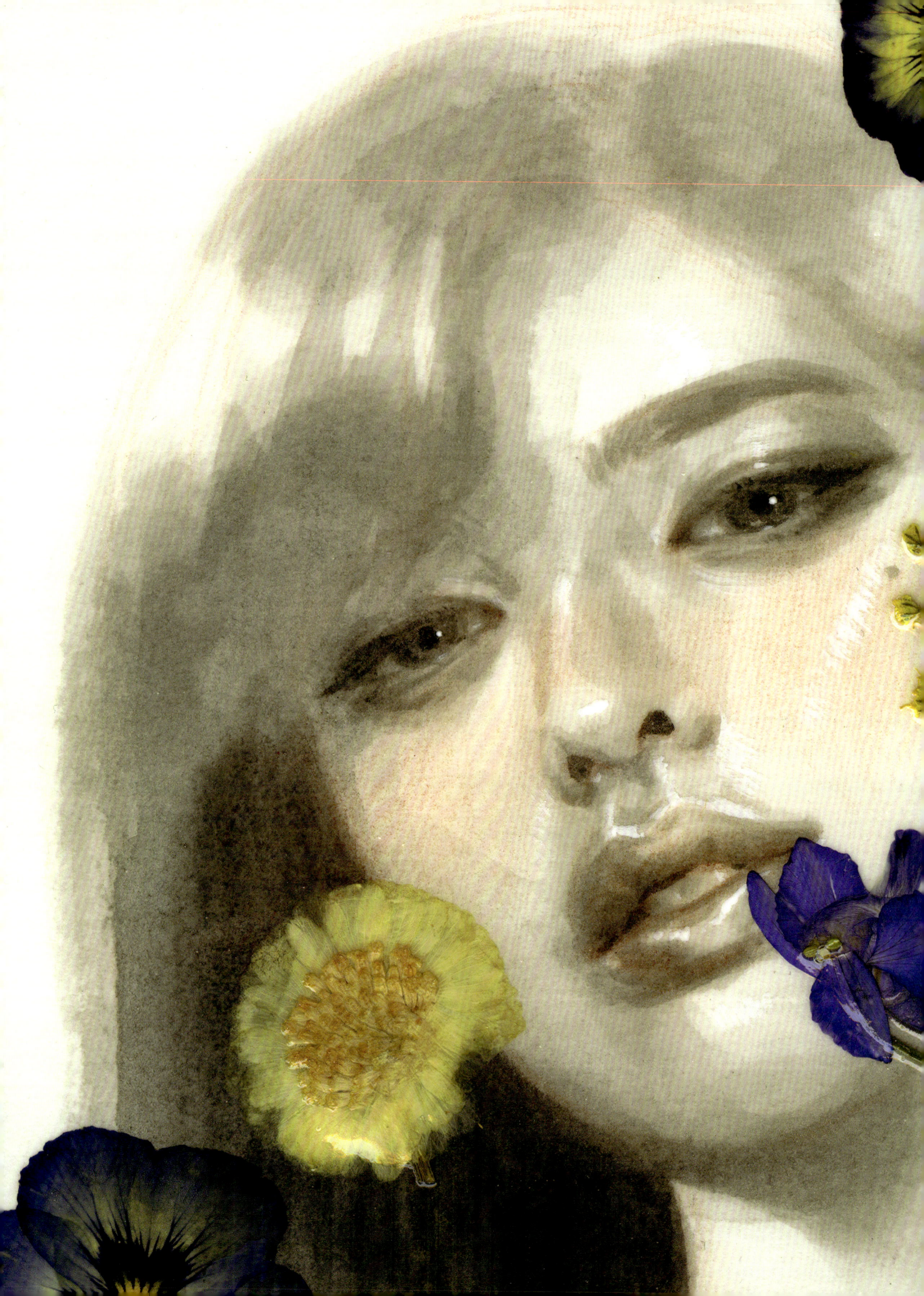

PRESSED NATURE

EXPERIMENTS WITH OBJECTS FOUND IN NATURE

My inspiration often derives from the interplay between nature and the feminine spirit. Many of the recurring motifs in my work are based on this, especially with the use of floral shapes and patterns. To further the viewer's interest, I started working with real flowers to incorporate this symbology.

After researching different styles of preserving plants collected in my local area, I began overlaying paintings with delicate pressed flowers. I arrange and rearrange the petals until there is a balance between paint and nature. Each bloom is unique in how it dries and interacts with wet-media pigments—differing in translucency, color and texture. Separating the flowers into smaller parts and adhering them to the composition helps to imbue it with an ephemeral beauty. I also utilize other objects, such as seashells and bird feathers. The marriage between botanical elements and strokes of paint celebrates my love for nature as an artistic theme.

STUDY NO. 43
acrylic, colored pencil & pressed flower, 5" × 7", 2016

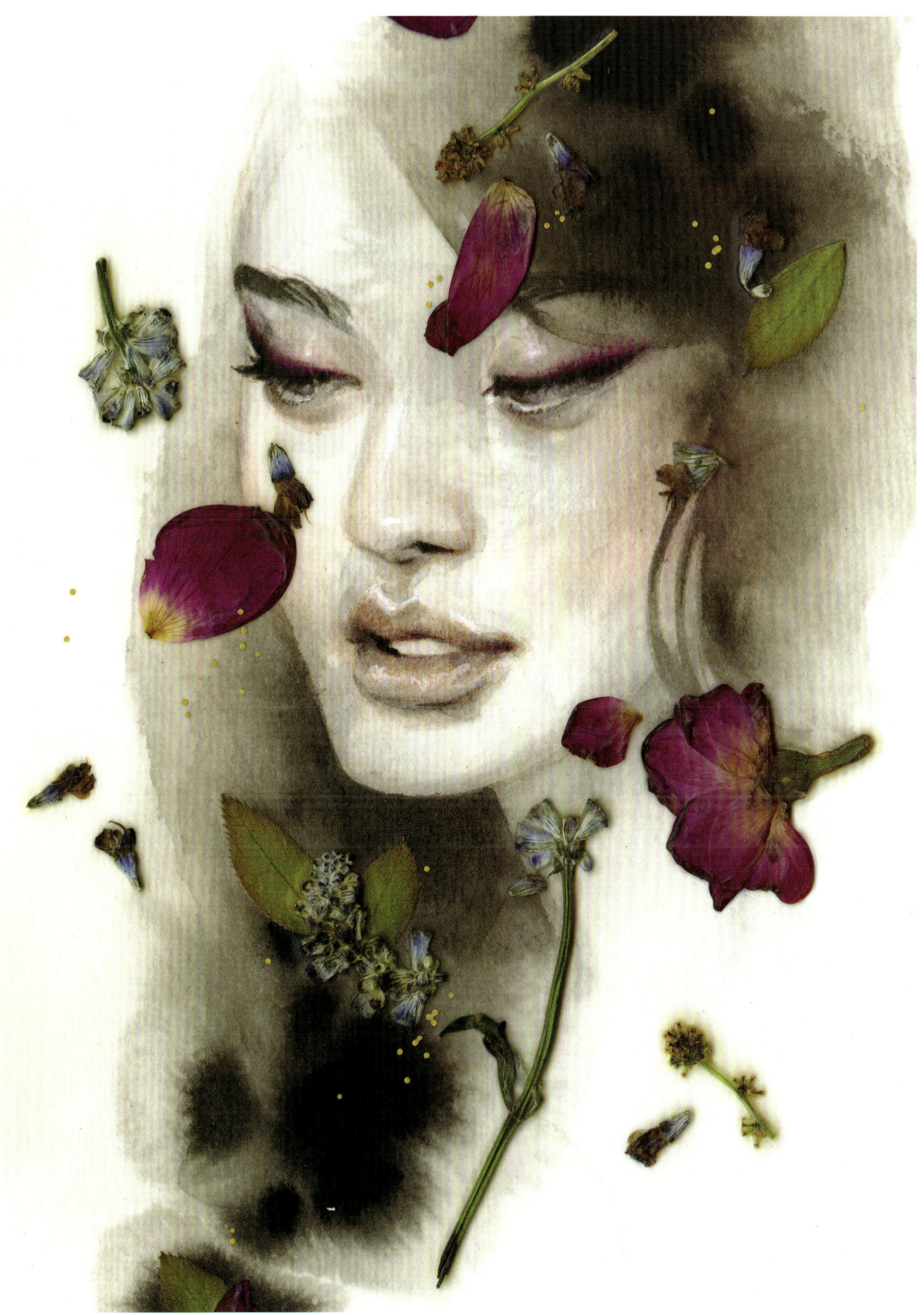

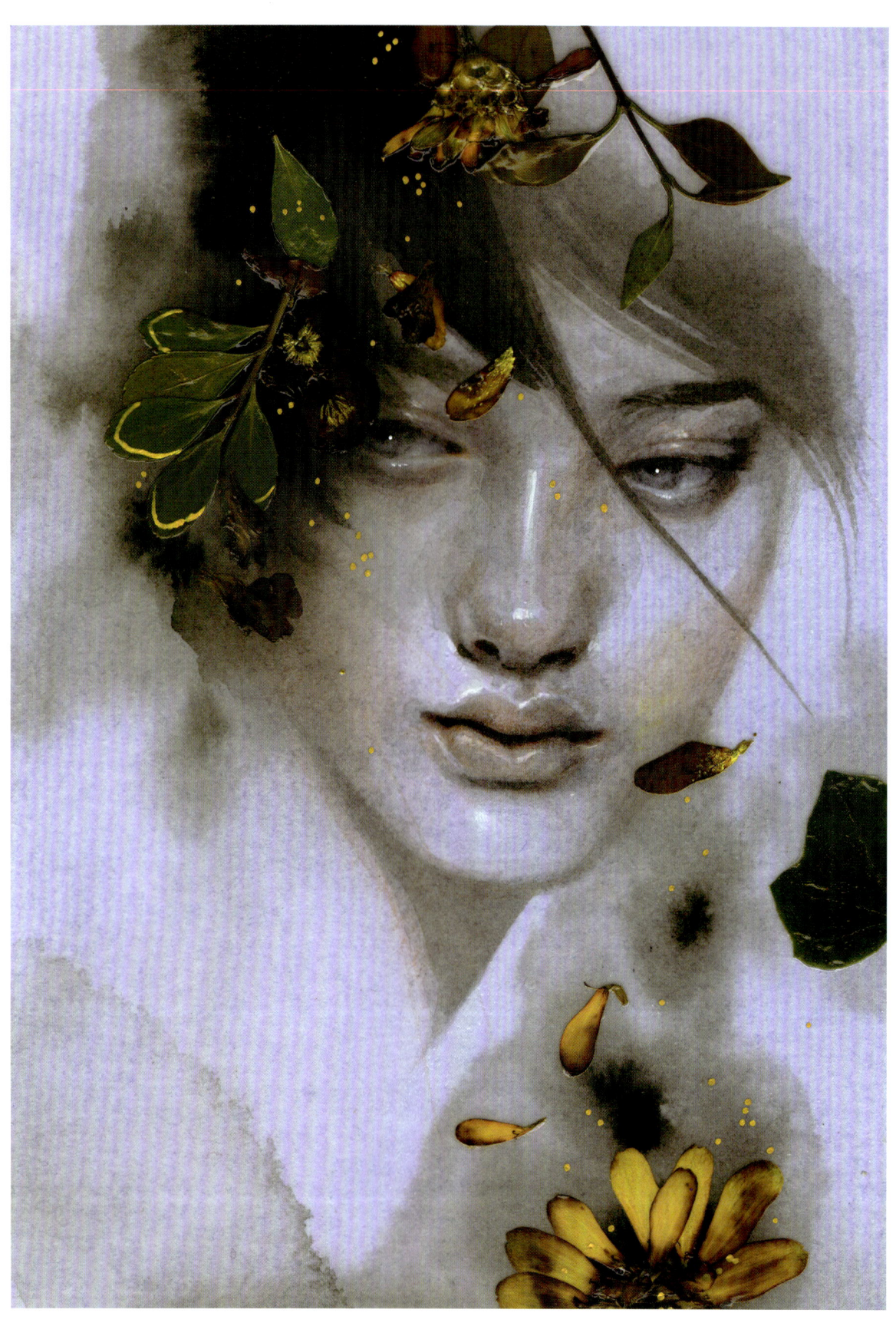

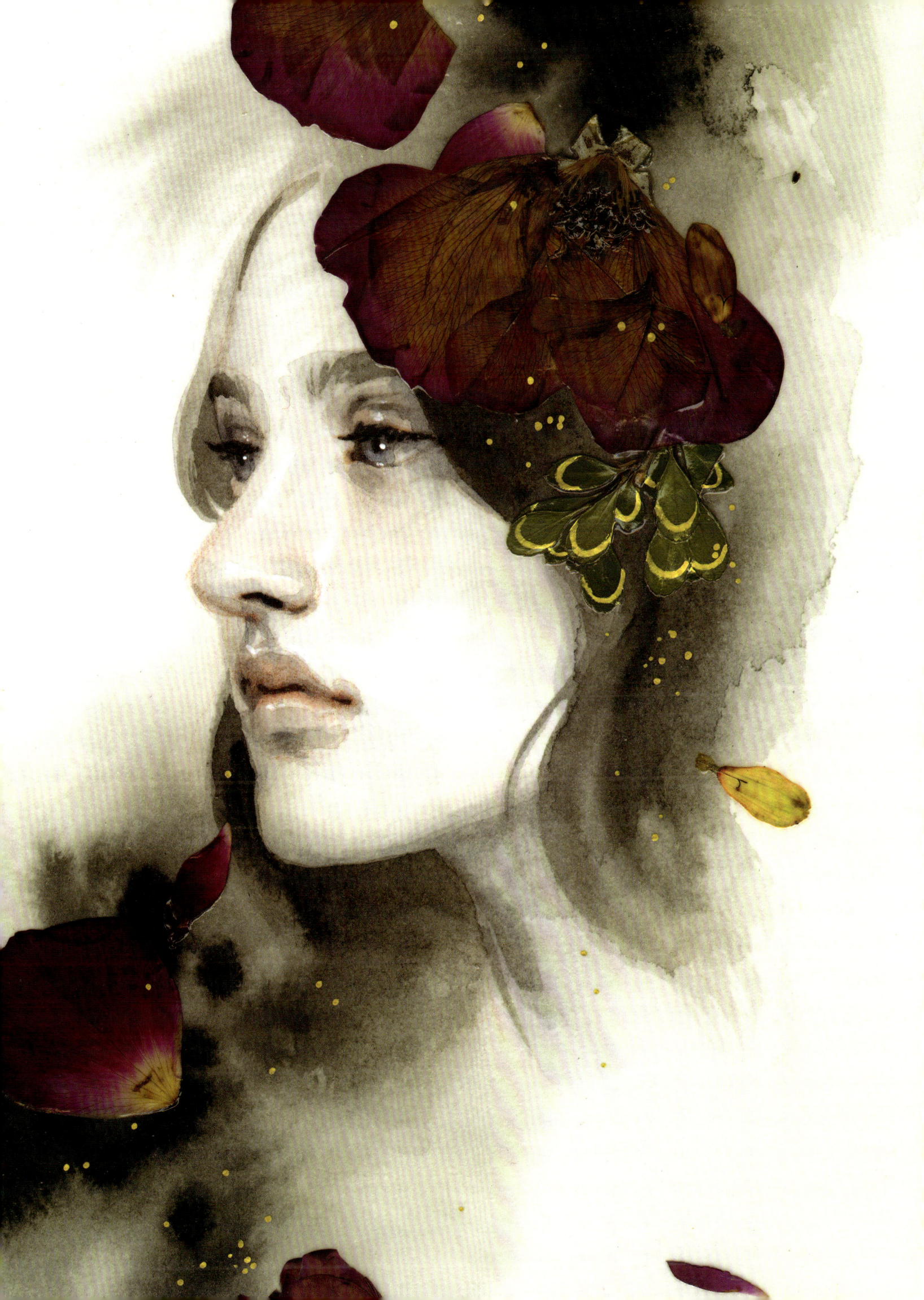

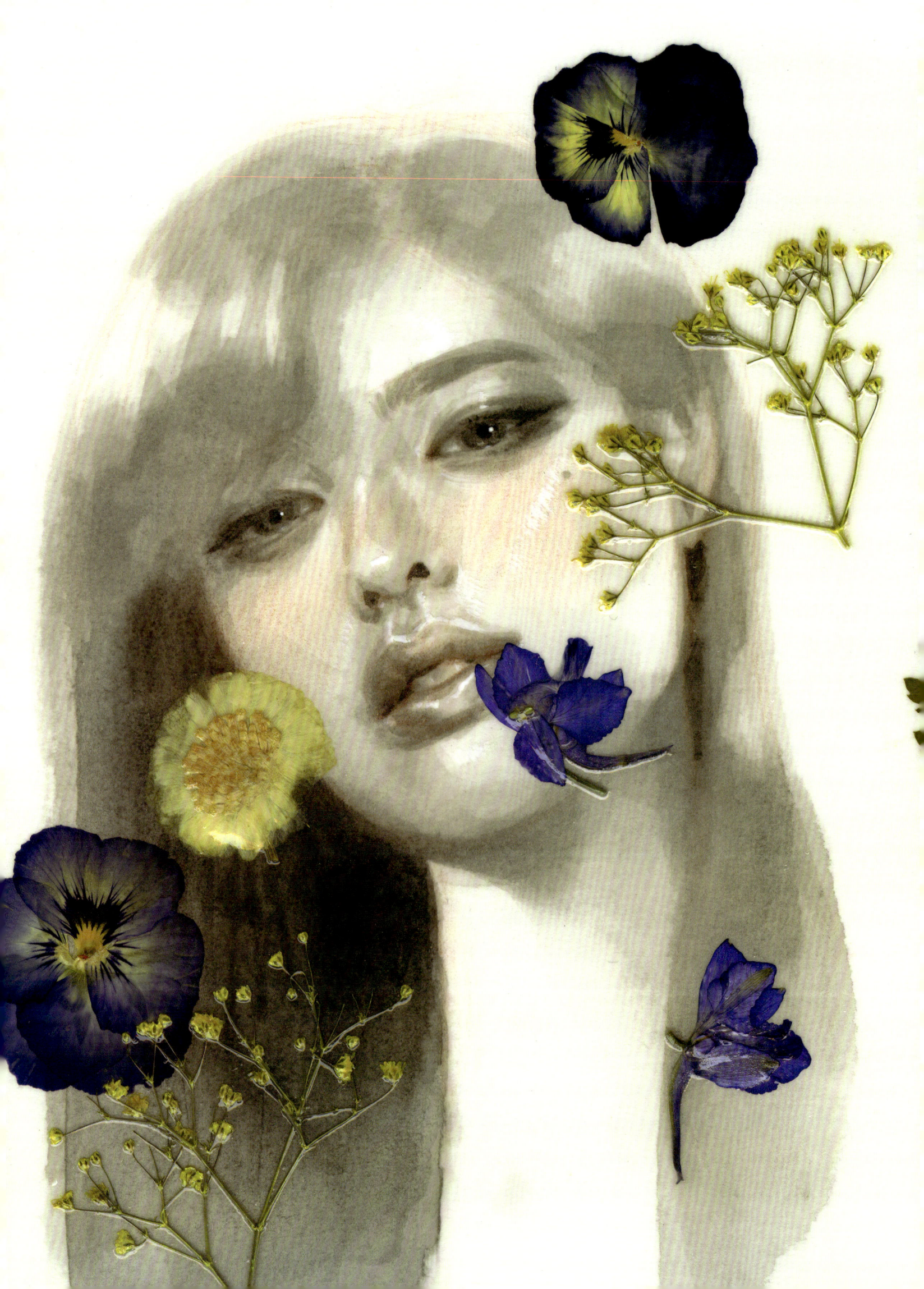

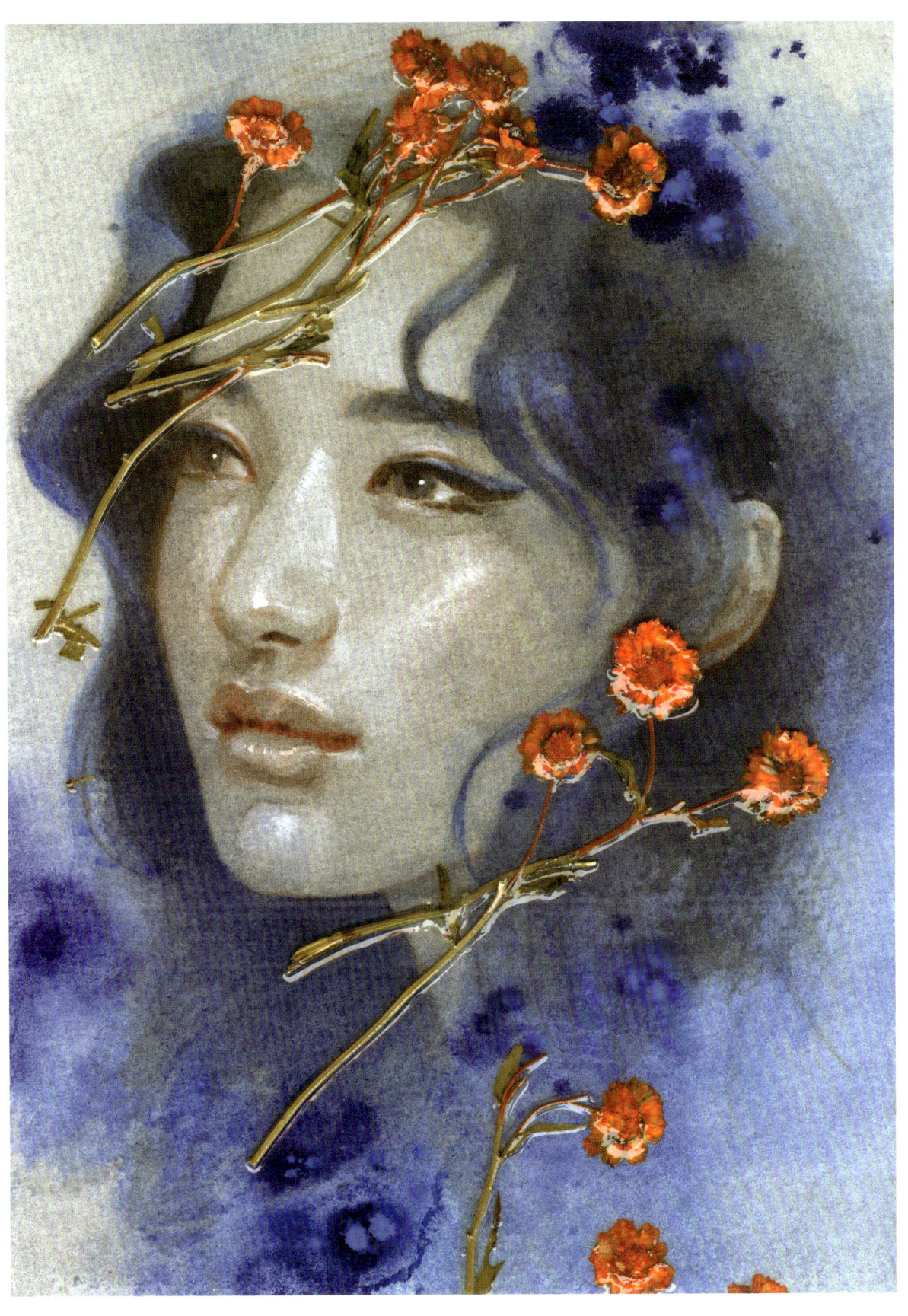

left
STUDY NO. 59
ink, colored pencil & pressed flower, 5.5" × 8.5", 2017

above
STUDY NO. 69
ink, acrylic & pressed flower, 5" × 7", 2018

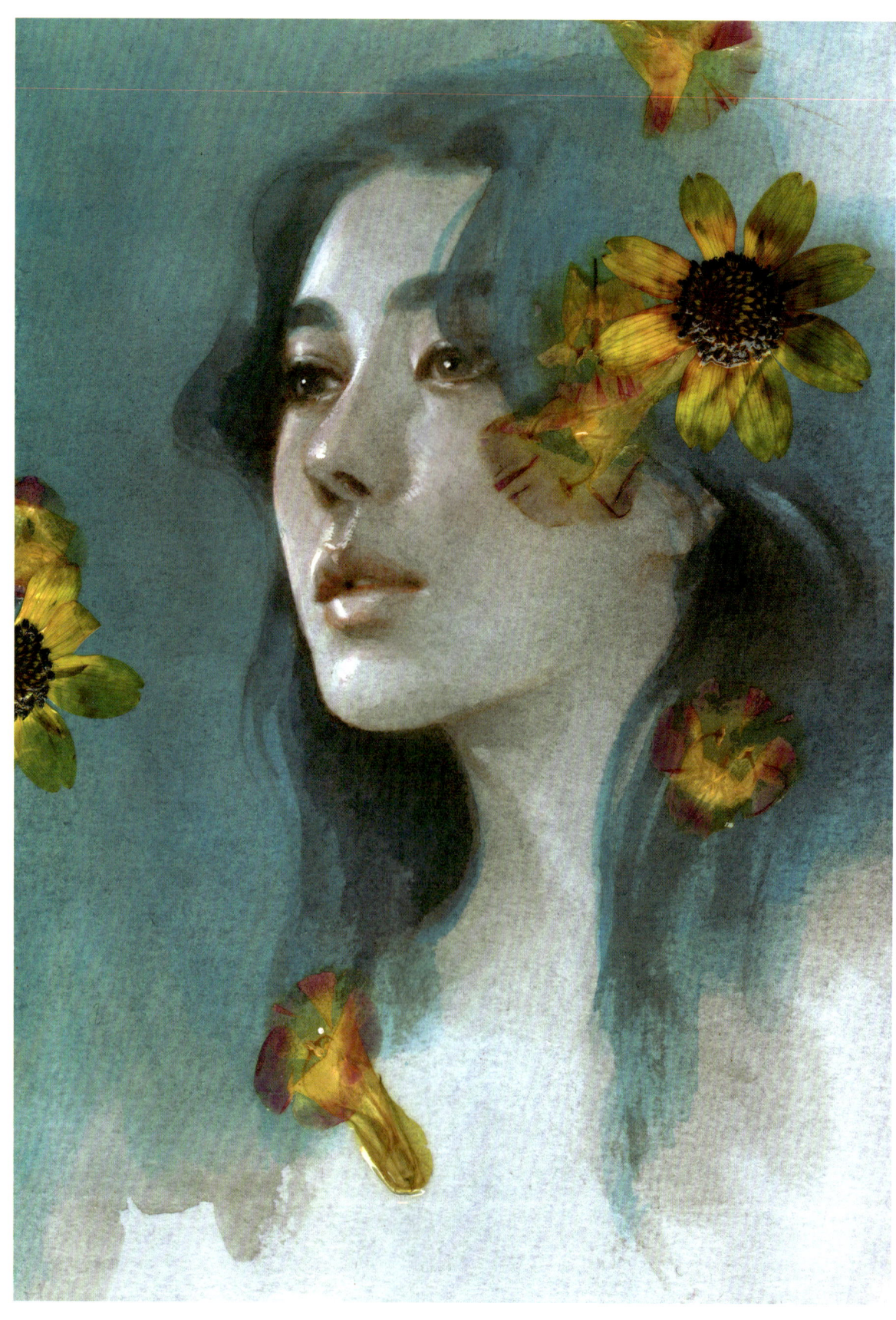

above
STUDY NO. 74
ink, acrylic & pressed flower, 5" x 7", 2018

right
STUDY NO. 80
watercolor, colored pencil & pressed flower 5.5" x 8.5", 2019

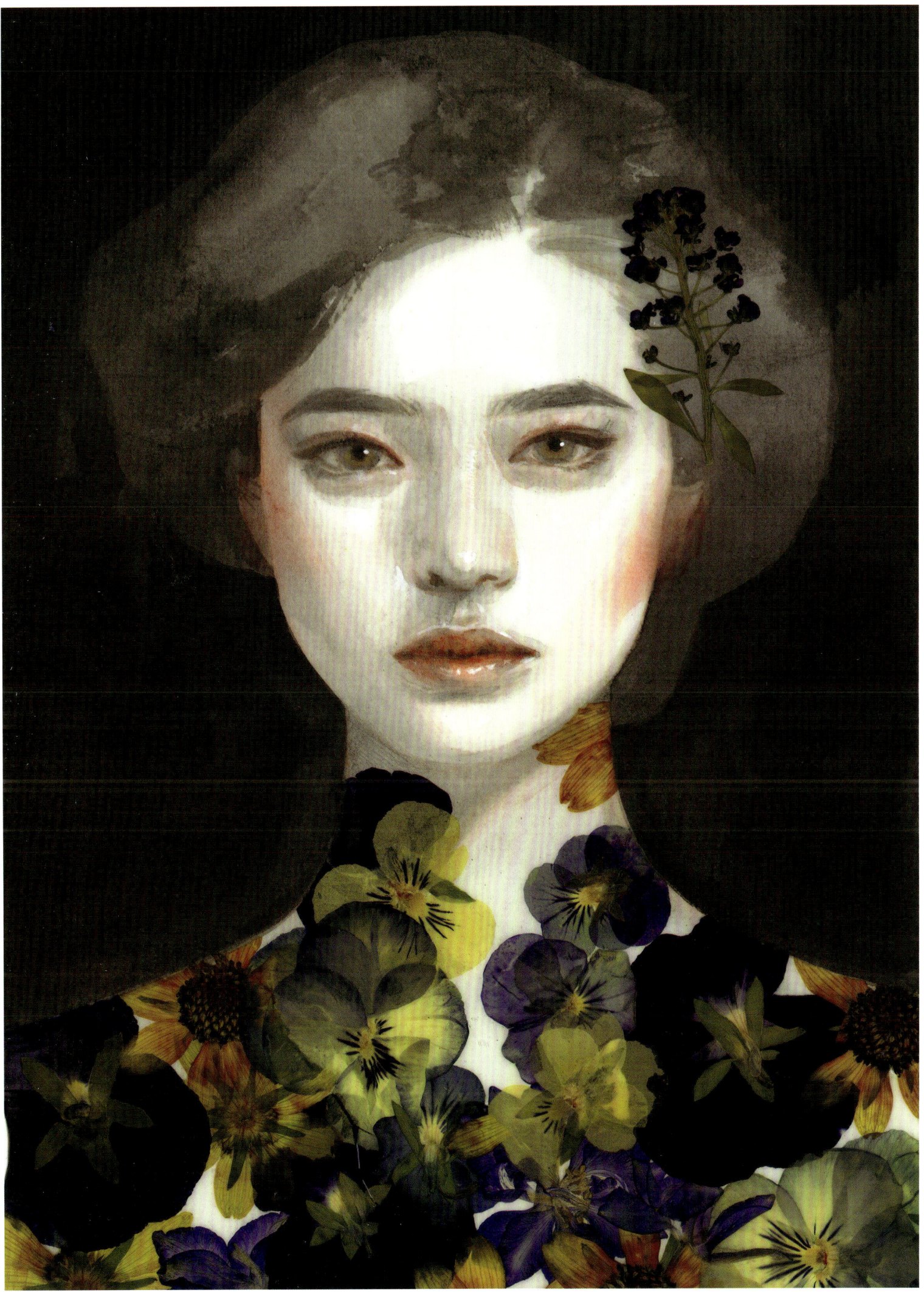

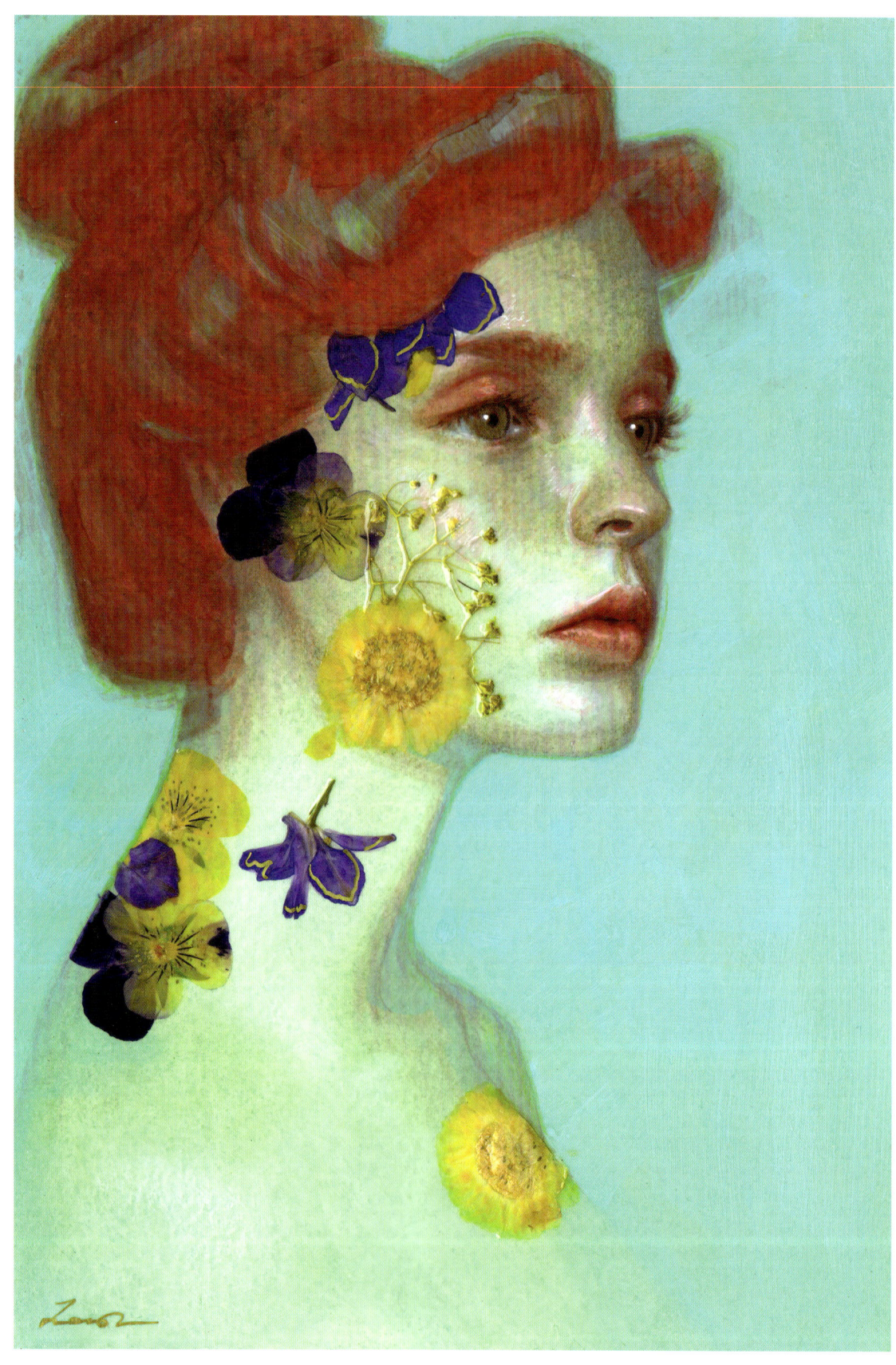

above
STUDY NO. 81
acrylic, colored pencil & pressed flower, 6" x 9", 2019

right
STUDY NO. 84
watercolor, colored pencil & pressed flower 5.5" x 8.5", 2019

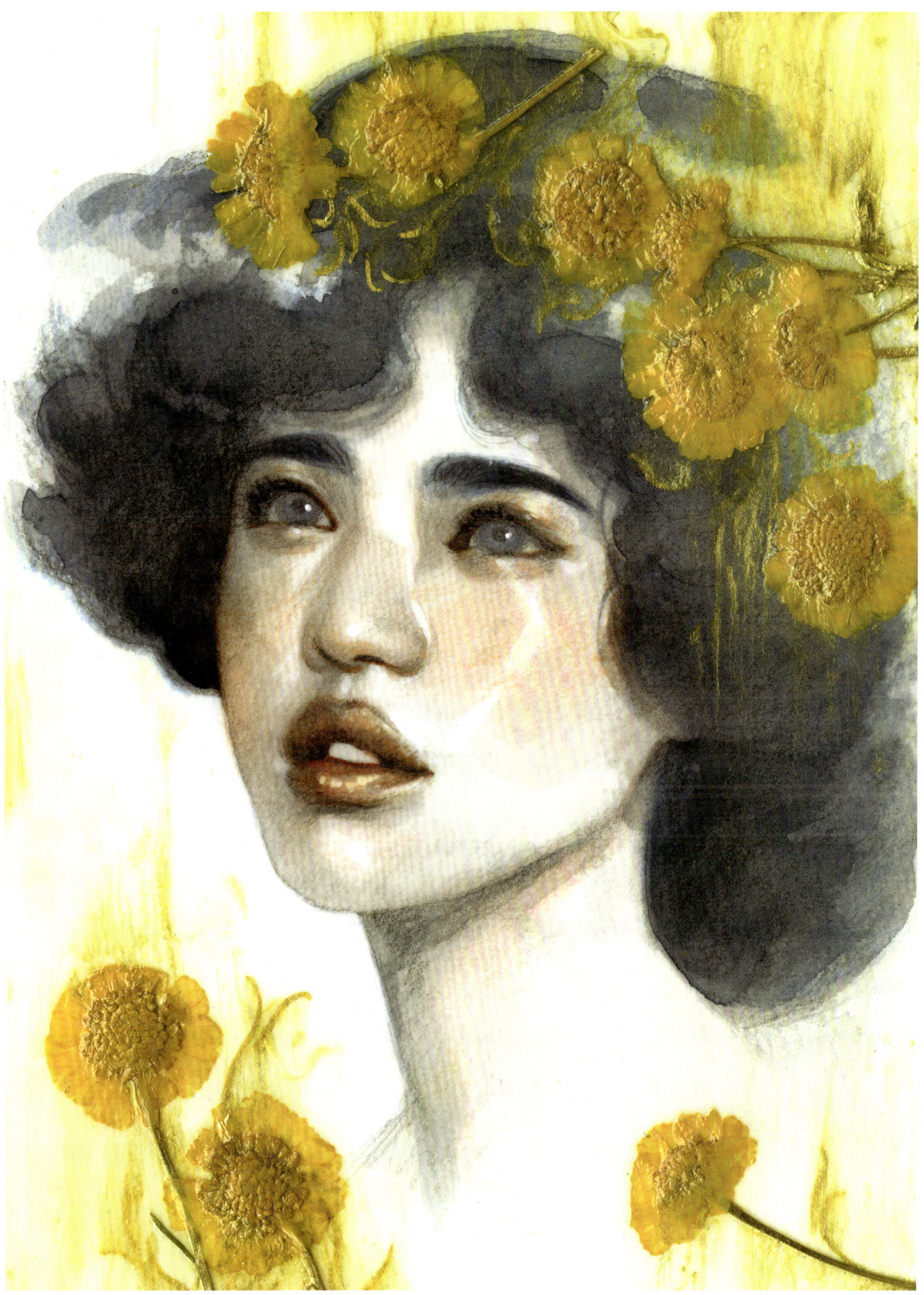

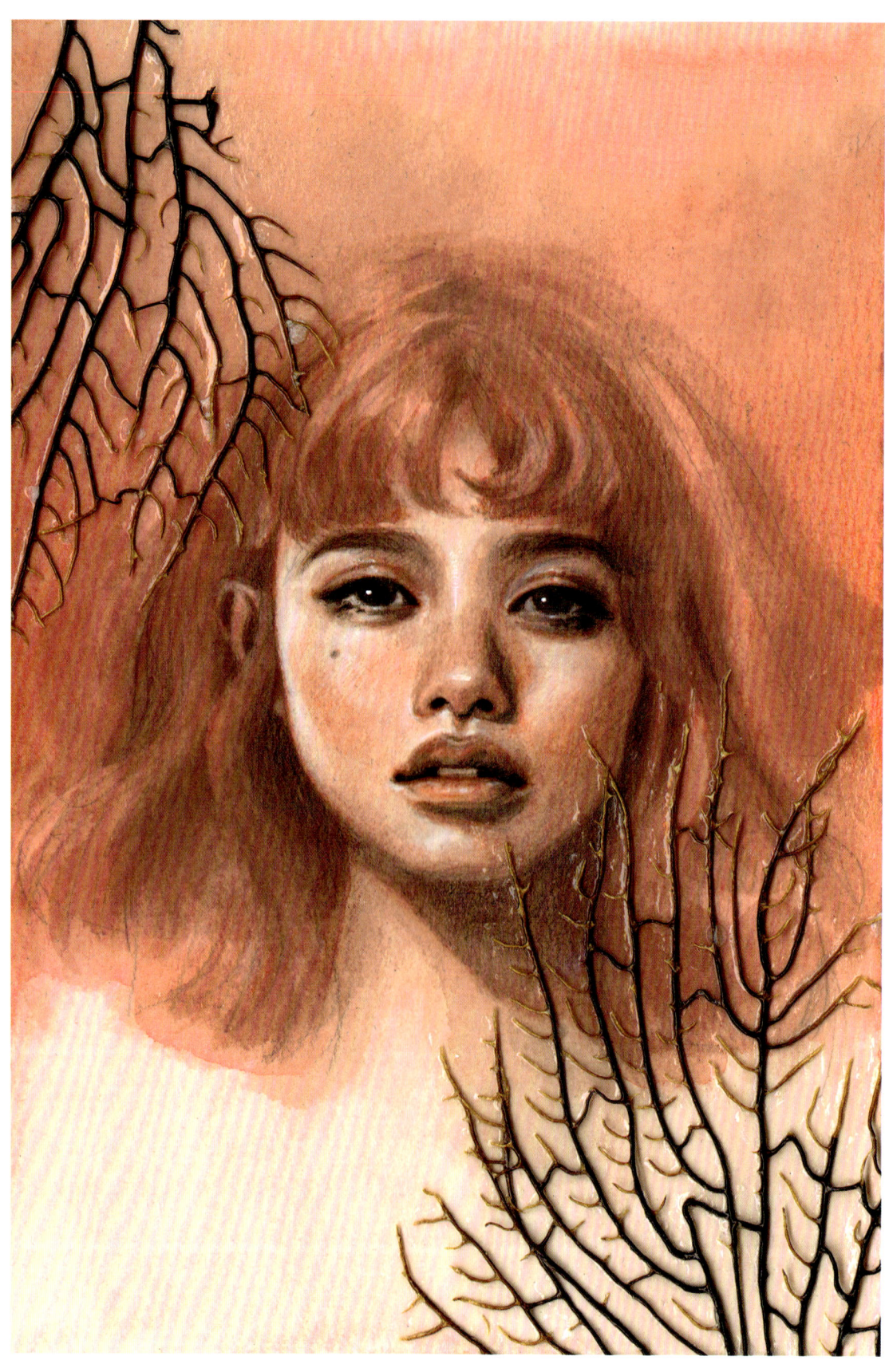

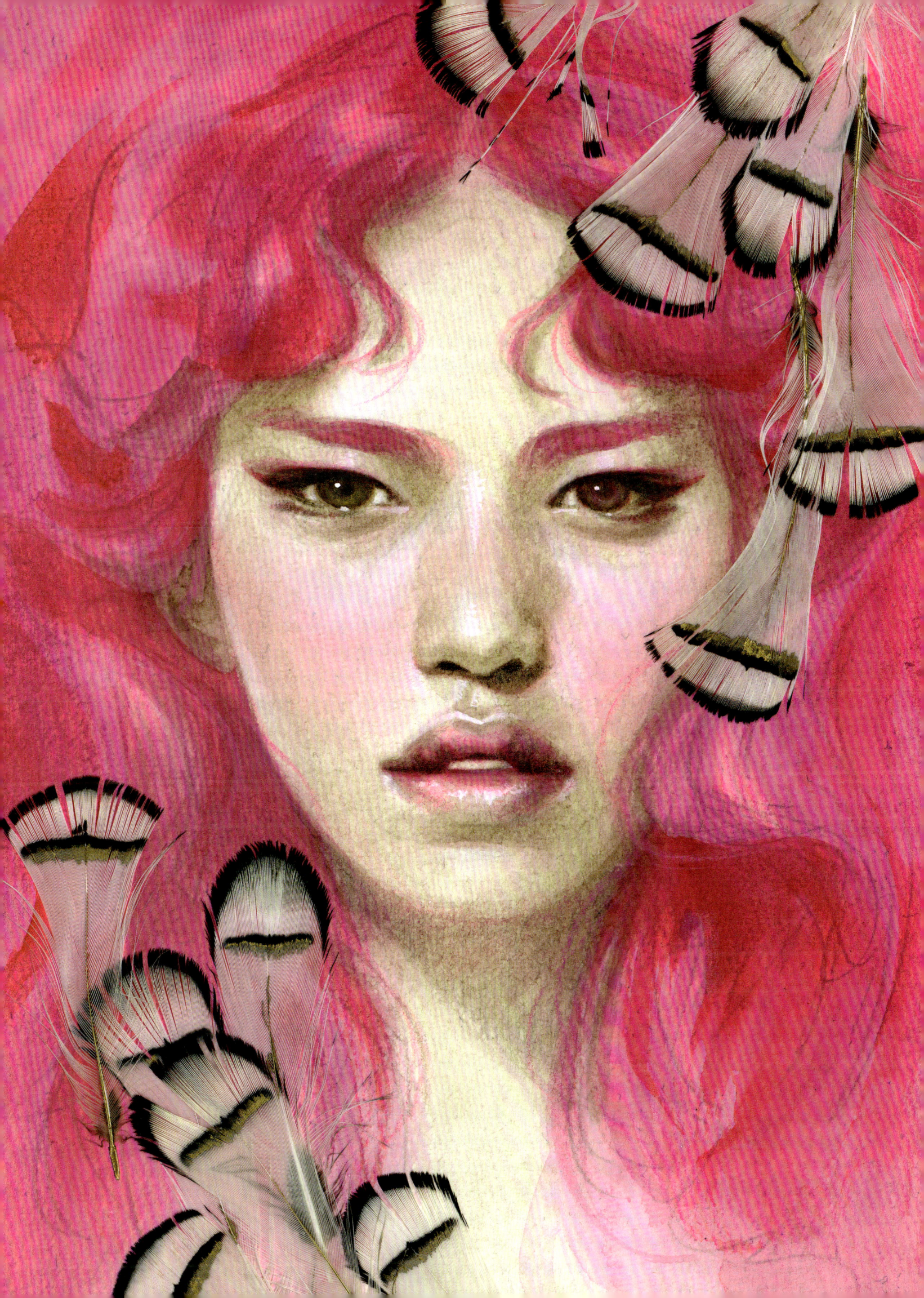

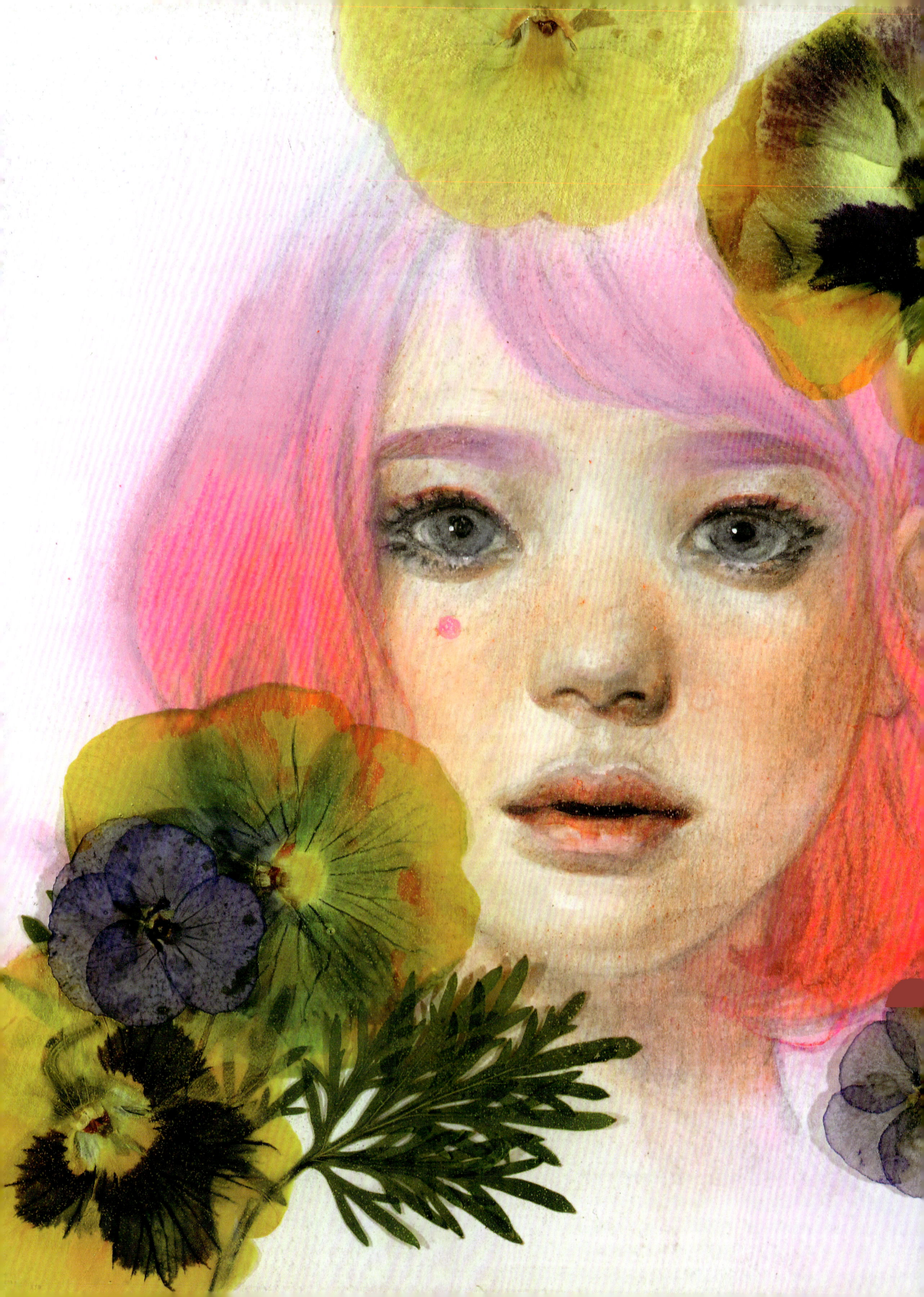

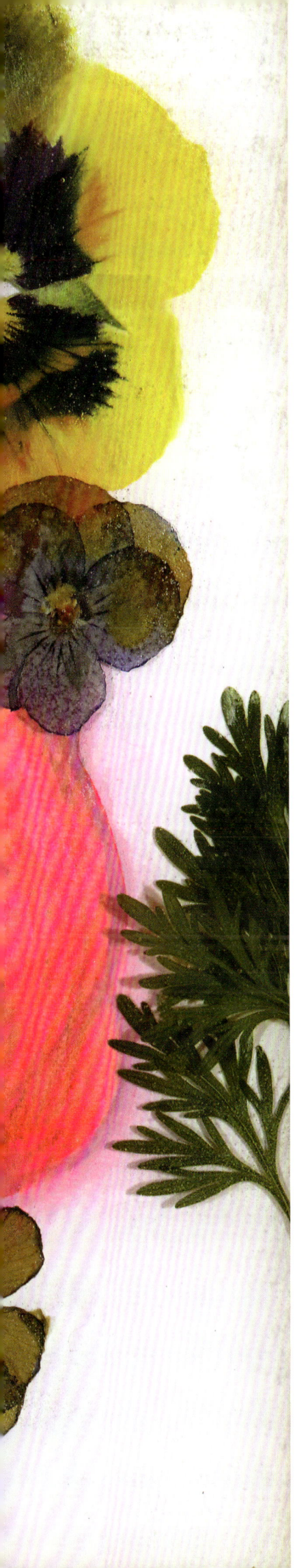

STUDY NO. 92
acrylic, colored pencil & pressed flower, 6" × 6", 2020

STUDY NO. 112
gouache, colored pencil & capiz shell, 6" × 9", 2022

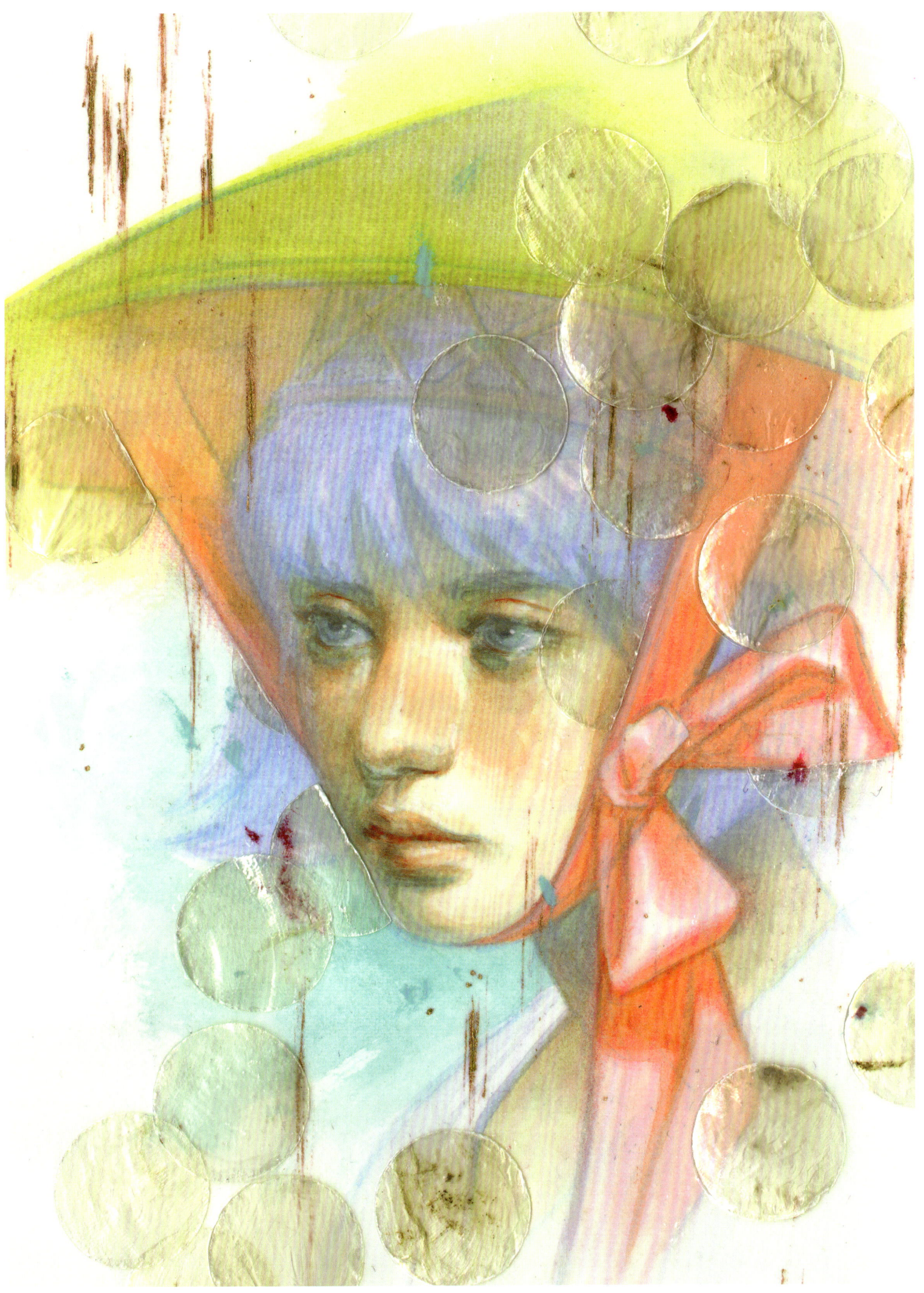

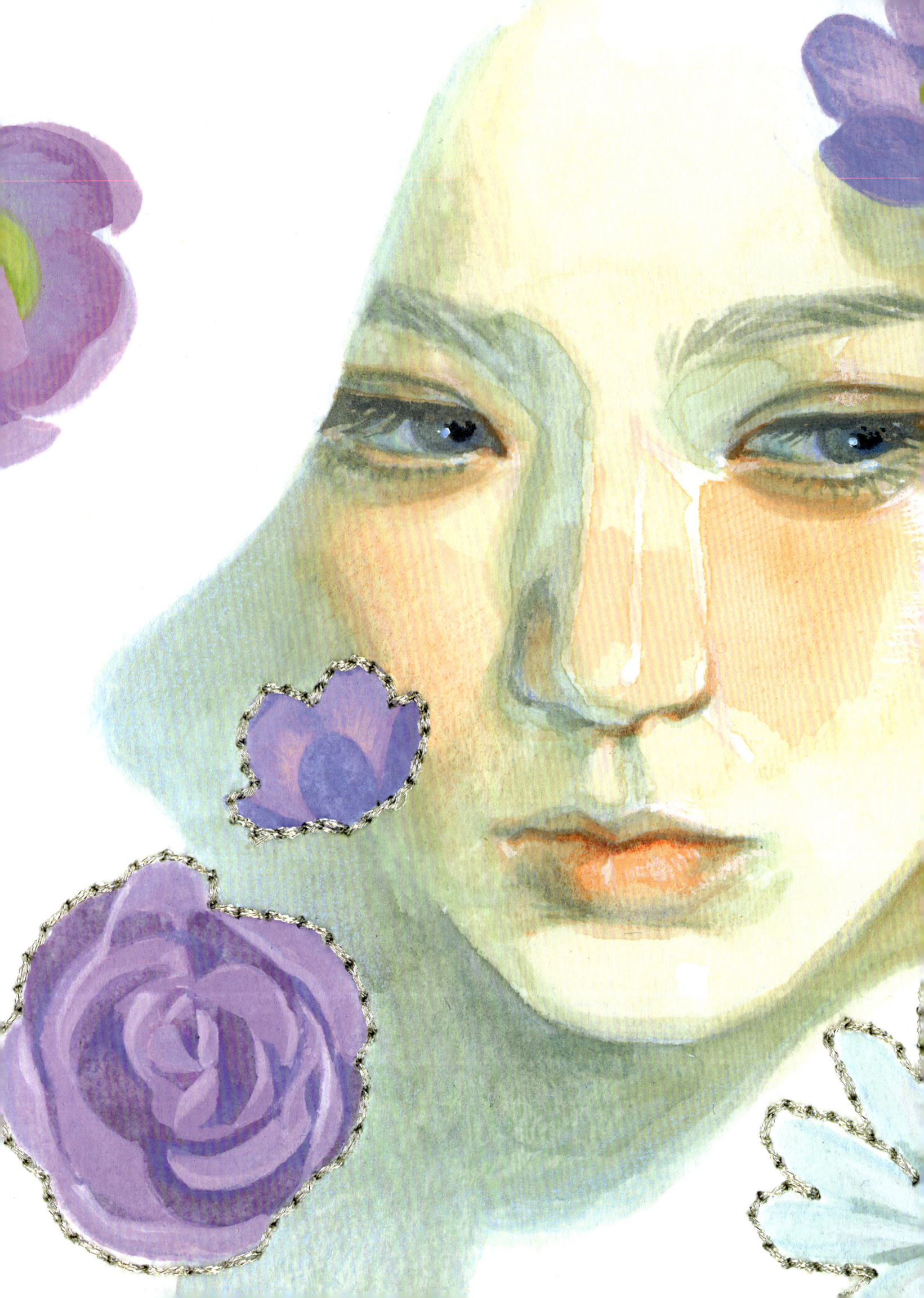

NEEDLE
AND THREAD

EXPERIMENTS WITH EMBROIDERY

Many of the women in my family who still reside in our home country work as seamstresses, making clothes such as the traditional Vietnamese dress called *áo dài*. An *áo dài* is often adorned with intricate needlework and embroidery. Designs such as these have fueled my interest in fashion, which I've started weaving together with my love for painting. The focused experiments in this section are the result of these two art forms' convergence.

The following are the most recent of my studies. Each subject's features and expression is captured with paint while the decorative needlework adds a tactile and textural element. Working with needle and thread, I plot out the embroidery design by poking holes in middleweight cotton paper. Then I connect the holes, with each stitch becoming a brushstroke in its own right. I implement a variety of stitching techniques, such as the back stitch, French knot, feather stitch and chain stitch. These small paintings are completed within a day, providing sufficient time for trial and error in my needlework exploration.

STUDY NO. 108
acrylic, colored pencil & embroidery, 6″ × 9″, 2022

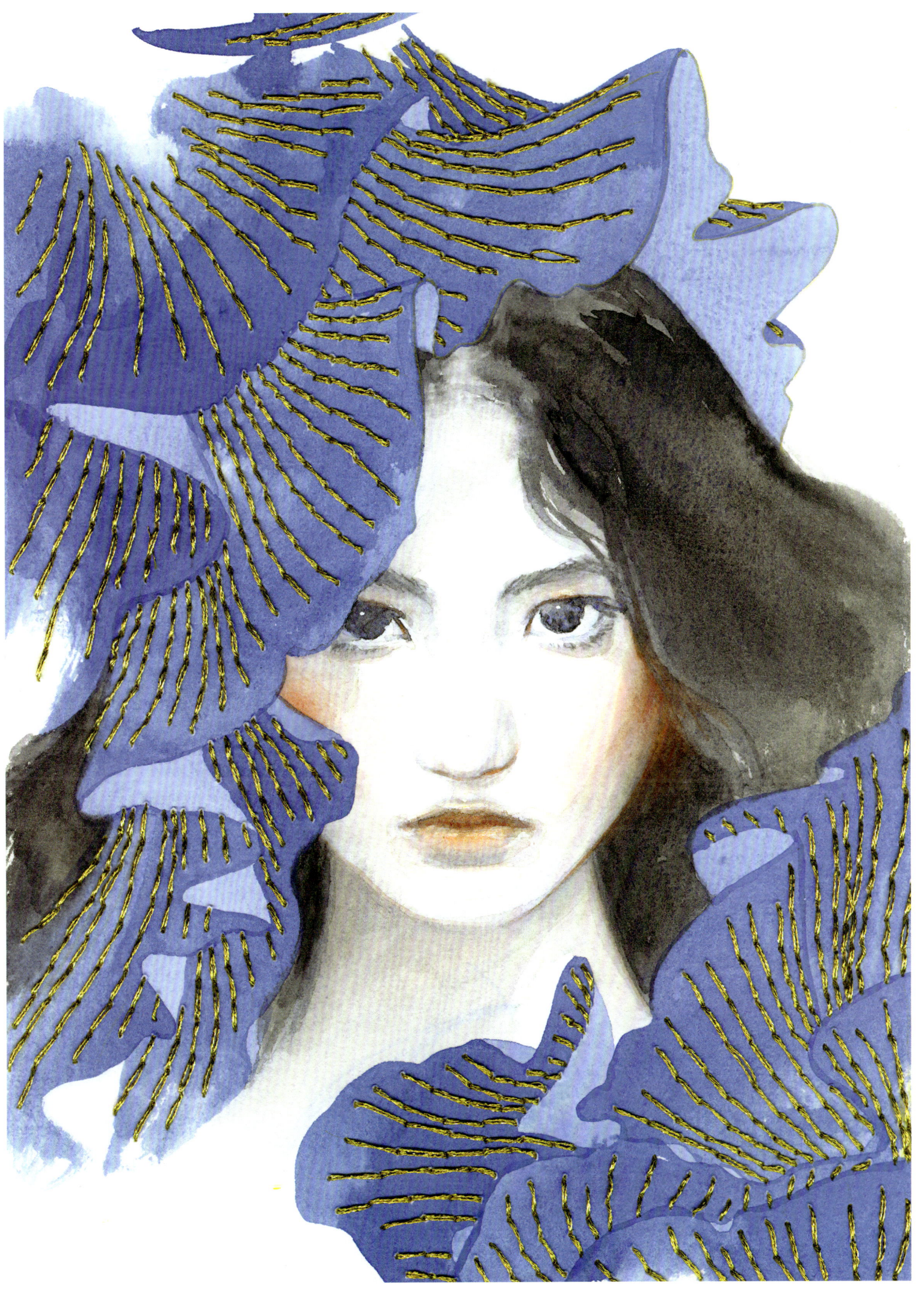

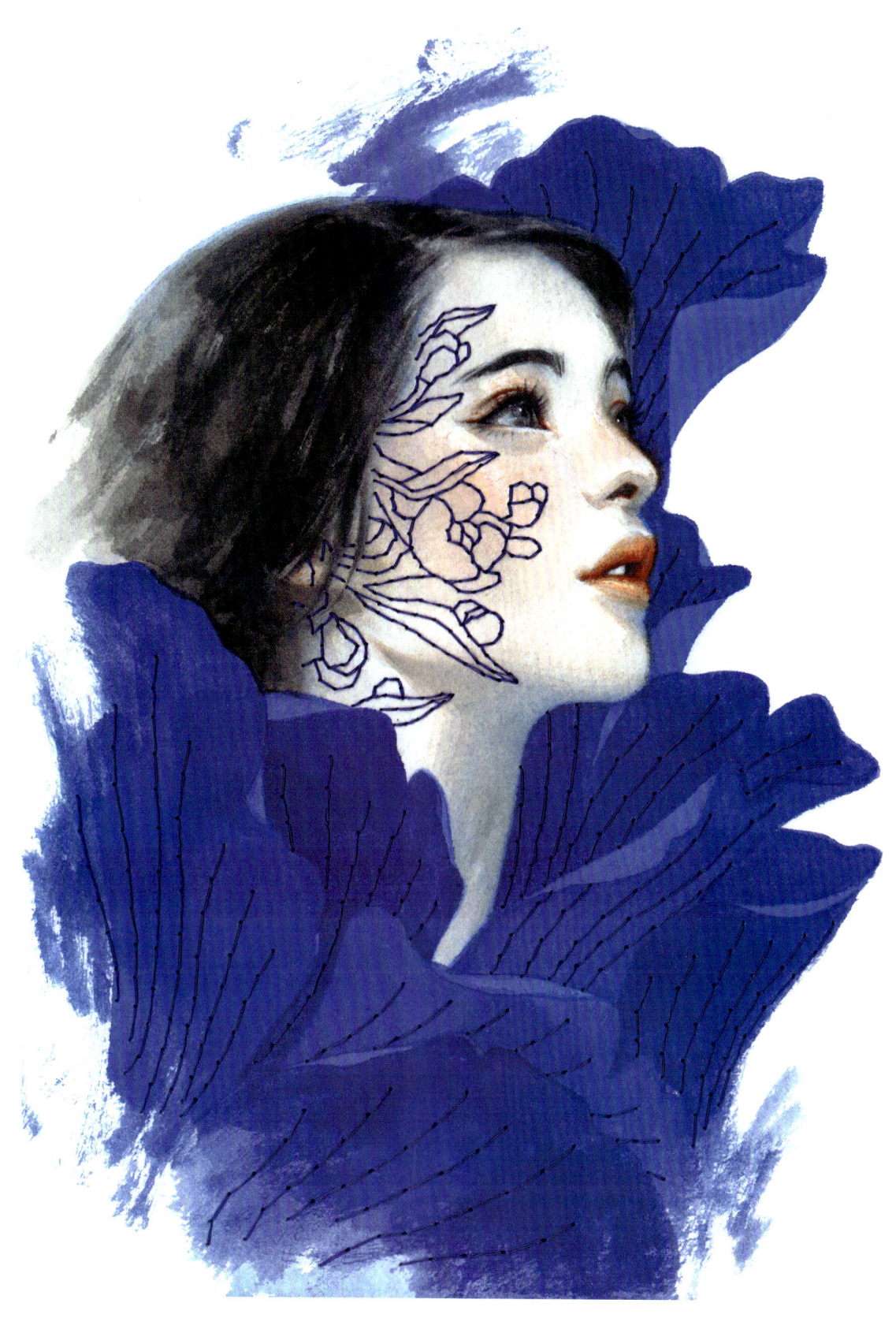

above
STUDY NO. 109
acrylic, colored pencil & embroidery, 6″ × 9″, 2022

right
STUDY NO. 110
gouache, colored pencil & embroidery, 6″ × 9″, 2022

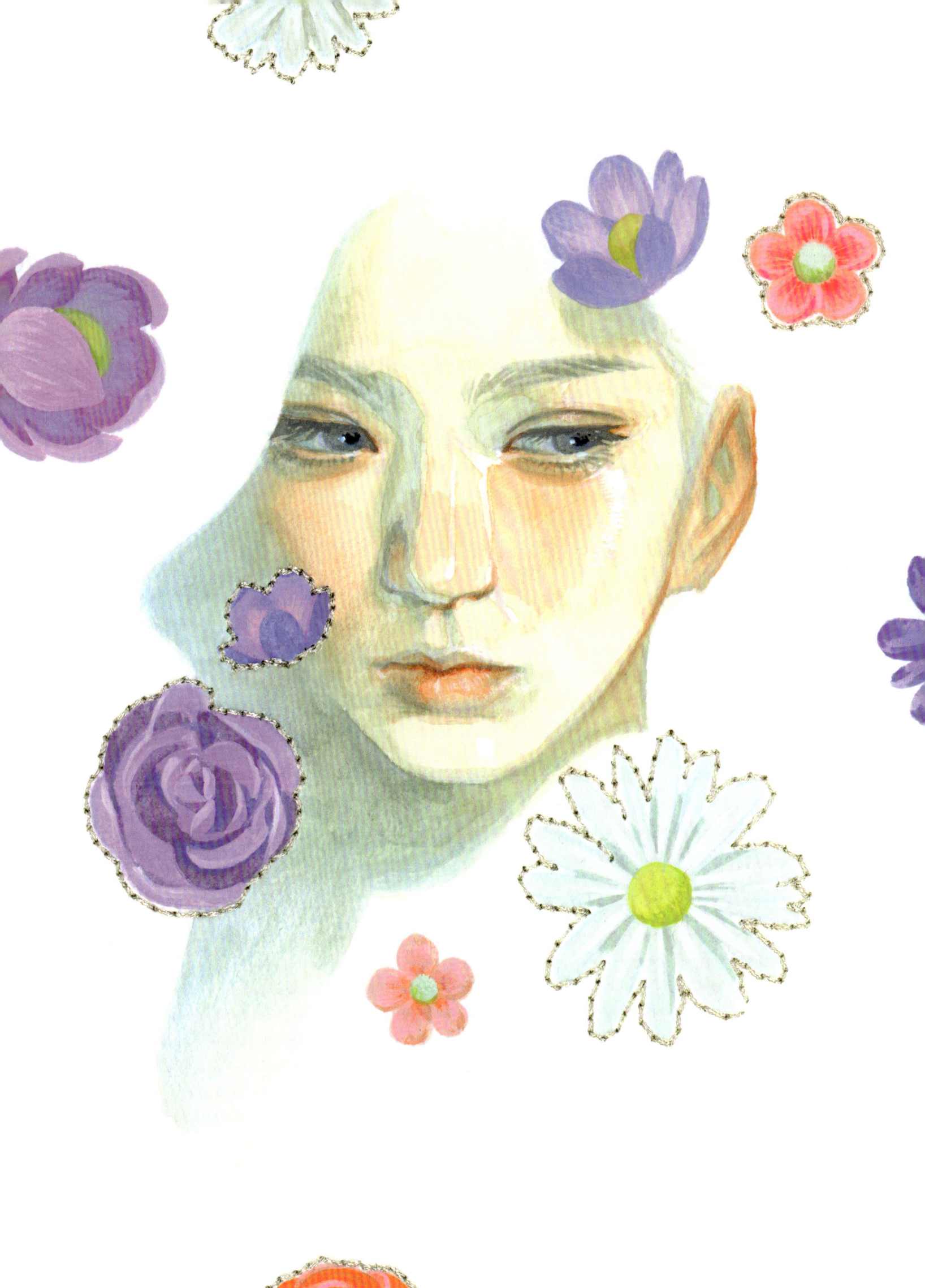

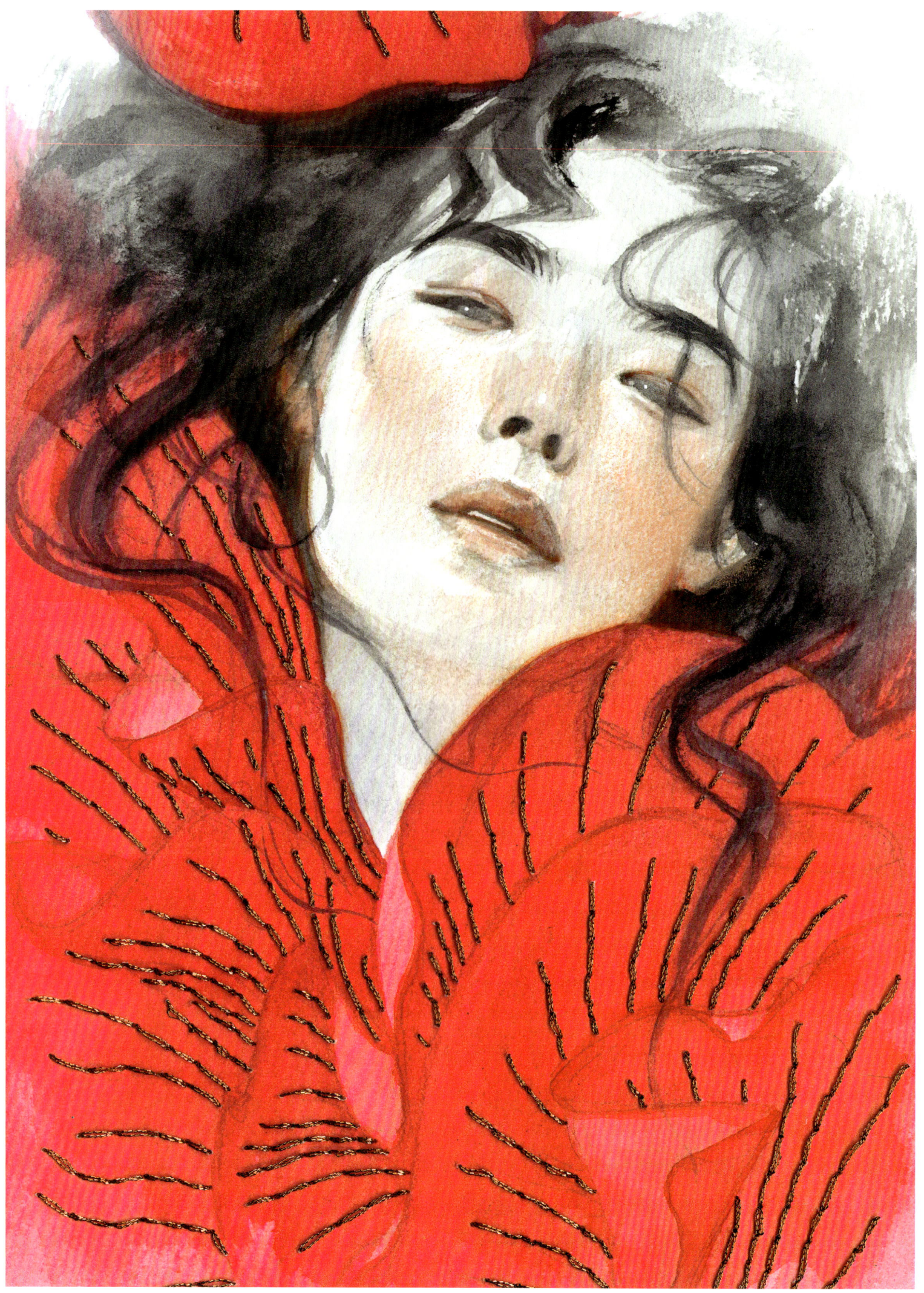

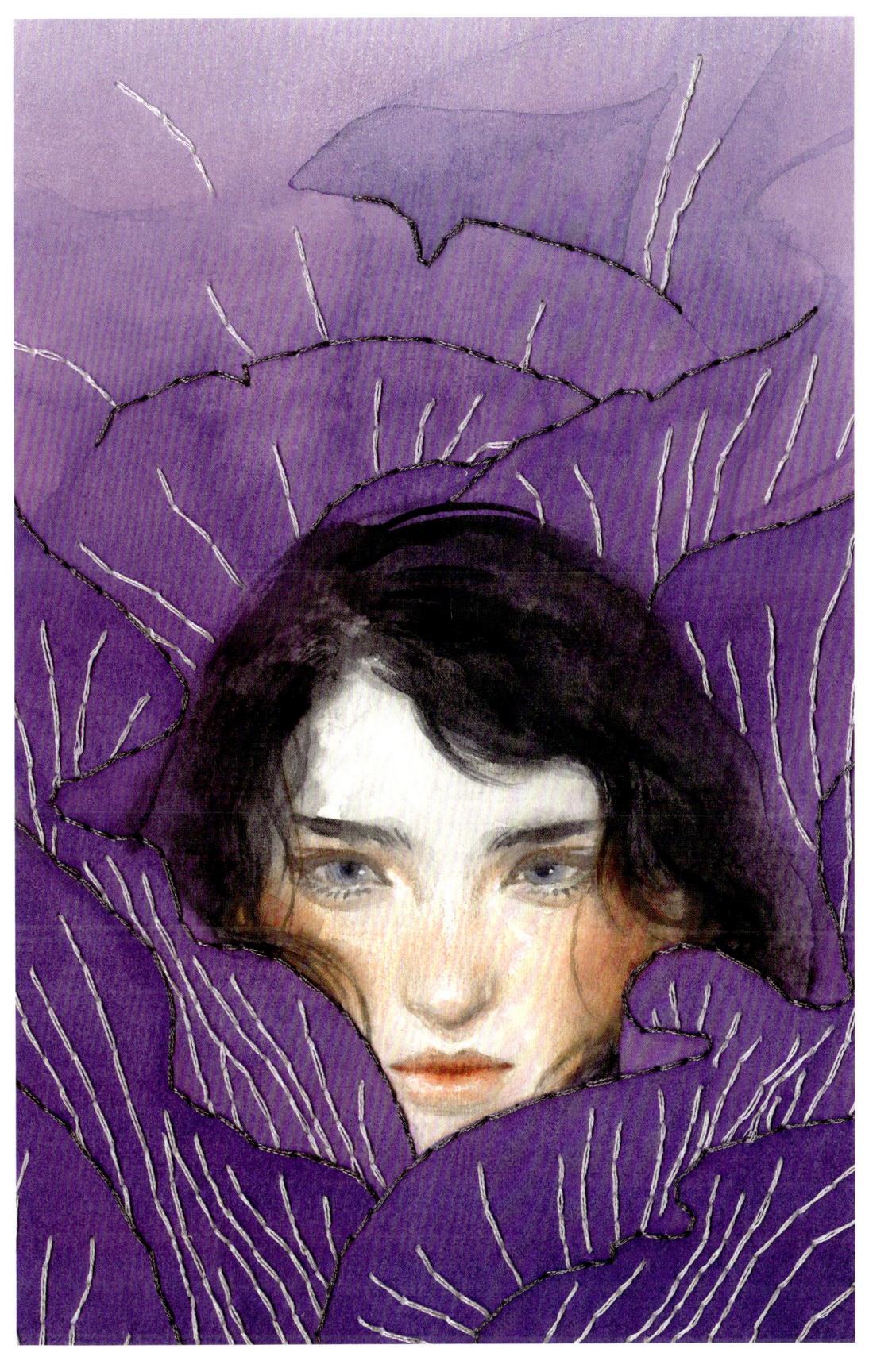

left
STUDY NO. 113
watercolor, colored pencil & embroidery, 6" × 9", 2022

above
STUDY NO. 114
watercolor, colored pencil & embroidery, 6" × 9", 2022

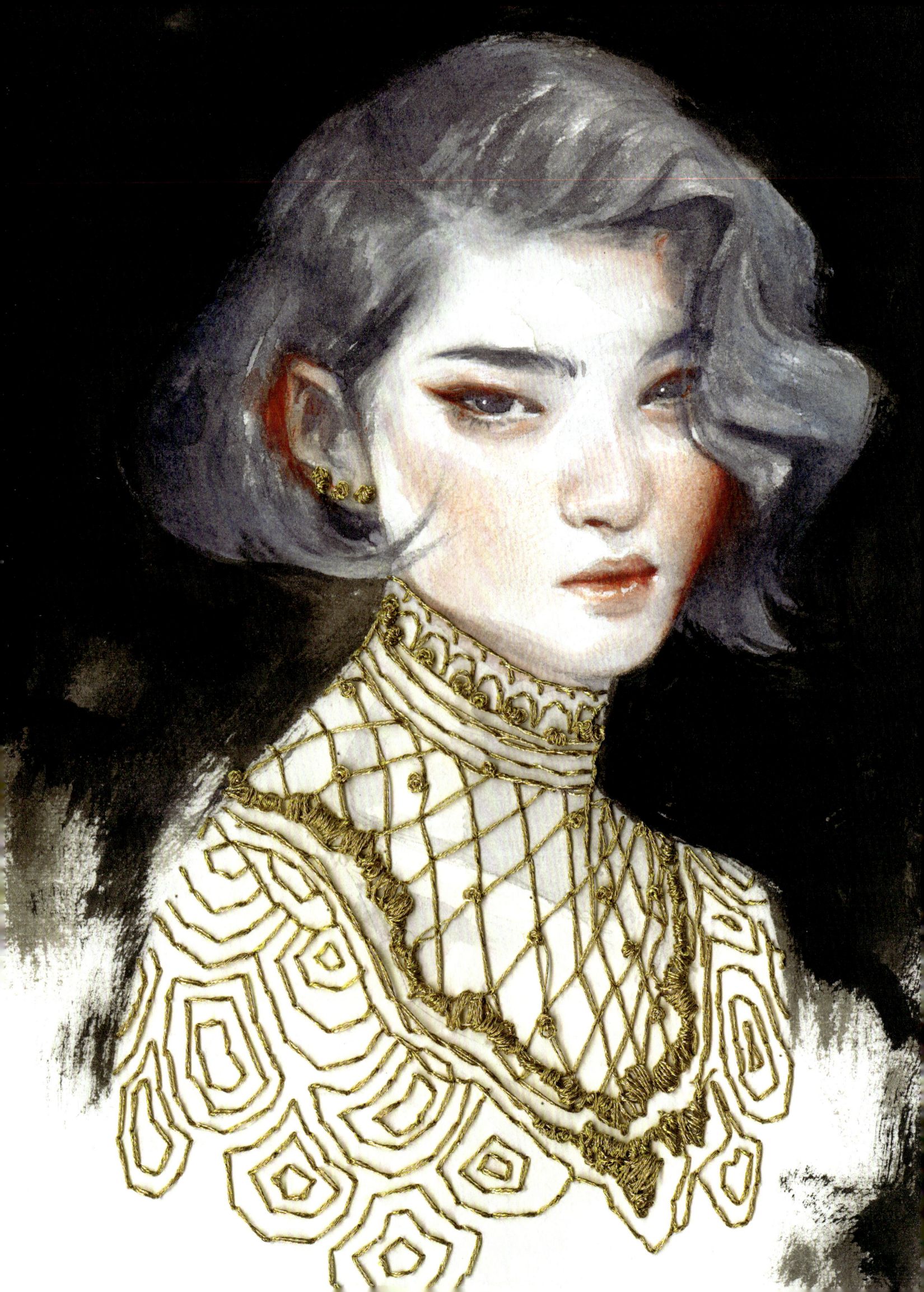

STUDY NO. 115
watercolor, colored pencil & embroidery, 6" × 9", 2022

STUDY NO. 116
gouache, colored pencil & embroidery, 6″ × 9″, 2022

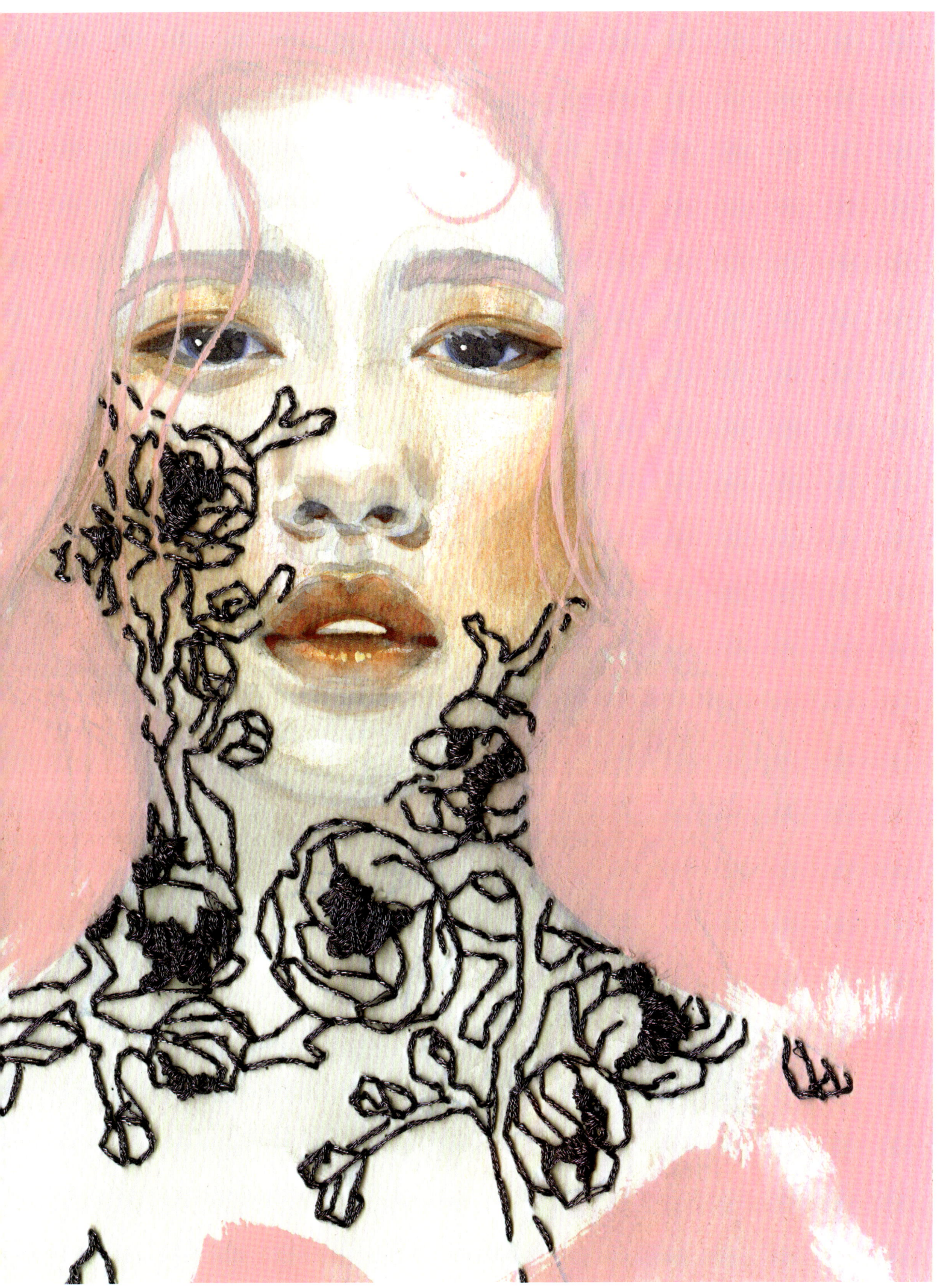

Tran Nguyen is a Vietnamese freelance artist currently residing in Atlanta, Georgia. She is best known for her book illustrations and fine art, which focus on figurative art, nature and the intricacies of the human condition.

Her work is painted traditionally with acrylics and colored pencil on watercolor paper, and it possesses an air of fantasy and surrealism. She has collaborated with clients such as Penguin Random House, Disney, Wizards of the Coast and *Smithsonian* magazine to bring their stories to life. More of her work can be found at *www.mynameistran.com*.

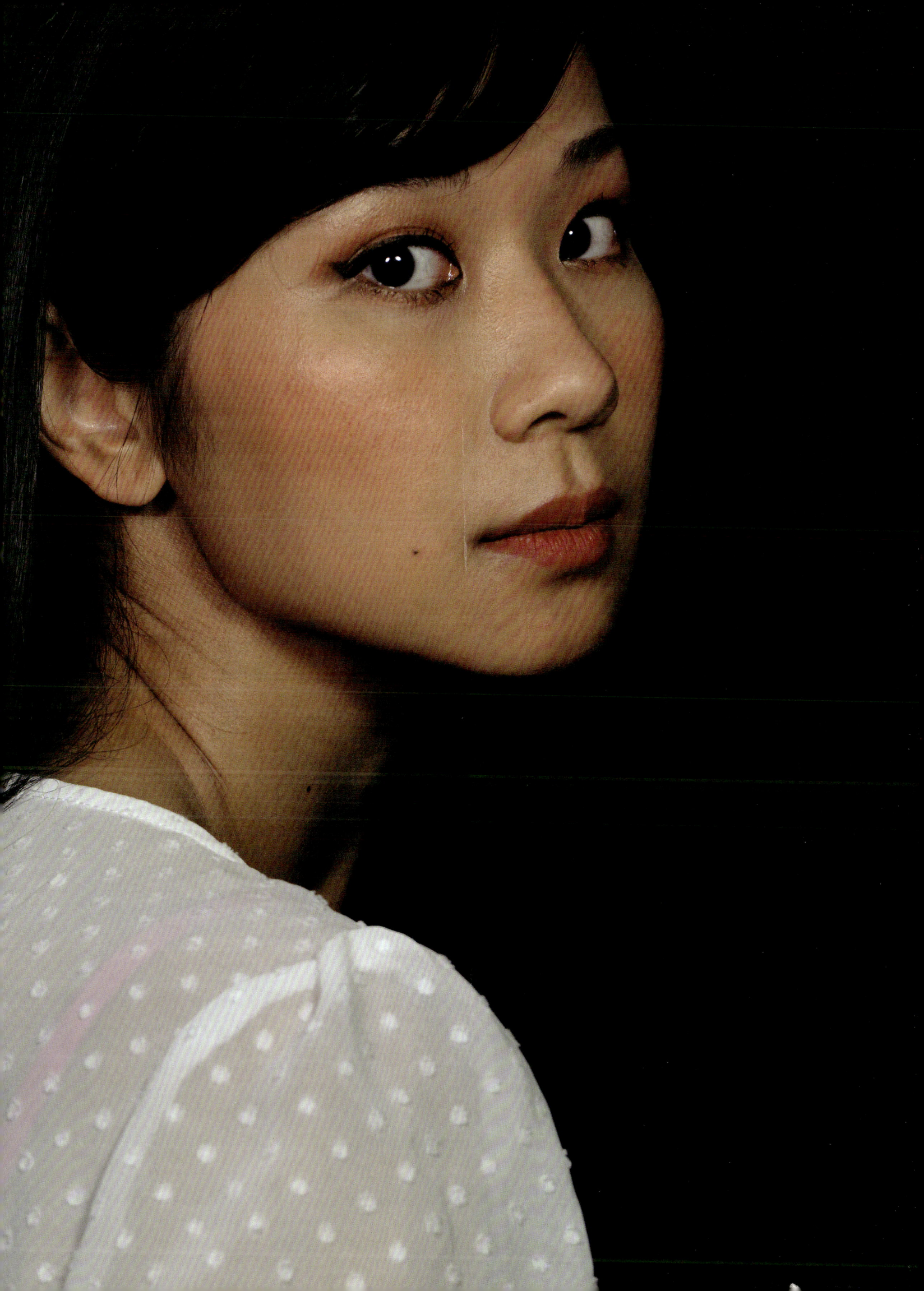

TO MY LITTLE BROTHER,

THE KINDEST SPIRIT OF US ALL.